COURT NOMINATIONS: ISSUES IN NOMINATIONS AND CONFIRMATION

COURT NOMINATIONS: ISSUES IN NOMINATIONS AND CONFIRMATION

PETER C. KESTERHOFF
EDITOR

Nova Science Publishers, Inc.
New York

For permission to use material from this book please contact us:
Telephone 631-231-7269; Fax 631-231-8175
Web Site: http://www.novapublishers.com

LIBRARY OF CONGRESS CATALOGING-IN-PUBLICATION DATA

ISBN: 978-1-60692-556-0

Available upon request.

Published by Nova Science Publishers, Inc. ✝ New York

CONTENTS

PREFACE

This new book sheds light on whether Senate processing of lower court nominations, particularly to the courts of appeals, has tended over recent decades to slow down in presidential election years. The book begins by reviewing recent debate, and historical events dating back to 1980, concerning whether the Senate and its Judiciary Committee customarily observe a practice referred to as the "Thurmond rule." Next, the book provides narratives on each presidential election year from 1980 to 2004, reviewing Senate and committee actions taken on court of appeals and district court nominations in each of the years. The book then compares these years quantitatively, examining the number and percent of nominations processed and the last dates of committee and Senate action taken. Findings include the following: Senators of both parties at different times have spoken of their expectations of a drop-off in processing of judicial nominations occurring earlier in presidential election years than in other years. However, there is no written Senate or Judiciary Committee rule — nor was any bipartisan agreement reached during the 1980-2004 period — concerning judicial nominations in presidential election years.

The Senate has, on average, confirmed fewer court of appeals nominees in presidential election years than in any other year of a presidential term between 1977 and 2007. In the presidential election years from 1980 to 2004, there was no consistently observed date after which the Judiciary Committee or Senate ceased processing lower court nominations; however, in the three most recent completed presidential election years, the Senate confirmed its last court of appeals nominee in July or earlier, while in the four preceding presidential election years, the Senate confirmed its final court of appeals nominee in October or later. On average, fewer court of appeals nominations received hearings, were reported, and were confirmed in the three most recent completed presidential election years

(1996, 2000, and 2004) than in the four preceding presidential election years (1980, 1984, 1988, and 1992).

From 1980 to 2004, the Senate confirmed, on average, more nominations (and a greater percentage of pending nominations) in years when the Senate majority was of the President's party than years in which partisan control of the presidency and the Senate was divided. The book also outlines relevant considerations for Senators in deciding whether to seek to speed or slow the judicial confirmation process in a presidential election year. These considerations include the public policy views of the incumbent President (and his successor), patronage considerations for Senators of both political parties, the appearance of a partisan judicial confirmation process, and whether a slowdown might greatly affect the judicial vacancy rate.

Chapter1 - Supported by the custom of "senatorial courtesy," Senators of the President's party have long played, as a general rule, the primary role in selecting candidates for the President to nominate to federal district court judgeships in their states. They also have played an influential, if not primary, role in recommending candidates for federal circuit court judgeships associated with their states. For Senators who are not of the President's party, a consultative role, with the opportunity to convey to the President their views about candidates under consideration for judgeships in their states, also has been a long-standing practice — and one supported by the "blue slip" procedure of the Senate Judiciary Committee.

Senators, in general, exert less influence over the selection of circuit court nominees. Whereas home state Senators of the President's party often dictate whom the President nominates to district judgeships, their recommendations for circuit nominees, by contrast, typically compete with names suggested to the Administration by other sources or generated by the Administration on its own.

Whether and how a state's two Senators share in the judicial selection role will depend, to a great extent, on their respective prerogatives and interests. Senators have great discretion as to the procedures they will use to identify and evaluate judicial candidates, ranging from informally conducting candidate searches on their own to relying on nominating commissions to evaluate candidates. Contact between a Senator's office and the Administration can be expected to clarify the nature of the Senator's recommending role, including the degree to which the Administration, in its judicial candidate search, will rely on the Senator's recommendations.

If a President selects a district or circuit court nominee against the advice of, or without consulting, a home state Senator, the latter must decide whether to oppose the nomination (either first in the Senate Judiciary Committee or later on the Senate floor). From the Senator's standpoint, opposition to the nomination might serve a number of purposes, including helping to prevent confirmation or influencing the Administration to take consultation more seriously in the future. On the other hand, various considerations might influence the Senator not to oppose the nomination, including the desirability of filling the vacant judgeship as promptly as possible and, if more home state vacancies are possible in the future, whether these might provide the Senator a better opportunity for exerting influence over judicial appointments.

In recent years, the role of home state Senators in recommending judicial candidates has given rise to various issues, including the following: What constitutes "good faith" or "serious" consultation by the Administration? Should home state Senators always have the opportunity to provide their opinion of a judicial candidate before he or she is nominated? How differently should the Administration treat the input of Senators, depending on their party affiliation? What prerogatives should home state Senators have in the selection of circuit court nominees? Should the policy of the Judiciary Committee allow a home state Senator to block committee consideration of a judicial nominee?

Chapter2 - This report seeks to shed light on whether Senate processing of lower court nominations, particularly to the courts of appeals, has tended over recent decades to slow down in presidential election years. The chapter begins by reviewing recent debate, and historical events dating back to 1980, concerning whether the Senate and its Judiciary Committee customarily observe a practice referred to as the "Thurmond rule." Next, the chapter provides narratives on each presidential election year from 1980 to 2004, reviewing Senate and committee actions taken on court of appeals and district court nominations in each of the years. The chapter then compares these years quantitatively, examining the number and percent of nominations processed and the last dates of committee and Senate action taken. Findings include the following:

- Senators of both parties at different times have spoken of their expectations of a drop-off in processing of judicial nominations occurring earlier in presidential election years than in other years. However, there is no written Senate or Judiciary Committee rule — nor was any bipartisan agreement reached during the 1980-2004 period — concerning judicial nominations in presidential election years.
- The Senate has, on average, confirmed fewer court of appeals nominees in presidential election years than in any other year of a presidential term between 1977 and 2007.

- In the presidential election years from 1980 to 2004, there was no consistently observed date after which the Judiciary Committee or Senate ceased processing lower court nominations; however, in the three most recent completed presidential election years, the Senate confirmed its last court of appeals nominee in July or earlier, while in the four preceding presidential election years, the Senate confirmed its final court of appeals nominee in October or later.
- On average, fewer court of appeals nominations received hearings, were reported, and were confirmed in the three most recent completed presidential election years (1996, 2000, and 2004) than in the four preceding presidential election years (1980, 1984, 1988, and 1992).
- From 1980 to 2004, the Senate confirmed, on average, more nominations (and a greater percentage of pending nominations) in years when the Senate majority was of the President's party than years in which partisan control of the presidency and the Senate was divided.

The chapter also outlines relevant considerations for Senators in deciding whether to seek to speed or slow the judicial confirmation process in a presidential election year. These considerations include the public policy views of the incumbent President (and his successor), patronage considerations for Senators of both political parties, the appearance of a partisan judicial confirmation process, and whether a slowdown might greatly affect the judicial vacancy rate.

Chapter3 - This chapter tracks nominations made by President George W. Bush to judgeships on the U.S. courts of appeals, the U.S. district courts, and the U.S. Court of International Trade — the lower courts on which, pursuant to Article III of the Constitution, judges serve "during good Behaviour." It lists and keeps count of all nominations made to these courts during the 110th Congress, including pertinent actions taken by the Senate Judiciary Committee and the full Senate. It also tracks the number of judicial vacancies on the courts (including vacancies classified by the federal judiciary as "judicial emergencies"), the number of nominations pending to fill the vacancies, and the names of the pending nominees. It presents the number of persons nominated by President Bush to each category of lower Article III court during his entire presidency (breaking down each total to show the number confirmed, pending, returned and not re-nominated, and withdrawn). Last, it provides tabular and graphical comparisons of President Bush's lower court nominee statistics with those of the four Presidents who immediately preceded him.

As of August 4, 2008:

- President Bush had nominated 21 individuals to the U.S. courts of appeals during the 110th Congress, with the Senate having confirmed 10 of them, and with three withdrawn by the President.
- President Bush had nominated 78 individuals to the U.S. district courts during the 110th Congress, with the Senate having confirmed 48 of them, and with one withdrawn by the President.
- There were 10 judicial vacancies on the U.S. courts of appeals, with eight nominations pending to fill these vacancies.
- There were 30 U.S. district court vacancies, with 25 nominations pending to fill these judgeships, and an additional four nominations pending to fill future district court vacancies.
- No vacancies had occurred on the U.S. Court of International Trade during the 110th Congress (and thus no nominations have been made to the court during the Congress).

During the entire presidency of George W. Bush (from January 20, 2001, to August 4, 2008), there have been 370 nominees to Article III lower court judgeships. Of the 370 total nominees, 37 are pending, 314 have received Senate confirmation, nine have been returned to the President in a previous Congress and not resubmitted, and 10 have been withdrawn by the President and not resubmitted.

For corresponding information about President Bush's appeals and district court nominations during earlier Congresses, see CRS Report RL3 1868, U.S. Circuit and District Court Nominations by President George W. Bush During the 107th-109th Congresses, by Denis Steven Rutkus, Kevin M. Scott, and Maureen Bearden.

In: Court Nominations
Editor: Peter C. Kesterhoff, pp. 1-85
ISBN 978-1-60692-556-0

Chapter 1

ROLE OF HOME STATE SENATORS IN THE SELECTION OF LOWER FEDERAL COURT JUDGES*

Denis Steven Rutkus

ABSTRACT

Supported by the custom of "senatorial courtesy," Senators of the President's party have long played, as a general rule, the primary role in selecting candidates for the President to nominate to federal district court judgeships in their states. They also have played an influential, if not primary, role in recommending candidates for federal circuit court judgeships associated with their states. For Senators who are not of the President's party, a consultative role, with the opportunity to convey to the President their views about candidates under consideration for judgeships in their states, also has been a long-standing practice — and one supported by the "blue slip" procedure of the Senate Judiciary Committee.

Senators, in general, exert less influence over the selection of circuit court nominees. Whereas home state Senators of the President's party often dictate whom the President nominates to district judgeships, their recommendations for circuit nominees, by contrast, typically compete with names suggested to the Administration by other sources or generated by the Administration on its own.

---

* Excerpted from CRS Report RL34405, dated March 6, 2008.

Whether and how a state's two Senators share in the judicial selection role will depend, to a great extent, on their respective prerogatives and interests. Senators have great discretion as to the procedures they will use to identify and evaluate judicial candidates, ranging from informally conducting candidate searches on their own to relying on nominating commissions to evaluate candidates. Contact between a Senator's office and the Administration can be expected to clarify the nature of the Senator's recommending role, including the degree to which the Administration, in its judicial candidate search, will rely on the Senator's recommendations.

If a President selects a district or circuit court nominee against the advice of, or without consulting, a home state Senator, the latter must decide whether to oppose the nomination (either first in the Senate Judiciary Committee or later on the Senate floor). From the Senator's standpoint, opposition to the nomination might serve a number of purposes, including helping to prevent confirmation or influencing the Administration to take consultation more seriously in the future. On the other hand, various considerations might influence the Senator not to oppose the nomination, including the desirability of filling the vacant judgeship as promptly as possible and, if more home state vacancies are possible in the future, whether these might provide the Senator a better opportunity for exerting influence over judicial appointments.

In recent years, the role of home state Senators in recommending judicial candidates has given rise to various issues, including the following: What constitutes "good faith" or "serious" consultation by the Administration? Should home state Senators always have the opportunity to provide their opinion of a judicial candidate before he or she is nominated? How differently should the Administration treat the input of Senators, depending on their party affiliation? What prerogatives should home state Senators have in the selection of circuit court nominees? Should the policy of the Judiciary Committee allow a home state Senator to block committee consideration of a judicial nominee?

INTRODUCTION

By long-standing custom, Senators of the President's party, as a general rule, have played the primary role in selecting candidates for the President to nominate to federal district court judgeships in their states.

They also generally have played an influential, if not primary, role in recommending candidates for federal circuit court judgeships associated with their states.

For Senators who are not of the President's party, a consultative role, with the opportunity to convey to the President their views about candidates under consideration for judgeships in their states, has been a longstanding practice as well.

In recent years, however, the role to be played by “home state Senators” in the selection process for lower court judges has periodically been the subject of debate.

With controversy frequently arising in the Senate over whether that body should confirm various of the President’s judicial nominees, [1] part of the contention sometimes has involved the question of whether, or to what degree, Senators should play a role in advising the President on whom to select as judicial nominees from their states. [2] To assist in examining that question, this chapter provides an analysis of the role that home state Senators, historically and in the contemporary era, have played in the lower court selection process.

Specifically, this chapter examines the role played by Senators in the selection of nominees to two kinds of lower court judgeships — to U.S. district court judgeships in the federal judicial districts lying geographically within the Senators’ states and to U.S. court of appeals judgeships in the judicial circuits of which the Senators’ states are a geographic part. [3] In separate sections the chapter discusses:

- the historical origins of the role of Senators recommending persons for nomination to lower court judgeships — particularly, the custom of “senatorial courtesy” and the Senate Judiciary Committee’s longstanding “blue slip” procedure;
- the effect of Senators’ political party affiliation on their role as recommenders of judicial candidates from their state;
- the lesser role that Senators generally play when recommending circuit court, as opposed to district court, candidates;
- the process by which Senators evaluate and select judicial candidates;
- Senators’ contacts with a President’s administration after they make their recommendations but before the President selects a nominee;
- the options available to home state Senators when the President selects a judicial nominee against their advice, or without consulting them; and
- issues that have arisen in recent years over the proper role, and degree of influence, for home state Senators in the selection of nominees for U.S. district and circuit court judgeships.

Background and Origins of Senators' Recommending Role

The Senate's Exercise of "Advice and Consent"

The President's appointments of judges in the federal court system are made subject to the approval of the Senate. [4] These appointments take place through a process, provided for in the Constitution, in which the President nominates and appoints persons to federal office "by and with the Advice and Consent of the Senate." [5] Exceptions to this rule are the relatively rare judicial appointments which the President alone makes, without the requirement of Senate approval, through his power, under the Constitution, to make temporary "recess appointments." [6]

The Senate most visibly exercises its "advice and consent" role with respect to judicial appointments when Senators vote on a nomination — either in committee (on whether to chapter the nomination to the Senate) or on the Senate floor (on whether to confirm). [7] Another significant, though less public, exercise of Senate "advice and consent" on judicial nominations, it can be argued, occurs when individual Senators provide actual advice to the President on whom to nominate to particular federal judgeships. By long-standing custom, dating back to the early 1800s, Senators of the President's party, in their capacity as home state Senators, have regularly provided Presidents such advice, recommending candidates for judgeships situated in their states or linked by tradition to their states. For Senators who are not of the President's party, a consultative role, with the opportunity to convey to the President their views about candidates under consideration for judgeships in their states, also has been a long-standing practice.

Role for Senators in Selecting Nominees Linked to Their States

Technically, each Senator is free to recommend candidates for any federal judgeship to be filled by presidential nomination. In reality, however, the ability of Senators to have their judicial recommendations heeded by a President will, in most cases, depend on the judgeship in question having a geographic link to the Senators' own state. A Senator, for instance, rarely will be able to exert influence on behalf of a judicial candidate for a geographically based court, such as a U.S. district court or a U.S. court of appeals, if the court is not geographically all or in part within the Senator's state. Similarly, most Senators, on any particular occasion, might have little basis on which to make judicial recommendations for a nationwide court of specialized subject matter jurisdiction (such as the Tax Court or the Court of Appeals for Veterans Claims), unless they are members of a Senate committee having jurisdiction over the court, have expertise in the court's subject matter, or have some other special interest in the court. [8]

By contrast, every U.S. Senator makes recommendations or in some way is consulted about potential candidates for judgeships in (1) the U.S. district court or courts which geographically fall within the Senator's state, and (2) the U.S. court of appeals "circuit" of which the Senator's state is a geographic part — provided the circuit judgeship historically has been filled by a resident of the Senator's state. [9] For these judgeships, long-standing Senate customs, as well as norms in Senate- presidential relations, govern, to a great extent, the role of individual Senators in the appointment process. The two most important of these customs arguably are "senatorial courtesy" and the "blue slip" practice of the Senate Judiciary Committee.

Senatorial Courtesy

Dating back to 1789, senatorial courtesy, as defined by one authority, is the "Senate's practice of declining to confirm a presidential nominee for an office in the state of a senator of the president's party unless that senator approves." [10] "In our day," another scholar has written, "senatorial courtesy has come to mean that senators will give serious consideration to and be favorably disposed to support an individual senator of the president's party who opposes a nominee to an office in his state." This scholar noted, however, that, as the practice of senatorial courtesy had evolved in the contemporary period, the Senate could not be expected to automatically support a Senator opposing a nomination if "his reasons are not persuasive to other senators or if he is not a respected member of the Senate...." [11]

The custom of senatorial courtesy provides the foundation for a special role in the nomination and confirmation process for a Senator of the President's party, whenever a presidential nomination is for a federal office in the Senator's state. The Senator's role is essentially a negative one in those relatively rare instances when the Senator opposes, and thereby seeks to block, a nominee's confirmation. In these situations, the Senator, by invoking senatorial courtesy, ordinarily can look to the rest of the Senate's Members to join the Senator in opposing the nomination. Much more frequently, however, the Senator's role is positive in nature when, periodically, he or she engages in making recommendations to the

President about whom to nominate to federal offices in the Senator's state. In these situations, the custom of senatorial courtesy, it can be argued, encourages the President to be receptive to the Senator's recommendations — rather than risk selecting nominees opposed not only by the Senator, but by the Senate as a whole, united in support of its colleague.

The precedent of senatorial courtesy, according to Joseph P. Harris, in his landmark study, The Advice and Consent of the Senate, [12] was set in 1789. Congress had been in session for only three months of its first term when the Senate rejected its first presidential nominee — one Benjamin Fishbourn, whom President George Washington had nominated to the post of naval officer of the Port of Savannah.

Though Fishbourn apparently had excellent qualifications for the position, the Senate rejected the nomination as a courtesy to the two Senators from Georgia, who had a candidate of their own. The next day, Washington withdrew the Fishbourn nomination and nominated the candidate desired by the two Georgia Senators.

In the Fishbourn episode, the courtesy that the Senate's members as a whole extended to their two colleagues from Georgia — by rejecting the nomination that the two Senators opposed — was an important precedent. As Harris explained:

> The Fishbourn case initiated the custom which requires the President to consult with the senators from the state in which a vacancy occurs, and to nominate a person acceptable to them; if he fails to do so, the Senate as a courtesy to these senators will reject any other nominee regardless of his qualification. The custom is usually invoked, however, only by senators of the same party as the President. It did not become firmly established in Washington's administration, for he continued to hold to the doctrine that the power of nomination belonged exclusively to the President and continued to consult widely in making his selections. Under later Presidents with less prestige, less force of character and less determination, the rule became firmly established with respect to senators of the same political party as the President. [13]

Harris, writing in 1953, described what was then the "well-established custom, which has prevailed since about 1840," wherein U.S. district judges "are normally selected by senators from the state in which the district is situated, provided they belong to the same party as the President." (By contrast, the President was said to have "a much freer hand in the selection of judges to the circuit courts of appeal, whose districts cover several states...." [14]) Another scholar, less than a decade earlier, in 1944, had described as near-absolute the power of home state Senators of the President's party to select district court nominees. The Senate, he maintained, had "expropriated the President's power of nomination so far as concerns appointments of interest to senators of the party in power; and the President has virtually surrendered his power directly to local party politics as to appointments in states where the senators are of the opposition." [15]

According to two other scholars, Senators, from the very beginning, "recognized that judgeships could be used effectively to reward loyal supporters back home." Senators also realized:

> that it would be damaging to their prestige if the President appointed to a judgeship within their own state someone of whom they disapproved. As a result, senators joined together to protect their individual interests in judicial appointments. The custom of "senatorial courtesy" grew out of these considerations. [16]

In the latter half of the 20th century, it continued to be common for Senators to regard their role in the appointment of U.S. district judges as more in the nature of selection than of recommendation. In 1977, former Senator Joseph W. Tydings (D- MD) wrote that selection of a U.S. district judge "is a power jealously guarded by many senators. It is an extremely important source of political patronage, and many senators consider judicial selection to be one of the duties they were elected to perform." [17] In 1989, similar sentiments were expressed by Senator Thad Cochran (R- MS) amid a controversy involving the reluctance of President George H.W. Bush to nominate to a Vermont district judgeship a candidate recommended by Senator James

M. Jeffords (R-VT). "As a matter of custom and tradition in the Senate," Senator Cochran declared, "the senators of the president's party's recommendations for district court judgeships have been tantamount to selection of that nominee," adding that selecting judicial nominees was "one of the few patronage positions that senators have" outside their staffs. [18] Echoing Senator Cochran's views, the Senate Republican Conference, it was reported, "went to Jeffords' defense with a resolution asking conference chairman John H. Chafee (R-R.I.) to advise President Bush of the senators' support for Jeffords' choice." [19] Ultimately, the candidate recommended by Senator Jeffords was nominated by President Bush and confirmed by the Senate by a voice vote. [20]

The view of many Senators, in other words, has been that the President should defer to Senators of the President's party in the selection of home state judicial appointees, rather than vice versa. This view is reinforced by the custom of senatorial courtesy, in which the Senate as a collegial body customarily supports Senators of the President's party in disputes with the President over judicial appointments in their state. [21] The custom serves as an inducement to the President to try to reach accommodation with home state Senators, rather than risk Senate rejection of a nominee whom they oppose. As a result, Presidents rarely go forward with a nomination for a district court judgeship if a home state Senator of the President's party has indicated beforehand a readiness to oppose the nominee in the Senate. [22]

The role of home state Senators of the President's party, however, is no longer one of unquestioned power to select district court nominees, as it has been generally portrayed in the past. A judicial appointments scholar observed in 1972 that "even granting that senators of the party in power may have 'owned' district judgeships at an earlier time in our history, they have not during the incumbency of the presidents since Truman." [23] In recent decades, Senators, when recommending judicial candidates, increasingly have found it necessary to accommodate new demands or calls from the President, which have made their selection power less absolute. For instance, recent Presidents have insisted that candidates whom Senators recommend for district judges, besides having necessary professional qualifications, meet other criteria of particular importance to the President [24] or that the Senators submit a number of candidates for a vacant judgeship, rather than only the name of the one candidate they most favor. [25] Further, one recent President (Jimmy Carter), through forceful advocacy, persuaded nearly all of the home state Senators of his party to establish nominating commissions for the selection of district court judges. In so doing, the Senators relinquished a substantial part of their traditional role in recruiting, evaluating, and recommending district court candidates. [26] Subsequent Presidents, however, have not insisted, as President Carter did, that Senators use nominating commissions to select district court candidates, and most Senators no longer do [27].

Blue Slip Policy of Senate Judiciary Committee

Senatorial courtesy, as has been shown, historically has contemplated a role for Senators of the President's party in providing advice to the President on nominees — but not necessarily a role for opposition party Senators. Nevertheless, even when neither of a state's Senators is of the President's party, a consultative role is contemplated, if not mandated, for them in the appointment process by means of the Senate Judiciary Committee's "blue slip" policy. Under the committee's blue slip policy, as it has evolved in recent decades, the Judiciary

Committee has come to expect that, as a courtesy, a state's Senators, no matter what their party affiliation, will be consulted by the Administration prior to the President nominating persons to U.S. district judgeships in the state as well as to U.S. circuit court judgeships historically associated with the state.

The blue slip policy of the Senate Judiciary Committee, as set by its chair, dates back at least to 1917. [28] Under this policy, the committee chair seeks the assessment of Senators regarding district court, circuit court, U.S. attorney, and U.S. marshal nominations in their state. In practice, the chair sends a blue-colored form to home state Senators regarding these nominations. If a home state Senator has no objection to a nominee, the blue slip is returned to the chair with a positive response; however, if a Senator has some objection to the nominee and wants to stop or slow committee action, he or she can decide not to return the blue slip or to return it with a negative response. [29] Some, but not all, chairs of the Judiciary Committee have required a return of a positive blue slip by both of a state's Senators before allowing consideration of a nomination.

For more than two decades, from 1956 through 1978, when a Senator returned a negative blue slip or failed to return a blue slip for a judicial nomination, it was the policy of the committee chair, in deference to the Senator, to decline to schedule a hearing or other committee action on the nomination. [30] In other words, a home state Senator, by not returning a blue slip or by returning it with a negative response, could halt all further action on a nominee from the state. This policy, in effect, gave Senators of either party, if they wished to exercise it through the blue slip, a veto over any home state judicial nomination to which they were opposed. [31] In so doing, the committee policy, some scholars have suggested, also had the effect of encouraging presidential administrations to consult beforehand with Senators of the opposition party, as well as of the President's party, to be sure that they would not oppose a person being considered for a judicial nomination in the state in question. [32]

Since 1979, however, deference to home state Senators using the blue slip to block or delay judicial nominees has not always been automatic. While some chairs of the Judiciary Committee, including Senator Patrick J. Leahy (D-VT) in the 110th Congress, have permitted committee action on a judicial nomination only when both home state Senators returned positive slips, the committee under other chairs, by contrast, has considered a judicial nomination with receipt of only one positive blue slip, [33] or on a few occasions, without a blue slip from either home state Senator." [34]

While the blue slip policies of various recent chairs of the Judiciary Committee have varied, nearly all policies, when articulated in writing, have communicated to the President the importance of pre-nomination consultation with both home state Senators. [35] Pre-nomination consultation, a 2003 analysis concluded:

> has been a key expectation of recent [Judiciary Committee] chairmen in the evaluation of negative blue slips. The President is now expected to consult and involve each home state Senator in the pre-nomination phase of the selection process. Without evidence of consultation by the White House, various chairmen have appeared, as a matter of policy, to accord greater value to a negative blue slip submitted by a non-consulted home state Senator. [36]

Moreover, the role contemplated for Senators not of the President's party, when engaging in pre-nomination consultation with the President, has been expanded. Official blue slip policy statements by recent chairs of the Judiciary Committee, for instance, have not only called for the opportunity for opposition party Senators to express opinions about judgeship candidates being considered by the Administration, but also the opportunity to propose their own candidates to the Administration. [37]

In sum, the Judiciary Committee's blue slip policy in recent decades, as applied in somewhat varying ways by different chairs, appears always intended to promote some measure of an advisory role for home state Senators of both parties in the judicial nominee selection process. Moreover, the contemplated advisory role has included the opportunity, if Senators wish, to make recommendations to the President about whom to nominate. As a caveat, however, it should be kept in mind that the blue slip policy is set by the committee's chair and is not a part of the committee's written rules. As a result, the policy's key elements, including the degree of importance placed on Administration consultation with home state Senators, is always subject to change, in keeping with the prerogatives of the committee chair.

Senators' Party Affiliations and Their Recommending Role

The political party affiliations of a state's Senators usually, if not always, are an important determinant of what role they play in the selection of federal judicial nominees in their state. As a general rule, a Senator who belongs to the President's party has the primary role in recommending candidates for federal district court judgeships in the home state, and an influential, if not the primary, role in recommending candidates for federal circuit court judgeships associated with the home state. These, as a general rule, are in contrast to the much lesser roles in recommending district and circuit court candidates played by a Senator who is of the opposite party. If both of a state's Senators are of the President's party, they usually, although not always, share the responsibility of recommending judicial candidates to the President. If neither Senator is of the President's party, some other official or officials in their state typically assume the primary role of recommending judicial candidates. Senators not of the President's party, however, sometimes are in a position to establish for themselves a more influential role in recommending judicial candidates than as just described. This particularly might prove to be the case if the Senators are perceived by the Administration as having the ability and likely inclination to block nominations in the Senate (either in committee or on the floor) unless afforded an enhanced role in judicial nominee selection.

When One Senator Is of the President's Party

As already discussed, [38] Senators of the President's party, by well-established custom, are the key persons who provide the President's Administration with recommendations for U.S. district court judgeships in their state. One authority on the judicial appointments process, writing in 1987, noted:

> A senator of the president's party expects to be able to influence heavily the selection of a federal district judgeship in the senator's state; indeed, most such senators insist on being able to pick these judges, and they expect judgeships on the federal courts of appeals going to persons from their states to be "cleared" by them.... [39]

When only one of a state's Senators is of the President's party, he or she alone, by custom, is entitled to select all candidates for district judgeships in that state. If the Administration has concerns about a Senator's recommendation, it is expected to resolve those concerns with the Senator. If the Administration continues to have a problem with a candidate, finding him or her unacceptable as a nominee, the Senator, and not any other official outside the Administration, is called on to provide a different recommendation. If the Administration prefers its own candidate, it in turn must persuade the Senator to agree to its choice. For the Administration to do otherwise, and push forward with a nominee objected to by the Senator, is to risk rejection by the Senate, given the custom of senatorial courtesy, discussed earlier. The latter scenario is very rare, however, for "[n]o administration deliberately seeks to alienate senators of their own party or to run the risk of a senator's sabotaging a nomination once it has been sent to the Senate." [40]

When only one of a state's Senators is of the President's party, that Senator will have almost complete discretion as to whether or how to consult with the state's other Senator about judicial nominations. There is no requirement that the former consult with the latter, and some Senators in such a situation may decline to consult with their home state colleague in any way. On the other hand, many Senators in such situations have consulted with their home state colleague, in various ways, and some have gone so far as to involve them in a joint or coordinated process of recommending judicial candidates to the President. [41] The following list notes some options available to a Senator of the President's party when considering whether or how to consult or cooperate with a home state colleague of the opposite party about judicial nominee recommendations. The options are not exhaustive but, rather, identify different degrees of consultation or cooperation about judicial candidates that can exist between home state Senators of opposite political parties:

- The Senator of the President's party makes recommendations to the Administration without consulting the other home state Senator at any stage — apprising the latter neither of persons under consideration early in the process nor of persons actually recommended later in the process.
- The Senator as a courtesy informs the other home state Senator of the person whom the former has recommended for a judicial nomination, without, however, soliciting the latter's views about the candidate or about other possible candidates.
- The Senator informs the other home state Senator of persons under consideration as potential judicial nominees, welcoming input from the latter about these candidates as well as suggestions as to other possible candidates.
- The Senator agrees to allow the other home state Senator to select a minority of the members of an advisory panel which evaluates and screens judicial candidates before the first Senator decides whom to recommend.
- The Senator shares the recommending function with the other home state Senator, allowing the latter to select candidates for a minority of the judgeships which become vacant in the state (for example, for every fourth judgeship).

- The two Senators work as co-equals in the selection process — for example, by using a completely bipartisan panel or commission to identify and screen applicants, and with all candidate recommendations to the President made by the Senators jointly.

These options, as mentioned, are almost entirely at the discretion of the Senator of the President's party, with his or her views about the judicial appointment process largely determining the extent to which there will be consultation or cooperation with the other home state Senator. Such views, in turn, may be influenced by the immediate political environment, including (1) the nature of working relations between the two Senators in general (e.g., strained or cordial); (2) the past practices of Senators in the state regarding judicial patronage (i.e., whether Senators in the state previously worked closely together on judicial appointments); (3) the degree of Administration support for consultation or cooperation between Senators of opposite political parties on home state appointments; [42] and (4) the extent to which the other Senator is perceived as able or inclined to block home state nominations either in committee or in the full Senate. [43]

When Both Senators Are of the President's Party

If both of a state's Senators are of the President's party, they may share the role of recommending judicial candidates to the President or, alternately, one of them may take the lead role. Senatorial custom, particularly in recent decades, provides ample support for both Senators having an active role in recommending judicial candidates in their states, if each wishes to participate in the process. [44]

In many states in which both home state Senators are of the President's party, both may be engaged in evaluating and selecting judicial candidates. One option within this arrangement is for both Senators to review and evaluate judicial candidates for every judicial vacancy that arises in their state. At their discretion, the Senators may use an informal process to select candidates, for example, relying on their personal knowledge of likely candidates or on input from close advisers or friends in the legal community. Alternately, they may use a more formal process, for example, relying on advisory panels to review applications, interview candidates and make recommendations for the Senators to choose from. At the end of the screening process, the Senators may agree on one or more candidates to recommend to the President for the judgeship, or, if they cannot reach agreement, they might combine their individual recommendations into one list to submit to the Administration.

Another option, by contrast, is for both Senators to be active in the judicial candidate selection process, but to take turns — alternating in the role every time there is a court vacancy in their state. Alternating, from the workload standpoint (in time required to screen judicial candidates), might appear more attractive for Senators in states having a relatively large number of district judgeships, where vacancies occur periodically. It, however, might appear less attractive for Senators in states having only a handful of district judgeships, where vacancies occur infrequently. Senators agreeing to alternate may decide, individually, to select candidates through either an informal or a formal process (as described in the previous paragraph). In cases where both Senators wish to rely on advisory panels to screen candidates, they have the choice of using joint panels (which serve on behalf of both Senators — with each Senator typically choosing some of the panel's members) or of using their own separate panels. At the end of such an alternating screening process, only the Senator involved submits a recommendation (or a list of recommendations) to the President for the vacant judgeship in question.

Sometimes, however, in a state having two Senators of the President's party, one Senator may opt out of an active role in recommending judicial candidates, leaving the task primarily to his or her home state colleague. A Senator might do so for a variety of reasons — lack of interest in judicial appointments, insufficient time available for the role (given other Senate responsibilities), or out of deference to the state's other Senator, due to the latter's seniority, interests, committee assignments, or greater experience in evaluating judicial candidates. In such cases, the more involved Senator, proceeding alone as the lead Senator, may review the backgrounds and qualifications of judicial applicants with informal support or input from others or, in a more formal arrangement, receive evaluations of the applicants, or recommendations, from an advisory panel established specifically on behalf of the Senator to screen judicial candidates.

At one or more points during the screening process, the lead Senator can be expected to consult with the other Senator — especially at the point at which the latter can be advised of the candidate or candidates whom the lead Senator believes should be recommended or who have received advisory panel recommendations. The lead Senator, before finalizing his or her choice of a candidate, will want the other Senator's approval — or, failing that, at the very least the other Senator's willingness not to object to the candidate's nomination later. [45] Once a candidate is selected, the actual recommendation may be made singly, by the lead Senator, or jointly, by both Senators. Likewise, a public statement noting a candidate's nomination by the President may be made solely by the lead Senator or jointly by both Senators.

If both of the state's Senators are of the President's party, the prospects for a district court candidate's nomination in that state are bolstered if both Senators have recommended that candidate to the President. A scholar on the judicial appointment process has noted:

> If there are two senators of the president's party from a particular state, [Justice] department arithmetic has it that the effect of two senators wanting a particular man for a district judgeship in their state is more than one plus one. The sum is more like infinity, for it would only be with great trepidation that the president's men would attempt to counter the will of both senators. [46]

When Neither Senator Is of the President's Party

If neither Senator in a state is of the President's party, each usually, by custom, plays at most only a secondary role in recommending judicial candidates for the President's consideration, with the primary role assumed by other officials from the state who are of the President's party. On occasion, however, exceptions to this rule do occur, with a President sometimes acquiescing to active senatorial participation in judicial candidate selection in states having two opposition party Senators. On other occasions, an agreed-upon arrangement in a state might be that while officials of the President's party would be the ones recommending judicial candidates, the state's opposition party Senators would exercise a veto power over any recommendations they found objectionable.

The Customary Model: Officials in the State Who Are of the President's Party Play the Primary Recommending Role. By custom, when neither of a state's Senators is of the President's party, the primary role in recommending candidates for district court judgeships is assumed by officials in the state who are of the President's party. Historically, in the absence of a Senator of the President's party, the state official or officials who most frequently have exercised the judicial "patronage" function have been the most senior member, or one of the most senior members, of the party's House of Representatives delegation, the House party delegation as a whole, the governor, or state party officials. In any given state, one of these officials may exercise the recommending function exclusively, or share it with one or more of the others.

A survey published in April 1993 illustrates the customary options used to select candidates for district judgeships in states not having Senators of the

President's party. The survey, by the interest group Alliance for Justice, was published shortly after the start of the presidency of William J. Clinton in January 1993. It was based primarily on interviews with staff members in the offices of Democratic Senators and House members, with additional information obtained through interviews of Democratic Party officials. At the time of the survey, there were 11 states in which neither Senator was a Democrat. In one of the 11 states, a judicial candidate selection process was not yet in place, and no judicial vacancies were pending there. In the other 10 states, according to the survey, judicial selection procedures were set or being put in place. The numerical breakdown of these 10 states, according to the type of Democratic official acting as the "chief sponsor" of judicial candidates, was as follows:

- 5 states — a House of Representatives Member;
- 2 states — the governor;
- 2 states — a House of Representatives Member and the governor;
- 1 state — the U.S. Department of Agriculture Secretary. [47]

In June 1993, a few months after the survey's publication, another state, Texas, joined the ranks of states in which neither Senator was of the President's party. (This occurred when a Republican was elected to a Senate seat in a special election, giving Texas two Republican Senators.) At that point, it was reported, "the traditional authority to make recommendations to the President fell to ... Texas's senior congressional Democrat" [48] (the state's senior Democratic House Member). [49]

Likewise, at the start of presidency of George W. Bush, a Republican, in January 200 1, the new Administration looked to other than senatorial sources for advice on judicial candidates in states having two opposition party Senators. The Legal Times reported that in "the 18 states where both senators are Democrats, Bush will be getting advice on potential nominees from a high-ranking Republican House member or the state's Republican governor." [50] Without listing the selection methods for each of the 18 states, the article noted, as examples, that in two of the states a senior Republican House member would be working together with the Republican governor on judicial recommendations, while in a third state a Republican House member expected to be the President's "point man on judicial nominations." [51]

By custom, the role of a state's Senators in judicial candidate selection, when neither is of the President's party, is secondary to the role of those officials discussed above, who actually choose candidates to recommend to the President. Customarily, in these circumstances, the state's Senators, if they are consulted by state officials of the President's party, are consulted for their reactions to candidates under consideration, but not for their own preferences. Where consultations of this sort are done in good faith, negative as well as positive feedback from the Senators would be welcomed, but typically they would not be called upon to make their own candidate recommendations. [52] As a scholarly study has noted, until recent decades:

> ... senators who were not of the president's party in any given administration played little or no role in district judge selection, except as permitted in informal agreements between senators and any given administration or by the Senate Judiciary Committee through the blue slip. Moreover, that role described above was generally a negative role: a senator who was not of the President's party from the state in which a judicial nominee would serve could delay or prevent confirmation of a nominee by refusing to return the blue slip, but the senator could not compel the President to choose his or her candidates. [53]

The secondary role of Senators in judicial candidate selection in states where both are of the opposition party was stated as formal Administration policy early in Ronald Reagan's presidency. In a March 1981 memorandum on judicial selection procedures, the Department of Justice discussed, among other things, the procedure that would apply in states with no Republican Senators. In these cases, the memorandum said:

> ... the Attorney General will solicit suggestions and recommendations from the Republican members of the congressional delegation, who will act in such instances as a group, in lieu of Senators from their respective states. It is presumed that congressional members in such cases would consult with Democratic Senators from their respective states. [54]

Exceptions to the Customary Model, Where Senators Play a Primary Recommending Role. Sometimes, however, in states having two opposition party Senators, Presidents agree to a more active form of senatorial involvement in judicial selection. In these cases, a more active role for a state's Senators might consist of actually serving as a primary source for judicial candidate recommendations or selecting at least some of the members of an advisory panel or commission, if one is established in cooperation with officials of the President's party to make judicial candidate recommendations.

In recent decades, various Presidents, in a limited number of situations, have allowed a state's Senators, when both were of the opposition party, an involvement in judicial candidate selection entailing more than simply being consulted during the selection process. For example, in states having two opposition party Senators, President John F. Kennedy, a scholar has written, was sometimes inclined to select persons of the opposition party for judicial appointments. In these situation:

> President Kennedy used Republican Minority Leader Everett Dirksen as a liaison between the White House and Republican senators. Dirksen was asked to solicit suggestions from the senators in those states which had two Republican senators, though suggestions of names made directly by the senators were accorded equal treatment. [55]

During the presidency of Gerald R. Ford, a Republican, Florida's two Democratic Senators increased their involvement in the selection of federal district judges in that state — through establishment of a commission to recruit and evaluate judicial candidates. The nine-member Federal Judicial Nominating Commission, which began operations in 1975, was created and chartered by the state of Florida, at the impetus of the two Senators, in conjunction with the state bar association. Under the charter, each of the three sponsors — the two Senators and the bar association — chose one commissioner from each of Florida's three federal judicial districts. [56] After evaluating applicants, the commission was to recommend not fewer than five candidates per vacancy to the Senators, who would then recommend one candidate for each vacancy. [57] In its first year of operation, the commission recommended candidates for nomination for two district court vacancies and one circuit court vacancy. President Ford and the Florida Senators cooperated to fill two of three vacancies with nominees selected from the commission's candidates. [58] In 1976, the second year of the commission's operation, and President Ford's last full year in office, the President continued to accept and select his nominees from the commission's candidates. [59] The Florida commission marked "the first time in more than 135 years" that Senators "who were not in the President's party played a substantial formal role at the stage before the official nominations of persons for district court judgeships." [60]

Other Senators of the opposition party also, on occasion, have successfully bargained for power over judicial patronage. During the presidency of Richard M. Nixon, a Republican, California's two Democratic Senators, it was reported, reached an agreement with the Administration that every third federal judgeship in that state would go to a judicial candidate suggested by the Senators. [61] More recently, in a number of states, the Administration of President William J. Clinton, a Democrat, spent "considerable time," according to one legal scholar, "treating Republican senators' demands that they be involved" in judicial candidate selection. [62] In a few of these states, Republican Senators "insisted that they be permitted to participate in choosing the candidates and even that they [were] entitled to propose nominees." [63]

Most recently, the Republican Administration of President George W. Bush, in a few cases, has accepted a formal role for a state's two Democratic Senators in judicial candidate selection. In at least four instances, the Bush Administration reportedly reached understandings with opposition party Senators to engage in a judicial selection process largely, if not entirely, reliant on candidate recommendations made by judicial nominating commissions from the Senators' states. These understandings were reached when the states involved — California, Florida, Washington, and Wisconsin — were represented by two Democratic Senators. [64]

In each of the aforementioned four states, the role of opposition party Senators in the selection process has entailed more than simply being consulted about possible nominees. In each state, a judicial nominating commission was established prior to, or during, the Bush presidency, to evaluate the qualifications of judicial candidates and to make nominee recommendations — with the Senators, in each case, responsible for selecting at least some of the commission's members. After a commission made its evaluations, its recommendations were forwarded to the Senators for their review. (A commission's recommendations, in some of the states, also were reviewed by House Members of the President's party.) In turn, the Senators were afforded the opportunity to indicate which candidates they preferred, before those names were forwarded to the President. [65]

In another kind of arrangement for a state, officials of the President's party would be the ones recommending judicial candidates, but with the state's opposition party Senators exercising a veto power over any recommendations they found objectionable. Such an arrangement, for instance, according to Illinois's two Democratic Senators, has been in place in their state during the current Bush Administration. [66]

Lesser Role for Senators When Recommending Circuit Court Candidates

Senators in general exert less influence over the selection of circuit court nominees than over selection of district court nominees. Whereas home state

Senators of the President's party often, if not always, dictate whom the President nominates to district judgeships, their recommendations for circuit court nominees, by contrast, typically compete with names suggested to the Administration by other sources or generated by the Administration on its own.

The lesser role for Senators, and the more independent role of the President, in the selection of circuit court nominees is well established by custom. In a landmark 1953 study of the appointment process, the President was said to have "a much freer hand in the selection of judges of the circuit courts of appeal, whose districts cover several states, than of district judges, who serve within individual states." [67] In 1971, during the presidency of Richard M. Nixon, a scholar wrote, "When it comes to making appointments to circuit courts, the balance of power shifts markedly [away from Senators] to favor decision-making by the President's men." [68]

In a 1977 analysis, a former U.S. Senator observed that, while many Senators had the "power" to select district court nominees from their states, "no single senator automatically controls" who is appointed to circuit judgeships. [69] The Senator's statement proved to be an understatement, for during the years of Jimmy Carter's presidency (1977-1980), his Administration relied almost entirely upon a circuit judge nominating commission to identify candidates for circuit court nominations. In so doing, the Administration largely excluded home state Senators of the President's party from the process of recommending persons for circuit judgeships. (The Senators, however, were consulted for their views about the commission's recommendations before President Carter actually selected a nominee.) [70]

President Ronald Reagan disbanded the circuit judge nominating commission created by President Carter, which restored for home state Senators a role in recommending circuit court candidates. [71] The role, however, was not a dominant one, for during the Reagan presidency, one scholar has written, the process for selecting circuit nominees was marked by "tight administration control over the screening process." [72]

At the start of the Clinton presidency, in 1993, a somewhat similar picture was portrayed of Senators playing a subordinate role to the Administration when identifying candidates for circuit court judgeships. In comparison with their role in recommending district court nominees, a report found, Senators were said to "have less influence over the President's selection of nominees to the 12 circuit courts" — with Senators free to "suggest [circuit] candidates to the White House," but with the President "traditionally not bound by such suggestions." [73] At the end of the Clinton presidency, an outgoing Department of Justice official noted that, while Senators usually "pretty much decided" who was nominated for district court judgeships, the appellate court selections were "primarily controlled, decided by the White House and the Justice Department, mostly the White House...." [74]

Subsequently, in the presidency of George W. Bush (2001-present), the role of Senators in recommending circuit court nominees continued, as a general rule, to be less significant than their role in recommending district court nominees: The names of circuit nominees have tended "to be generated more by the Administration" than by Senators, [75] with instances of Senators having President Bush select their candidates for circuit judgeships being exceptions to the rule. [76]

Eleven of the 13 U.S. circuit courts of appeals, [77] it will be recalled, are geographically based courts encompassing three or more states. In each of these circuit courts, many of the seats on the bench have traditionally been linked to a particular state. "And historically, overwhelmingly," one scholar has observed, "the majority of replacement appointments for appeals court vacancies have, indeed, gone to judges from the state in which the vacancy arose."78 Hence, each time one of these judgeships is vacated, Senators of the state involved usually can be expected to cite the tradition of the "state seat" and seek, through their own candidate recommendations, to preserve the judgeship for a nominee from their state.79 For their part, Presidents in recent decades usually, but not always, have been inclined to make a circuit court appointment in keeping with the "state seat" tradition, by selecting a nominee from the same state as the vacating judge. [80]

While Presidents usually observe the traditions of state seats on the circuit courts, in most cases they are not required to do so. A President will be required to select a resident from a particular state for a circuit court vacancy only when necessary to assure that the court is represented by at least one appointee from that state. [81] In all other circumstances, a President is free to appoint a resident from any state within the circuit to a judgeship, in spite of any historical association a particular state might have with the judgeship. This latitude of the President, to select a circuit court nominee from candidates in more than one state, prevents Senators from being able to assert an absolute claim for their state over any circuit judgeship (unless the judgeship's vacancy would leave the Senators' state without representation on the circuit). When a President selects a different state to be represented by a circuit judgeship, he in effect gives the senatorial prerogatives associated with the judgeship to a different pair of Senators.

While Senators usually are not the dominant or decisive players in the process of selecting circuit court nominees, they, nonetheless, do enjoy certain prerogatives in the process. Once a judgeship in a circuit becomes vacant, Senators in states falling within the circuit are free to suggest names to the

President's Administration regarding possible nominees. If the Administration has indicated which state it wants the judgeship to represent — whether in keeping with a traditional state seat or in a break with that tradition — the Senators of that state, if they are of the President's party, customarily are among those who recommend candidates for the judgeship. Senators of the President's party, one authority has written, "expect judgeships on the federal courts of appeals going to persons from their states to be 'cleared' by them...." [82] If the home state Senators are not of the President's party, they nonetheless have expectations — based on the Senate Judiciary Committee's long-standing blue slip policy — that they, too, will be consulted by the Administration for their views about the prospective nominee.

Perhaps the most forceful input Senators can provide to a President's Administration regarding potential circuit court nominees is strong disapproval of a particular candidate from their state. If the candidate is nominated in spite of their objections, the Senators, whether of the President's party or not, will have important Senate traditions in their favor if they decide to oppose the nominee in the Senate. If they are of the President's party, the Senators know (and the Administration will know as well) that they have the tradition of senatorial courtesy to call upon. As one scholar has noted, Senators can invoke senatorial courtesy effectively against a circuit court nominations, provided they are of the President's party and the nominee is a resident of their state. [83] Hence, input from such Senators in forceful opposition to the candidate amounts to a "negative recommendation" that the Administration should take very seriously, to avoid Senate rejection of the candidate based on senatorial courtesy.

Senators who are not of the President's party, by contrast, ordinarily would not be expected to invoke senatorial courtesy to oppose a circuit court nominee from their state. They, however, can take advantage of the Senate Judiciary Committee's blue slip procedure to bolster their opposition. In the event a candidate objectionable to them is nominated, the Senators, as discussed above, may register their disapproval at the committee stage by declining to return a blue slip or returning a negative blue slip to the Judiciary Committee. Such action by a home state Senator, experience has shown, can jeopardize or doom a nomination, depending on the blue slip policy of the committee's chair.

During some chairmanships in recent decades, the policy of the Judiciary Committee has been to allow, in some instances, committee consideration of a judicial nomination receiving a negative blue slip, or no blue slip, from one or both of the nominee's home state Senators. [84] When such a policy is in effect, a Senator's negative blue slip, or failure to return a positive blue slip, does not foreclose the possibility of the committee reporting the nomination to the Senate.

It, however, at the very least, draws the committee's attention to the concerns of the home state Senator and to the question of what degree of courtesy the members of the committee owe that Senator's concerns.

A nomination is much more in jeopardy when the Judiciary Committee policy in effect is not to consider any nomination for which a home state Senator has not returned a positive blue slip. When such is the committee's policy, a home state Senator's opposition to a judicial nomination, through use of the blue slip, eliminates any chance of its being reported out of committee (in effect killing the nomination), unless the Senator can be persuaded to drop his or her opposition.

Accordingly, when both of a state's Senators are of the opposition party and they object to a circuit court candidate from their state, their opposition might persuade the President not to nominate the candidate. In turn, the Senators also might succeed in influencing the President to nominate another individual from their state who is more acceptable to them. However, a President, if dissuaded from nominating the candidate objected to by the Senators, may then consider nominating an individual from another state in the circuit. In the event the President chooses this option, the Administration will no longer have to engage in consultation with the same Senators regarding the vacant judgeship, because they would no longer be the nomination's home state Senators. The home state Senators, with whom the Administration would be expected to consult, would now be the Senators of the state of the new circuit court candidate. [85]

SELECTING JUDICIAL CANDIDATES TO RECOMMEND LEARNING OF THE VACANCY

For a home state Senator, the process of selecting a lower court judicial candidate typically begins when the Senator's office learns that a judgeship is, or soon will become, vacant. A judicial vacancy is created when a judicial officeholder vacates the office (for example, by retirement, resignation, elevation to a higher court, or death) or when legislation is enacted creating a new judgeship. Depending on the circumstances, a current or future judicial vacancy will be brought to the attention of a home state Senator by the outgoing judge, by the Administration, or on the initiative of the Senator's office. The typical practice of circuit and district judges is to give notice of their planned retirements months in advance [86].

Sometimes Senators learn of an upcoming judicial vacancy when a circuit or district judge from their state, as a courtesy, alerts the Senators beforehand of the judge's intention to retire. White House or Department of Justice officials responsible for advising the President on judicial appointments also can be expected to notify a Senator's office of a judicial vacancy in the Senator's state — particularly if the Senator is of the President's party — and to invite the Senator to make recommendations of candidates to fill the judgeship. In this initial contact, or soon thereafter, the Administration might also inform the Senator of its preferences concerning candidates and the selection process: These preferences, for example, might include the number of recommendations the Senator is expected to submit, the qualification standards that the Senator's candidates must meet, and the time frame in which the Senator is expected to submit recommendations to the Administration. Also, in this preliminary outreach to the Senator, the Administration might discuss paperwork requirements, such as the background questionnaires that eventually will have to be filled out by any candidate that the Senator selects.

A Senator, however, does not have to wait to hear from outgoing judges or the Administration to be informed of current or upcoming judicial vacancies. On its own initiative, a Senator's office can visit the federal judiciary's Internet website [87] to identify district and circuit court judgeships which currently are vacant or are scheduled to be vacated in the future. Within the judiciary's website are hypertext links to several vacancy lists, including one of current court vacancies, and another of future court vacancies, both arranged by judicial circuit. [88] In both lists, a Senator or the Senator's staff will readily find, under the heading of the judicial circuit in which the Senator's state is located, any circuit judgeships, as well as any district judgeships within the Senator's state, which are currently vacant or are scheduled to be vacated at a specified future date.

Of course, a Senator is free, if he or she chooses, to initiate a judicial candidate selection process, or to compile a list of prospective judicial candidates, before learning that a judgeship is vacant or scheduled to become vacant. Some Senators, particularly those representing a state having many lower federal court judgeships — where vacancies might be expected to occur periodically — might find it advantageous to be ready at any time, with names of judicial candidates to recommend.

Relationship with the Other Home State Senator

A key variable affecting the role of a Senator in selecting candidates for federal judgeships will be the state's other Senator. As discussed above, the extent to which the two Senators will share the judicial selection role will depend, to a great extent, on their respective prerogatives and interests in this area. One Senator might have more prerogatives to select judicial candidates than the other, particularly if he or she is of the President's party and the other is not. Further, if one Senator has far more experience or expertise in selecting judicial candidates, the other Senator might be inclined to defer to the more senior colleague in recommending persons to federal judgeships. In addition, one Senator might be very interested in the judicial selection process, while the other might, because of other priorities in the Senate, have less interest in this area. If the prerogatives and interests of a state's Senators in selecting judicial candidates are roughly equal (e.g., they are both of the President's party, have about the same amount of Senate seniority, and are both interested in recommending judicial candidates to the President), sharing the candidate selection role in some way seems almost inevitable.

First Option: Only One Senator Would Be Actively Involved in Selecting Judicial Candidates. Within this approach, the other Senator, if he or she wished, could be afforded the opportunity to clear or review any candidate selections, prior to their being recommended to the Administration, as well as to join the selecting Senator in formally recommending candidates. This option might be suitable not only in various situations where only one home state Senator is of the President's party, but also where both Senators are of the President's party yet only one wishes to be actively involved in the judicial selection process.

Second Option: The Two Senators Apportion between Themselves the Selection of Candidates. This option could be taken by alternating the selection role, with the Senators taking turns selecting a candidate each time a lower court vacancy arises in their state. A variation on this approach would be for one Senator to select candidates for a majority of the judgeship vacancies that occur and for the other Senator to select candidates for a minority (for example, for every third or fourth judicial vacancy); this arrangement, as noted earlier, might be suitable in situations where a Senator of the President's party is willing to share the candidate recommending role with a home state Senator of the other party. Also, Senators in states having more than one federal judicial district could apportion between themselves the selection of judicial candidates according to judicial district — for example, with candidates in one district selected by one Senator and candidates in the second district selected by the other Senator.

Third Option: The Two Senators Work Together in Selecting Each Candidate. This arrangement could consist of active involvement of both Senator's offices in each phase, or in most phases, of the candidate selection process, for example, announcing vacancies and inviting candidates to apply, reviewing candidate applications, interviewing applicants, and selecting one or more candidates to recommend to the Administration. Alternately, if the Senators were too busy to involve themselves with each phase of the candidate selection process, and did not wish to assign their personal office staff to selection process tasks, they could delegate much of the selection role to an outside screening committee, panel, or commission. [89] In such a delegated arrangement, the Senators might be most involved in the earliest and latest phases of the selection process — in the beginning, when they would share in appointing members to the screening panel, and at the end of the process, when they both would weigh the panel's candidate recommendations.

Criteria Used to Select Judicial Candidates

Senators might use a number of criteria to determine the fitness of persons from their state who seek to be recommended for U.S. district or U.S. circuit court judgeships. Ordinarily, two sets of criteria can be expected to be most important in governing the Senators' choices — first, the standards explicitly set by the Administration for judicial candidates, and second, the personal criteria that the Senators themselves are inclined to use when deciding whether prospective candidates merit recommendation to the President.

In recent decades, various Presidents have issued guidelines or made public statements regarding the qualification standards that their judicial nominees must meet. Virtually every President has emphasized the importance of a nominee meeting high professional standards and having the ability to be impartial as a judge. At the same time, each President has underscored that judicial nominees must conform with the basic values or ideals that the President believes are inherent in the Constitution, as well as with the President's views of what a judge's fundamental role and priorities should be in our nation's constitutional system. Such perspectives on the Constitution have tended to vary somewhat from one President to the next — with some Presidents, for example, emphasizing the limited role of a judge in our constitutional system (i.e., whose role is to "interpret" rather than to "make" the law) and others emphasizing the role of judges in safeguarding constitutional and legal protections of citizens' rights.

Further, some Presidents also have set various representational standards or goals for Senators to meet when selecting judicial candidates, endorsing, for instance, the goal of increasing the representation of women and persons of minority ethnicity in the lower federal courts. Elaboration of what qualities an administration looks for in judicial candidates also can come from White House or Department of Justice officials who are involved in the judicial selection process.

A Senator seeking to select judicial candidates acceptable to the President will necessarily want to take into account any qualification requirements expressed by the President or other key Administration officials.

Senators also will have their own considerations or criteria to guide them in selecting judicial candidates. Ideally, in nearly all cases, a fundamental starting requirement for a Senator engaged in the search for judicial candidates will be that any person selected have the professional qualifications, integrity, and judicial temperament needed to perform capably as a federal judge. Forming a backdrop to each Senator's search will be "the custom to appoint lawyers who have distinguished themselves professionally — or at least not to appoint those obviously without merit." [90] Accordingly, in many cases, a judicial candidate will, as part of the Senator's selection process, be evaluated or rated by a local or state bar association or some other kind of informal or formal panel of lawyers called upon specifically to evaluate the candidate's professional qualifications. A Senator should be mindful that, once he or she has recommended a judicial candidate to the President, the candidate's qualifications will be closely investigated by Administration personnel involved in advising the President on whether the candidate should be nominated. The nominee's qualifications also will be exhaustively examined by the American Bar Association's Standing Committee on the Federal Judiciary, either in the selection process prior to nomination or immediately after the nomination is made. [91]

Finally, the nomination will be scrutinized yet again, by staff of the Senate Judiciary Committee, upon Senate receipt of the nomination from the President.

Also, a Senator likely will be guided by at least some political party considerations in the judicial candidate search. Traditionally, the overwhelming majority of all federal judicial nominees come from the same party as the nominating President, with more than half of all federal judges having been "'politically active' before their appointments." [92] The tradition of selecting candidates having the same party affiliation as the President is linked to political patronage concerns of home state Senators of the President's party. In this context, a home state Senator in some instances might regard a judgeship recommendation, at least in part, as "a reward for major service" to the party, the President or the Senator. [93] A scholarly study of the judicial appointment process cites two reasons why most nominees for judicial office "must have some record of political activity....":

> First, to some degree judgeships are still considered part of the political patronage system; those who have served the party are more likely to be rewarded with a federal post than those who have not paid their dues. Second,

> even if a judgeship is not given as a direct political payoff, some political activity on the part of a would-be judge is often necessary, because otherwise the candidate would simply not be visible to the president or senators(s) or local party leaders who send forth the names of candidates. If the judicial power brokers have never heard of a particular lawyer because that attorney has no political profile, his or her name will not come to mind when a vacancy occurs on the bench [94]

A Senator also may evaluate the suitability of a judicial candidate according to whether certain groups or constituencies are adequately represented on the district or circuit court in question. Among the representational considerations a Senator might take into account are a candidates's ethnicity, religion, gender, and place of residence. For instance, at the time a particular judicial vacancy occurs, a Senator might be concerned with increasing the representation of a certain ethnic group on that court, to make its membership more representative of the population of the Senator's state, or of that part of the state in which the judicial district is situated. Another concern of the Senator, for example, might be to assure that membership in the district court or courts in the Senator's state represent all of the state's geographic regions.

Senators, as well, may sometimes use philosophical or ideological criteria to evaluate judicial candidates. In applying such criteria, a Senator might be concerned with what values — legal, constitutional, political, social, economic, and philosophical — would underlie a candidate's reasoning and decision making as a judge, and whether, in light of these values, the candidate would approach cases with impartiality or with prejudgment. A Senator also might be concerned with gauging how the candidate ultimately might decide certain kinds of legal or constitutional issues (especially any issues about which the Senator personally feels strongly), or in what general direction the candidate might move a court if joined with judges of similar views. Applying such criteria, a Senator might find a judicial candidate acceptable if his or her orientation appeared sufficiently compatible with the Senator's. The exact philosophical or ideological criteria applied would vary among Senators, reflecting their individual views regarding the courts, the Constitution, and public policy. [95]

Procedures Used to Identify and Evaluate Candidates

Senators have great discretion as to the procedures they will follow in identifying and evaluating candidates for appointment to federal judgeships.

These may range over a wide spectrum of options — from procedures that are extremely informal, unstructured, and totally dependent on a Senator's individual judgment, to those formalized, structured, and reliant on judgments of others beside the Senator. A Senator, for instance, may view his or her role in selecting a judicial candidate as essentially making a personal choice, with any input from others being informal in nature and not in any way limiting the Senator's involvement in the search for candidates. By contrast, at the other end of the spectrum, a Senator may use a formally constituted advisory body of individuals, such as a nominating commission, not only to identify and evaluate judicial candidates, but also to make recommendations that would be binding on the Senator or that the Senator ordinarily would be expected to follow.

A Senator, as well, may take a procedural approach that falls somewhere between the two just described or that has elements of each. For instance, a Senator may use the services of a formal committee of expert advisers to identify and evaluate judicial candidates, but with the understanding that the committee's recommendations are advisory only, and not in any way binding on the Senator. [96]

In a November 12, 2003, floor speech, a Senator illustrated, from his own experience, the discretion and flexibility Senators have to tailor their own personal approach to judicial candidate selection. In the speech, made during an extended Senate debate on judicial nominations, [97] the Senator stated that, over the course of his Senate career, he saw himself as bearing the following responsibility — that if "you are going to make [judicial] recommendations to the President of the United States, do so with care." [98] He described two somewhat different approaches that he had taken during his tenure to identify candidates for lower court judgeships in his state. In the first 25 years of his Senate career, he noted,

> I appointed a nominating committee ... made up principally of very distinguished attorneys and judicial figures for whom I had respect and from all over my state.
>
> I knew these people commanded respect, and they were very helpful in identifying, each time a judicial vacancy occurred, several nominees.
>
> Without fail, I presented all of these nominees to the president, and his staff sifted through them and in each case came up with one of the nominees, frequently the one recommended first by the panel. [99]

In 2002, however, upon learning that two U.S. district court judges in his state would be retiring, the Senator took a different approach to identifying judicial candidates. [100] On this occasion, he said, he wrote letters to the press throughout his state. In the letters, he outlined all the of the qualifications he saw needed for a federal judge and invited "every well-qualified person to apply." Over the course of four months, "15 serious candidates emerged." After reading all of their applications, he interviewed five of the candidates — with a principal interest in their professional skills, as well as in their "characterization of how they would fulfill their responsibilities." From the five interviewed candidates, the Senator submitted three names to the White House, and two of those persons were nominated by the President (and subsequently confirmed by the Senate). [101]

As mentioned above, another option for Senators is to delegate all or some of their power to evaluate and recommend candidates for federal judgeships to judicial nominating commissions (sometimes also referred to as "merit commissions"). Such commissions are ordinarily created by Senators for the specifically stated purpose of identifying and recommending highly qualified persons for federal judicial appointment. [102] While the structure and operations of nominating commissions vary, most have the following features in common:

- They have been formally, and publicly, constituted by one or both of their state's Senators (or by predecessor Senators of their state).
- They have a specific number of members, who have been publicly identified.
- Each commission has a clearly defined mission.
- Each publishes notices of judicial vacancies and invites applicants.
- The applicants fill out a standard application form or questionnaire and are evaluated according to procedures that are the same for each application.
- Applications must be submitted, and the commission's evaluation of applications completed, by specified deadlines.
- The commission recommends not one but several candidates for a judicial position (forwarding the names either to the home state Senators or directly to the President).
- Typically, commission memberships include prominent attorneys in the state or local bar, and sometimes leaders of other community groups, and they often, if not always, represent both political parties. [103]

The advent of widespread use of nominating commissions to identify candidates for federal judgeships came with the presidency of Jimmy Carter, who, at the start of his Administration in 1977, urged every Democratic senator to establish a commission for the selection of candidates for U.S. district judge positions. [104] By 1980, the last full year of the Carter presidency, senatorial commissions were operating in 31 states. [105]

Although President Reagan in 1981 disbanded the commission created by President Carter to identify circuit court candidates, [106] his Attorney General urged Republican Senators to use commissions (as Democratic Senators had done during the previous four years) to screen candidates for district court judgeships. [107] While senatorial use of nominating commissions is no longer widespread, a Brookings Institution study in November 2007 reported that "[t]oday, 16 senators in eight states use them; in five both senators are Democrats." The study found that most of the present-day commissions had bipartisan memberships, a circumstance attributed to political necessity:

> Bipartisan commission membership is essential in this period of polarized politics, with both majority and minority senators ready and able to contest nominations. Realizing this, the Democratic senators who use commissions today appoint some Republican members, named either by themselves or by state Republican leaders, similar to what Republican senators did during the Carter administration. [108]

Senators who use nominating commissions to identify and evaluate judicial candidates often, if not always, require their commissions to follow clearly defined rules of procedure. In Wisconsin, where its two Democratic Senators have chartered a commission to advise them in the selection of candidates to fill U.S. district court vacancies in that state — as well as for vacancies for U.S. attorneys in Wisconsin and U.S. circuit court judgeships "which are appropriately considered Wisconsin seats" — the charter lays out the rules of procedure in detail. The charter provides that the commission shall consist of 11 members in the case of district court and U.S. attorney vacancies, or 12 members in the case of a circuit court vacancy. The number of members that each Senator may appoint to the commission varies, depending on whether the Senator is of the same political party as the President. [109] When a court vacancy occurs, the charter provides specific timetables for seeking candidates and accepting applications, as well as for evaluating the candidates' qualifications. Further, the charter sets organizational and voting procedures for the commission's members, including a quorum requirement and the number of affirmative votes required to recommend a candidate for nomination. Finally, it states that after the commission has designated not less than four nor more than six individuals as best qualified to fill a vacancy, the commission shall immediately notify the state's Senators as to the names of the individuals. [110]

In the above example, use of a nominating commission can be seen as largely removing Senators from the initial search for judicial candidates as well as from the evaluation of all of the candidates who initially submit applications. The arrangement, however, retains for the Senators the opportunity to evaluate the smaller number of applicants who ultimately are recommended by the commission. Further, the Senators are not required by the language of the commission's charter to forward to the President every commission recommendation that they receive. Absent a commitment to be bound by a merit panel's recommendations, Senators retain the discretion to further inquire, on their own, into the qualifications of persons recommended by the commission and to pass along to the President only those recommendations that they find acceptable. [111]

Interaction with Administration during Nominee Selection Process

Administration Entities and Their Roles

In every presidential Administration in recent decades, there has been an office assigned principal responsibility for consulting with Senators regarding judicial appointments in their state. When a federal judgeship in a Senator's state becomes vacant, or there is the imminent prospect of a vacancy occurring, a frequent scenario will find the Senator or top aides to the Senator in contact with, or contacted by, this office. In some recent Administration, the role of consulting with Senators about judicial appointments was performed primarily by officials in the Department of Justice. During the presidency of George W. Bush, however, the White House counsel's office has played the primary liaison role with Senators regarding judicial appointments. [112] As the primary consultative link with Senators, it is this office that ordinarily receives Senators' recommendations of specific individuals for judicial appointment.

In recent presidencies, the task of evaluating the background and qualifications of judicial candidates has been performed by an informal committee of staff persons from the White House counsel's office and the Department of Justice. The committee, aided by the research of subordinate White House or DOJ staff, as well as by investigations of the Federal Bureau of Investigation (FBI) into the backgrounds of judicial candidates, decides which candidates to recommend to the President for nomination. In recent presidencies, the selection process has consisted of a number of basic preliminary steps, including, for any given Administration, all or nearly all of the following:

- At the outset, the names of judicial nominee candidates are identified (as recommended by Senators or others outside the Administration or as generated from within the Administration).
- The candidates fill out various forms and questionnaires, including a personal background information form for the FBI, a financial disclosure form, a White House questionnaire, and a questionnaire from the Senate Judiciary Committee. (Sometimes, the Administration waits until it has narrowed down the nominee search to one candidate, requiring only that candidate to fill out the aforementioned forms.)
- An initial evaluation (or "preliminary vetting") of the candidates is conducted, which includes interviewing some or all of the candidates (either by phone or in person) and reviewing publicly available information about them (such as their published writings and news media accounts of their past activities in public life). [113]
- The candidates also might, or might not, be asked by the Administration to fill out a questionnaire of an American Bar Association committee, which evaluates and rates the professional qualifications of nominees for federal judgeships. [114]
- The search is narrowed down to one candidate, who is recommended to the President for more intensive evaluation;
- The President clears the candidate for this more intensive evaluation, known as "detailed vetting."

The detailed vetting phase of the selection process, for any given Administration in recent decades, has included all, or nearly all, of the following steps:

- The FBI conducts a confidential background investigation of the candidate, which typically takes four to six weeks.
- The ABA Standing Committee on the Federal Judiciary, if informed by the Administration of the candidate under consideration (and upon receipt of an ABA questionnaire filled out by the candidate) also conducts an investigation of the candidate.115
- Simultaneously with the FBI investigation (and with the ABA committee investigation as well, if that committee is involved in the pre-nomination

selection process), executive branch staff from the Department of Justice or the White House or both carefully review the candidate's written opinions or other legal writings (depending on whether the candidate is a judge or a practicing attorney), as well as the forms and questionnaires filled out by the candidate, and interview persons in the legal community who have had past contact with, or have knowledge about, the candidate.

- A follow-up interview of the candidate is conducted (either in person or by telephone) to address any new questions or confirm new information arising out of the detailed vetting process.
- Judicial selection staff in the Administration evaluate the results of the detailed vetting effort and recommend to the President whether to nominate the candidate.

In the Administration of President George W. Bush, the above steps in the selection process have been directed by a judicial selection committee consisting of staff from the White House counsel's office and the Department of Justice's Office of Legal Policy (OLP). Under the committee's direction, OLP staff have had primary responsibility for investigating the background and qualifications of prospective nominees. The sole responsibility for liaison with U.S. Senators, on the other hand, has resided with the White House counsel's office. Staff in this office receive input from Senators regarding judicial candidates and consult with Senators or their staff at different steps in the judicial candidate evaluation process. Consultation can be expected to include apprising Senators of the status of their recommended candidates and indicating how far along the Administration has progressed in narrowing its search for a nominee.

Clarifying the Senator's Role

Initial contacts between an administration and a Senator's office regarding judicial appointments can be expected to clarify the nature of the Senator's recommending role. [116] A principal question to be addressed in these contacts will be the degree to which the Administration, in its judicial candidate search, will rely on recommendations from the Senator. The Senator, for instance, will want to know whether the Administration will give sole or primary consideration to candidates that the Senator recommends for a particular judgeship — and, further, whether the Administration, if not comfortable with the Senator's candidates, will seek, and rely primarily on, additional recommendations from the Senator (rather than on recommendations coming from others). This role typically might be expected when the Senator is the only Senator in the state of the President's party, or if the state's other Senator is also of the President's party and the two are making joint recommendations, and if the vacancy to be filled is on a district court.

Under different circumstances, however, the Administration, might intend the Senator to have a lesser role. The Administration, for example, might welcome recommendations from the Senator, while also encouraging recommendations from other sources and while conducting its own search for candidates. This role might often be the case if the Senator is of the President's party but the appointment in question would be to a circuit court. In a third type of arrangement, it might be understood that the Senator would not be regarded as a primary source for candidate recommendations; however, as a courtesy, the Administration would consider any recommendations the Senator might make, apprise the Senator of judicial candidates under serious consideration, and invite the Senator's opinions about those candidates before one were selected as a nominee. This often might be the case when the Senator is of the opposition party, regardless of the kind of judgeship in question, and sometimes might be the case when the Senator is of the President's party and the appointment in question is to a circuit court.

Another question to be addressed in preliminary consultations between a Senator's office and the Administration will be the number of persons, if any, that the Senator is expected to recommend for a single judicial vacancy. In recent presidencies, the Administration practice usually has been to request that a Senator supply the names of at least three candidates for a judgeship, affording the President more options in making a final choice than would be possible with only one candidate under consideration. If multiple recommendations are requested by the Administration, a Senator might wish to establish whether this is a preference or a requirement. If a requirement, the Senator might wish to inquire into the Administration's possible willingness to initially evaluate only the Senator's first choice and, if finding that choice acceptable, to dispense with evaluating the other recommended candidates. [117]

Also a topic of possible discussion would be the Senator's relationship with the other state's Senator and the extent to which the two Senators would be coordinating or sharing the role as recommender. If one Senator would be taking the lead, to what extent would that Senator, or Administration officials, assume the responsibility for consulting with the other Senator regarding the search for, and evaluation of, judicial candidates? If an advisory panel were to be used, would it serve that Senator alone, or would the panel's recommendations, before being forwarded to the Administration, be cleared by the other Senator as well? If neither Senator were of the President's party, would designated officials in the President's party having a judicial recommendation role in that state be making recommendations to the Administration in close consultation with the Senators or apart from them?

The long-standing practice of presidential administrations ordinarily has been to give the primary recommending function to Senators of the President's party (or to House Members or state officials of the President's party when there are no Senators from the states of the vacancies) if the vacancy to be filled is that of a district judgeship. For circuit court nominations, by contrast, the Administration's usual practice (especially so with the most recent presidencies) has been to center its consideration on candidates whom it selected on its own, rather than on persons recommended by home state Senators [118].

An administration, however, sometimes might be amenable to altering its usual practices. It might, for example, be amenable to allowing home state Senators not of the President's party, in some circumstances, a greater than usual role in recommending district court candidates, or to allowing home state Senators of either party a greater than usual role in identifying circuit court candidates for the Administration to consider. Further, even if afforded only a marginal role in recommending candidates at the outset, a home state Senator, regardless of party affiliation, ordinarily can expect to be consulted by the Administration subsequently during the selection process. The typical purpose of such consultation will be to apprise the Senator of candidates that the Administration is seriously considering and to afford the Senator an opportunity to express his or her views concerning the candidates [119].

Accordingly, a home state Senator presumably will want to use his or her initial contact with the Administration, at the very least, to clarify the Administration's general policy regarding the recommending role of Senators in the selection of lower court nominees. In some cases, the Senator, during this initial or subsequent contact, might also wish to explore whether he or she can play a larger recommending role than ordinarily contemplated by Administration policy. Further, the Senator might want to clarify, when a home state judicial vacancy arises, how often and for what purpose the Administration would intend to consult with the Senator until a nominee were actually selected.

Consultation at Different Stages of the Process

Consultation between a Senator and the Administration over the selection of a judicial nominee can take different forms, depending on the stage reached in the selection process. Early in the process, as already noted, consultation may consist primarily of the Senator providing input to the Administration. The input in many cases will be in the nature of recommending a particular candidate or list of candidates for a judgeship. If providing more than one name, the Senator might or might not rank the candidates in order of the Senator's preferences. The input in some cases might also take a negative form, with the Senator expressing opposition to particular candidates or kinds of candidates. (A Senator might provide this kind of input if he or she understood that the Administration would be relying on its own internally generated list of candidates or on recommendations from sources other than the Senator).

In some instances, a Senator may convey recommendations directly to the President — for example, in an in-person meeting, by telephone, or by letter — without White House or senatorial staff functioning as intermediaries. A Senator, or an aide on the Senator's behalf, also may submit recommendations to the President indirectly, by transmitting them, for example, in written or other form to the Administration office charged with serving as liaison to Senators on judicial appointment questions.

As the selection process moves forward, the onus for engaging in further consultation shifts to the Administration, to apprise the home state Senator where things stand. The point at which this first occurs may vary somewhat, depending on the particular judicial position to be filled or on the understandings reached earlier between the Administration and the Senator. Often, however, renewed consultation can be said to come when the Administration is close to concluding, or has concluded, its preliminary evaluation of a candidate or candidates for a judgeships. Based in part on its interviews of the various candidates (if there is more than one candidate) and on a preliminary examination of the available record of the candidates, the Administration at some point will be in a position to apprise the home state Senator whether one candidate has emerged as the clear favorite.

Various policy statements made in recent decades by chairs of the Senate Judiciary Committee have expressed the view that home state Senators should be informed when an administration has narrowed its list of candidates for a judgeship to one candidate. The expectation of the policy statements has been that the home state Senators will be so apprised before the President approves that candidate for a more intensive "formal clearance" — before the candidate undergoes a complete FBI background investigation and other aspects of the "detailed vetting" process discussed earlier. If the Administration is considering the selection of someone other than a candidate recommended by the Senator, the Administration at this point may apprise the Senator of this fact, affording the

Senator an opportunity to express any opinions or concerns about the candidate, including whether the Senator might oppose the candidate if nominated. In some instances, a preliminary review of candidates recommended by a Senator might result in the Administration deciding that none would be acceptable. At that point the Senator might be called on to provide additional recommendations for the Administration to consider (or, perhaps less often, be informed that Administration staff have decided on a candidate of their own to recommend to the President).

If a judicial candidate under consideration for "formal clearance" is a person recommended by the home state Senator, such clearance, when it occurs, of course, ordinarily will meet with the Senator's wholehearted approval. The subsequent "vetting" of the candidate, as already discussed, will involve a comprehensive FBI investigation of the candidate and might also include a review of the candidate's past rulings or legal writings, and the questionnaires he or she filled out, as well as an initial or follow-up interview of the candidate, and interviews of persons in the legal community who have had past contact with, or knowledge about, the candidate. During this investigation, Administration consultation with the home state Senator might entail little more than providing routine status reports on the progress of the clearance process, particularly if nothing problematic about the candidate is found.

By contrast, if a candidate under consideration for formal clearance has not been recommended by a home state Senator, subsequent Administration consultation with the Senator might, or might not, take place at several points. If it acts in keeping with the kind of consultative process called for in past policy statements of the Judiciary Committee, the Administration might notify the Senator that it is preparing to begin a formal clearance process for a particular candidate, affording the Senator an opportunity to provide feedback, before it actually initiates the clearance process. Subsequently, if the Senator, in providing feedback, objects to the candidate, the Administration, might in turn, as a courtesy (and in accord with past Judiciary Committee policy statements), notify the Senator that the formal clearance process is being initiated despite the Senator's objections.

If, at the conclusion of the clearance process, the President decides to nominate the candidate, consultation again can be expected, particularly if the home state Senators are of the President's party. Specifically, the Administration, if it acts in keeping with past Judiciary Committee statements, will notify home state Senators (whether or not they recommended the person involved) before the nomination is actually made. The Administration, however, is not obliged, by any rule or longstanding custom, to engage in all of the consultative steps just discussed. In the absence of any requirements to engage in pre-nomination consultation, a President's Administration might not always notify home state Senators of judicial candidates it is considering.

When a Nominee Is Selected against the Advice of, or without Consulting, a Senator

Sometimes, as noted, a President might select a district or circuit court nominee against the advice of one or both home state Senators. On other occasions, the Administration might provide a home state Senator little or no opportunity to provide any feedback before a candidate is selected by the President as a judicial nominee. In either situation, the Senator will then face the question of whether to oppose the nomination, either first in the Senate Judiciary Committee or later on the Senate floor.

Option of Opposing the Nomination in Committee or on the Senate Floor

From the standpoint of a Senator, opposition to a lower court nomination in his or her state may serve a number of purposes, including the following:

- Preventing confirmation. The Senator's opposition, if successful, will prevent the nomination from receiving Senate confirmation. Opposition by the Senator will succeed if it causes the nomination to fail to be reported out of committee or to receive Senate consideration or a Senate vote to confirm.
- Averting a similar kind of nomination. Successful opposition to the President's nominee (preventing Senate confirmation) might dissuade the President from making a new nomination to the judgeship of someone else as objectionable to the Senator as the original nominee.
- Causing the Administration to take consultation more seriously. A Senator's opposition to a judicial nominee, based all or in part on an alleged lack of Administration consultation with the Senator, might persuade the Administration to consult more closely with the Senator when selecting future home state judicial nominees.

- Preserving the appointment for a later President or Congress. Successful opposition to the judicial nomination might, in some situations, delay the filling of the judgeship in question until a new President is in office or until a new Congress is convened (where, in either case, the Senator might have more influence over the selection of home state judicial appointments).
- Drawing attention to policy differences with the Administration. The inability of the Administration and the Senator to agree on a judicial nominee might suggest that they have different policy objectives for judicial appointments, or use different criteria in evaluating judicial candidates. In such situations, a Senator might wish to publicize, rather than conceal, these differences, to promote his or her own policy preferences and call those of the Administration into question.

If the Senator decides to oppose the nomination, the first available recourse will be to exercise the prerogatives afforded to a home state Senator by the blue slip policy of the Senate Judiciary Committee. As already discussed, the blue slip policy determines what effect the disapproval of a home state Senator (indicated by the return to the committee of a negative blue slip or by the non-return of the blue slip) will have on the prospects for a nomination to be considered by the committee. The blue slip policy is set by the chair of the Judiciary Committee, usually at the outset of a Congress. Over the years, particularly when the majority party in the Senate has changed (resulting in a new chair of the Judiciary Committee), or when an outgoing President has been succeeded by a President of the opposite party, the committee's blue slip policy also has changed — sometimes barely noticeably, but other times in more controversial ways.

The most important difference between various blue slip policies applied over the years, it can be argued, concerns whether, under a particular policy, a home state Senator may block committee consideration of a nomination simply by returning a negative blue slip (one expressing opposition to the nomination) or declining to return the blue slip. The blue slip policy of some committee chairs, including the one in effect during the 110th Congress, has been to afford that basic veto power to the home state Senator. When the committee's policy is to consider a nomination only if both home state Senators have returned positive blue slips, a refusal of one of the Senators to do so will block the nomination. The Senator, in such a situation, might initially have been unsuccessful in trying to prevent the President from nominating a particular person. Nevertheless, under the committee policy in effect in the 110th Congress, the Senator ultimately can succeed in preventing Senate confirmation of the nominee, by using the Judiciary Committee's blue slip procedure to stop the nomination in committee.

The policy of some other chairs of the committee, by contrast, has been not to allow a negative blue slip, or non-return of a blue slip, by itself to automatically block consideration of the nomination in committee. For instance, the policy sometimes has been applied to allow consideration of a judicial nomination when one or even (in very rare instances) both home state Senators have declined to return positive blue slips, or to allow a negative or unreturned blue slip to block committee consideration only if the Administration, in the view of the committee chair, did not consult in good faith with a home state Senator prior to selecting the nominee. [120]

When the Judiciary Committee's blue slip policy is not to allow a single home state Senator to block committee consideration of a lower court nominee, the next recourse available to the Senator is to convey to the committee his or her objections about the nominee, if and when it considers the nomination. The Senator might have objections based on concerns about the fitness of the nominee to be a federal judge, or about the nature or lack of consultation that the Administration engaged in with the Senator prior to the selection of the nominee. The Senator might wish to convey these concerns as an argument to the committee against voting on the nominee or, in the event of a vote, that the vote be to reject. Even if the Senator anticipates that the committee will vote to report the nomination, the Senator might wish to put his or her concerns about the nominee on record with the committee, to set the stage for making the same case again, before the full Senate.

Another tactical option for the Senator will be to try to persuade one or more members of the Judiciary Committee to engage in a filibuster in committee — in an effort to prevent the committee from voting on the nomination. [121] Rule IV of the Judiciary Committee's rules of procedure provides that debate on a matter before the committee shall be terminated if a non-debatable motion is made to bring the matter "to a vote without further debate," and it "passes with ten votes in the affirmative, one of which must be cast by the minority." [122] Depending on how the chair of the Judiciary Committee interprets Rule IV, a Senator opposing a nomination might, or might not, succeed in preventing a committee vote on it (and thus block it in committee). The Senator will succeed in a filibuster against the nominee, for instance, if none of the minority members of the Judiciary Committee votes in favor of a motion to terminate debate and if the chair of the committee interprets Rule IV as "providing the minority with a right not to have debate terminated and not to be forced to a vote without at least one member of the minority agreeing." [123] The Senator, however, will not succeed, if the chair wishes to bring the nomination to a vote and views the committee chair as having "the inherent power to bring a matter to a vote." [124]

If the Judiciary Committee votes to report the objected-to nomination, the home state Senator's opposition strategy then shifts to the Senate floor. At this point, the Senator, if so inclined, may inform his or her party leader that the Senator wants to place a "hold" on the nomination. This action would have the effect of preventing or delaying Senate action on the nomination, if the majority leader honors the request for a hold. Alternately, the Senator may request the leader to place a hold on another nomination or on an important Administration-backed bill, in order to pressure the President to withdraw the objected-to nomination. The effectiveness of the hold is grounded in the difficulty for the Senate, under its rules, of getting to a final vote on a nomination if a single Senator objects. Such an objection, voiced on behalf of the home state Senator, would indicate that a hold had been placed on the nomination [125] and that the Senator placing the hold might be prepared to filibuster the nomination. [126] To end delay on the nomination and allow for an eventual vote on it may require three-fifths of the entire Senate membership, or 60 of 100, to vote in the affirmative under the cloture procedure of Senate Rule XXII. [127]

As long as the Senate majority leader honors the hold placed by the home state Senator, the nomination will not receive floor consideration. [128] (The Senator's hold will prevent confirmation if it succeeds in pressuring the President to withdraw the nomination or if it is honored by the majority leader until an adjournment of the Senate for more than 30 days, at which point, under Senate rules, the nomination may be returned to the President.) However, if the majority leader decides to schedule action on the nomination, the Senator must decide whether to filibuster it (as well as whether to enlist the support of other Senators in this effort). For their part, Senators supporting the nomination, in response to a filibuster (or in anticipation of one), may file a cloture petition (signed by 16 Members) to end debate. If three-fifths of the Senate's membership votes in favor of cloture, a maximum of 30 hours of additional debate on the nomination would remain. After 30 hours, unless less time were used, the Senate would vote on whether to confirm.

The success of a Senator's strategy to defeat the nomination by filibuster will be determined by the Senate's vote on any cloture motion that might be filed. [129] If fewer than three-fifths of the Senate's Members vote to invoke cloture, the Senator (and other Senators voting against cloture) will have succeeded in preventing a Senate vote on the nomination, at least at that time.

Option of Not Opposing the Nomination

Sometimes, a home state Senator might choose not to oppose a judicial nominee selected by the President with little apparent regard for the views of the Senator during the nominee selection process. Various considerations might influence the Senator to take this position.

One consideration for not opposing the nominee might be the desirability of filling the vacant judgeship in question as promptly as possible. To successfully oppose the nomination in the Judiciary Committee or the full Senate would compel the President to make a new nomination for the judgeship at a later point in time. The Senator's opposition, in other words, would prolong the time in which the judgeship was vacant. Hence, a Senator, in some situations, might consider filling the vacancy with a nominee in whom he or she found fault (or about whom the Senator had been inadequately consulted) to be a "lesser evil" than prolonging the vacancy indefinitely by successfully opposing the nominee in the Senate.

In some situations, another consideration for not opposing a nomination might be the nominee's qualifications for the judgeship — particularly if the nominee appeared highly qualified. This consideration, it could be argued, might be a reason for a Senator not to oppose the nominee unless the Senator thought his or her own candidate search would likely produce an even more qualified nominee.

A Senator also might not wish to oppose a particular nomination if it might project to the public a picture of the Senator as "obstructionist" or unduly antagonistic in relation to the Administration. Particularly, under certain circumstances, opposing a President's judicial nomination might be seen as unduly negative. For instance, if the Senator's objections to the nominee are purely procedural in nature (in essence, that the Administration afforded the Senator little or no opportunity to provide input prior to the candidate's being nominated), the Senator might see the merits of opposing the nominee on these grounds as outweighed if the Senator finds no fault with the nominee and if the public is also likely to look favorably or sympathetically upon the nominee.

Sometimes a consideration not to oppose a home state judicial nomination might be the likelihood of more judicial vacancies arising in the Senator's state in the near future. A Senator might see these future vacancies as providing a better opportunity for exerting senatorial influence over judicial appointments than is possible by opposing someone whom the President has already nominated. Further, by not opposing a particular home state nomination, the Senator might be in a position to gain goodwill with the Administration, from which the latter might well be moved to afford the Senator a more enhanced role in the selection process for future home state judicial nominees.

A final consideration for not actively opposing a judicial nominee is that this option would not necessarily preclude the Senator from expressing criticisms of the current nominee or of the process used in his or her selection. While refraining from opposing the nominee, the Senator would be free to call on the Administration to "do better" with its next judicial nomination from the Senator's state. The Senator also could suggest ways of improving the consultative process between the Senator and the Administration in the search for future lower court nominees, as well as the kind of qualities that the Senator deemed important for the future nominees to possess. This approach, it could be argued, would put the Administration on notice that public criticism of, and possible opposition to, the next judicial nominee from that state could be expected, if more attention were not paid in the future to the Senator's views during the nominee selection process.

Current Issues and Concluding Observations

Wide Acceptance of Importance of Pre-Nomination Consultation

Home state Senators have long played an important role in providing advice to Presidents on judicial appointments. Historically Presidents have generally been more receptive to such advice when it has come from Senators of their own party rather than of the opposition party. Nevertheless, presidential administrations have long recognized that pre-nomination consultation with opposition party home state Senators also is important, serving, at the very least, as a means to learn Senators' views about potential nominees (and whether they would be likely to return positive blue slips to the Judiciary Committee if certain candidates were nominated).

In recent decades, despite periodic controversies over judicial nominations, the idea that there should be consultation on judicial appointments between an administration and home state Senators, regardless of their party, appears to have gained widespread acceptance. As discussed earlier, various chairs and other members of the Judiciary Committee, in correspondence with the White House between 1989 and 2001, declared the importance of such consultation. [130] Specifically, these letters expressed the expectation that the Administration engage in consultation with home state Senators of both parties that is "in good faith," "serious," and two- way. Senators, the letters said, should not only provide feedback on judicial candidates under Administration consideration but also have the opportunity to make their own candidate recommendations. The letters also called for consultation to include a number of specified sequential steps, to keep Senators informed and involved throughout the Administration's judicial selection process. Recent administrations have not publicly challenged these expectations; indeed, the White House counsel to President George W. Bush, in a 2001 letter, indicated his general acceptance of them. [131]

Recent Controversies over Administrations' Consultation with Senators

During the nation's two most recent presidencies, however, Senators, usually of the opposition party, have sometimes questioned the adequacy of Administration consultation with home state Senators in the lower court selection process. In 1997, for instance, during the presidency of William J. Clinton, Senator Orrin G. Hatch (R- UT), then-chairman of the Judiciary Committee, drew attention to questions that he said had been raised about the Clinton Administration's "level of consultation" with home state Senators on lower court appointments:

> While we are on the subject of judicial nominations, I would like to respond to some of my colleagues who have come to me to express their frustration that they have not received the level of consultation that they have expected, and typically received, regarding nominees from their states. It has long been the policy of the Senate, and of the Committee, that a fair, efficient and cooperative confirmation process is best achieved when the Executive Branch engages in genuine, good faith consultation with home state senators in the process of determining whom to nominate for judicial positions. [132]

Several years later, Senator Hatch, who had been chairman of the Judiciary Committee during the last six years of the Clinton Administration, explained what had happened to some of the judges nominated by President Clinton who were not confirmed. "Seventeen of those," Senator Hatch said, "lacked home state support, which often resulted from the White House's failure to consult with home state senators. There was no way to confirm those nominations without completely ignoring the senatorial courtesy we afford to home state Senators in the nomination process." [133]

During the current presidency of George W. Bush, Senators, mostly along party lines, have periodically debated whether the Administration has adequately consulted with home state Senators before President Bush selected his nominees.

Democratic leaders in the Senate have asserted that the Bush Administration frequently has not consulted with, or heeded the advice of, their party's home state Senators before the President made judicial nominations. As a result of not receiving senatorial input, or receiving but not heeding it, the President, they maintained, has made unwise, controversial nominations, provoking Democratic opposition in the Senate. [134] Senate Republicans, by contrast, have defended the Bush Administration, portraying it as having regularly consulted with Senators regarding judicial nominations in their states, while faulting opposition party Senators for seeking, through the consultative process, the power to select whom the President nominates, rather than solely making recommendations or expressing opinions about candidates under presidential consideration [135]

During two Congresses coinciding with the Bush presidency (the 108th and the 109th) Congresses), the President's party, the Republicans, had majority control of the Senate. During the 108th Congress, the blue slip policy of the Senate Judiciary Committee then in effect did not prevent committee consideration of, or action on, five circuit court nominations that were ultimately reported to the Senate in spite of opposition by Democratic home state Senators. [136] In the Senate, however, in the face of significant opposition from Democratic Members, none of the five nominees received final confirmation votes [137] (although three were subsequently confirmed, during the 109th Congress). [138] Also during the 108th Congress, long-running consultations between the White House and one state's Democratic Senators failed to reach an agreement over whom from that state to nominate for circuit judgeships. The President was criticized by Senate Democrats, [139] but defended by Senate Republicans, [140] for not agreeing to a proposal offered by the two home state Senators as a compromise. Under their proposal, a bipartisan judicial nomination commission would be established, with the President selecting circuit court nominees from names recommended by the commission.

During the 109th Congress, with Republicans again in the Senate majority (but with the Judiciary Committee under a different chair), no instances were reported of district or circuit nominations receiving committee action in the absence of favorable blue slips returned to the committee by home state Senators. Senate Republicans and Democrats, however, clashed over other judicial nominations and over the propriety of using filibusters on the Senate floor to prevent Senate votes on those nominations. [141] In May 2005, leaders of the Senate's Republican majority announced their intention, if Senate Democrats continued to seek to prevent confirmation votes on several circuit court nominees, to change the chamber's rules or precedents to require the vote of only a simple Senate majority to end Senate debate on judicial nominations. [142]

A Senate confrontation over judicial filibusters was averted on May 23, 2005, when an agreement was reached by a coalition of seven Democratic and seven Republican Senators. As part of the agreement, the Senators in the coalition pledged not to lend their support to filibusters against judicial nominations except under "extraordinary circumstances," and not to support any change in the Senate rules to bar filibusters against judicial nominations, as long as the "spirit and continuing commitments made in this agreement" were kept by all of the Senators in the coalition. [143] As a result of this agreement, some, but not all, of the President's most controversial circuit court nominations, which previously had been blocked on the Senate floor, were confirmed [144].

The agreement, in the form of a "memorandum of understanding," also called on the President to consult with Senators, regardless of their party, on prospective judicial candidates. Specifically, on this point, the memorandum stated:

> We believe that, under Article II, Section 2, of the United States Constitution, the word "Advice" speaks to consultation between the Senate and the President with regard to the use of the President's power to make nominations. We encourage the Executive branch of government to consult with members of the Senate, both Democratic and Republican, prior to submitting a judicial nomination for consideration.
>
> Such a return to the early practices of our government may well serve to reduce the rancor that unfortunately accompanies the advice and consent process of the Senate [145].

Throughout most of the first Congress coinciding with his presidency (the 107th), President Bush's party was not the majority party in the Senate, and it is not the majority party in the 110th Congress. In the Judiciary Committee during the 107th Congress, five lower court nominees opposed by home state Senators were among a larger number whose nominations did not advance to the committee hearing stage. [146] Likewise, under the blue slip policy in effect in the 110th Congress, the Judiciary Committee will not consider or act on a judicial nomination if a home state Senator declines to return a positive blue slip. [147] Further, the chairman of the Judiciary Committee, on various occasions, has criticized President Bush for failing to "work with" Senators of several specified states in making judicial nominee selections for those states [148] and for selecting nominees who have not received support from their home state Senators in the form of positive blue slips [149].

In another instance during the 110th Congress, the President has nominated someone to a circuit judgeship who was not on the list of five candidates recommended jointly to the judgeship by the two home state Senators, one a

Republican and the other a Democrat. (The nominee, however, had been on the list of candidates recommended by the Republican Senator earlier, in the 109th Congress.) Immediately, upon announcement of the nomination, the two Senators criticized the White House for ignoring their recommendations,150 with the Democratic Senator reportedly stating there was "no way" he would return a positive blue slip to the committee needed for Judiciary Committee consideration of the nomination. [151] Eventually, the nominee, citing "press reports" that he was unlikely to receive a hearing before the Judiciary Committee, requested that President Bush withdraw his nomination [152].

Specific Issues Concerning the Recommending Role of Home State Senators

In recent years, the role to be played by home state Senators in the selection process for lower court judges has periodically been the subject of debate. Specific issues concerning the Senators' recommending role have included the following:

What Constitutes "Good Faith" or "Serious" Consultation? Various Judiciary Committee policy statements, discussed earlier, have prescribed specific consultative steps between an administration and home state Senators as requisite elements in consultation conducted seriously and in good faith. The statements, however, did not address how seriously the Administration should consider the Senators' judicial candidate recommendations or their objections to other candidates under Administration consideration. In various controversies over particular judicial nominations during the Bush presidency, Democratic home state Senators asserted that the Bush Administration did not engage in good faith, serious consultation with them during the judicial nominee selection process, an assertion denied by the Administration. The Administration view, in these controversies, appeared to be that it engaged in good faith, serious consultation with a home state Senator on judicial nominations if it considered the input of a Senator, even if it ultimately made a decision (in the selection of a judicial nominee) contrary to the Senator's express wishes. On the other side, by contrast, the view of opposition party Senators appeared to be that good faith, serious consultation was shown not to have occurred when the President selected a judicial nominee over their strong objections or with evident disinterest in candidates that they might have proposed.

Should Home State Senators Always Have the Opportunity to Provide Their Opinion of a Judicial Candidate Before He or She Is Nominated? Over the years, the Bush Administration's stated practice has been one of welcoming home state Senators' views about who should or should not be nominated to fill federal court judgeships in their states. [153] The Administration, however, appears not always to have informed home state Senators, prior to announcing the selection of a nominee, of all candidates under consideration or of the candidate finally chosen to be the nominee. For example, in at least one such instance, a circuit court nominee allegedly was selected without prior consultation with the home state Senators. A spokesperson for one of the Senators criticized the President for acting in an "uncooperative unilateral manner," which, he said, broke "sharply from the cooperative process in which previous nominees were chosen. [154]

How Differently Should the Administration Treat the Input of Senators, Depending on Their Party Affiliation? Historically, as a general rule, Presidents, as already discussed, have been much more accepting of judicial recommendations from Senators of their own party than from Senators of the opposition party. When neither of a state's Senators are of the President's party, the recommending role has traditionally been filled by another state official of the same party as the President, such as the governor or the most senior U.S. Representative of the President's party from the state. If only one of the state's Senators is of the President's party, the role of providing recommendations traditionally has belonged to that Senator alone, to the exclusion of any significant consultative role for the opposition party Senator.

Like many of his White House predecessors, however, President George W. Bush has selected some lower court nominees from among candidates recommended by opposition party Senators. In these situations, the Administration might make special accommodations with opposition party Senators for reasons unique to the state in question — for example, to be in keeping with an established practice in the state for its two Senators, regardless of their party, to make recommendations to the President; to minimize potential conflict with particular Senators whose support for, or opposition to, the President's judicial nominations, might be regarded as of strategic importance for confirmation purposes; or to minimize the chances of opposition party Senators using the Senate Judiciary Committee's blue slip procedure to block home state nominations in committee.

In the 110th Congress, with the Democrats in the Senate majority, and thus able, if voting along party lines, to defeat a judicial nominee in committee or on the Senate floor, an issue for the Administration is whether to accord a primary recommending role to opposition party Senators in additional states. Many opposition party Senators presumably would welcome such a role. Nonetheless, there would appear to be powerful political and policy incentives for a President not to confer this role on opposition party Senators in general. In states without a Senator of the President's party, other officials of the President's party, based on tradition, can claim a role in the judicial selection process, and they might well be offended if required to share this role with (or relinquish it to) opposition party Senators. Further, the President presumably would wish, as much as possible, to draw upon judicial nominee recommendations from persons who are sympathetic to his philosophical views about the judiciary; this concern would be an incentive for him to rely as much as possible on input from officials of his own party, rather than on opposition party Senators.

What Prerogatives Should Home State Senators Have in the Selection of Circuit Court Nominees? As already discussed, [155] home state Senators of the President's party by custom exert less influence over the selection of circuit court nominees than of district court nominees. Such Senators may, and frequently do, recommend circuit court candidates, but with the usual understanding that the Administration will be considering other candidates as well — with the distinct possibility of the President selecting a nominee from the latter group. Home state Senators of the opposition party are also free to recommend candidates for circuit court nominations (as they may for district court nominations). By custom, however, such recommendations (in large part because they come from the Senators of the opposition party) are ordinarily not at the top of the list among candidates under Administration consideration. (The rare exceptions to this, where recommendations by an opposition party Senator are a major consideration in the selection of circuit court nominees, have usually occurred when the recommendations were made jointly with a Senator of the President's party or in accord with the recommendations of a bipartisan judicial nominee selection panel established in the Senators' state).

Throughout the presidency of George W. Bush, Administration sources have indicated an openness to receiving circuit nominee recommendations from home state Senators, without, however, being under any obligation to follow the advice given. President Bush's disinclination to cede selection power to home state Senators of his party in the area of circuit court appointments seemed to be borne out by various news media accounts in 2007, which reported on public disagreements between the Bush Administration and a number of Republican Senators over whom to nominate to fill certain circuit judgeships. A Washington Post story, reporting on these disagreements, quoted "one conservative who is close to the nominating process" (and who would speak only on the condition of anonymity) as saying, "There has been a long-standing practice in Republican administrations that courts of appeals nominees are the president's prerogative, period" [156].

Controversy also has arisen periodically, throughout the Bush presidency, over how much influence home state Senators of the opposition party should have on the President's selection of circuit court nominees. The controversies usually have occurred when President Bush selected nominees who were objectionable to the Senators, doing so apparently uninfluenced by the Senators' pre-selection input aimed at dissuading him from making these choices. Rather than "working with" the home state Senators to select nominees who would be acceptable to both sides, the President, his Senate critics have alleged, selected nominees without regard to the Senators' nominee preferences or concerns.

The Bush Administration, as of early March 2008, has not publicly stated, as a matter of general policy, what it regards as the proper degree of influence for opposition party home state Senators to have on the selection of circuit court nominees, or to what degree the President should accommodate opposition party Senators in these selections. However, if it chose to do so, the Administration arguably could defend decisions by the President to make circuit nominee selections against the advice of opposition party Senators on at least these two grounds: First, it could be argued, if the President typically does not give primary consideration to the circuit court recommendations from home state Senators of his own party, why should he do so for home state Senators of the other party? Second, it arguably is appropriate, given the importance of the rulings of the circuit courts (in setting precedents that are binding on all the district courts within their circuits), that a President be concerned with selecting circuit court nominees who have a judicial philosophy that is compatible with his own. From the President's standpoint, opposition party Senators, who have frequently been in public conflict with his Administration over the criteria to use in selecting judicial nominees, cannot realistically be regarded as providing the most suitable circuit candidate recommendations for the President to consider.

In the 110th Congress, however, a new consideration for the President has come into play, one favoring a more important role for opposition party Senators in the circuit nominee selection process than they traditionally have been afforded. This consideration is that a circuit or district court nomination has a reduced chance of being confirmed by the Senate during the 110th Congress if it is opposed by a home state Senator, which was not necessarily the case in previous Congresses.

After being the minority in the Senate during the 108th and 109th Congresses, the Democrats in the 110th Congress now have majority control of the Senate and its Judiciary Committee. As already discussed, under the blue slip policy of the Judiciary Committee now in effect, a circuit or district court nomination in a state will not be considered by the committee if both of the state's two Senators have not returned positive blue slips. For the Bush Administration, the consequences of this policy appear to be as follows: If the President selects a circuit (or district) court nominee over the objections of a home state Senator of the opposition party, or in spite of the Senator's recommendations that someone else be nominated, the Senator, by declining to return a positive blue slip, can block the nomination in the Judiciary Committee. Where an opposition party Senator is able and inclined to block a home state judicial nomination unless the President selects a nominee acceptable to the Senator, the Administration may have to make some accommodation with the Senator — if it hopes to see the nomination confirmed. The accommodation would consist, in some way, of affording the Senator a greater, more influential role in the nominee selection process than typically has been afforded opposition party Senators in the past.

Should the Policy of the Judiciary Committee Allow a Home State Senator to Block Committee Consideration of a Judicial Nominee? In recent decades, the blue slip policy of the Senate Judiciary Committee, as already discussed, has often varied, depending on the committee chair. The blue slip policy of the Judiciary Committee under its current chair is that a judicial nomination will not receive a hearing unless both home state Senators return a favorable blue slip to the committee. [157] Several home state Senators in the 110th Congress have indicated their displeasure with the Administration for not having consulted with them more actively in a cooperative effort to select circuit court nominees from their states. [158] Decisions by any of these Senators not to return positive blue slips for judicial nominees from their states, it has been noted, would prevent Judiciary Committee consideration of the nominees during the 110th Congress. [159] For its part, the Administration has described its judicial nominees as "people who are qualified to serve and should be on our courts," [160] calling for action on all of the nominations already sent forward, "with fair and open hearings and swift votes by the full Senate" [161].

Throughout the Bush presidency, the Judiciary Committee's blue slip policy has often been at the center of Senate debate over judicial nominations. In this debate, Senators have differed in their view of exactly how the policy has been applied in the past and how much control over lower court nominations the policy should confer on home state Senators. The latter issue, of whether the Judiciary Committee should consider a district or circuit court nomination if a home state Senator has not returned a favorable blue slip, is of continuing relevance in the 110th Congress. The Administration position (as indicated by the above quote calling for "swift votes" by the Senate on all pending nominations) is that the Judiciary Committee should consider each nomination, regardless of whether a blue slip has been returned. A rationale for this position was laid out in an April

2003 letter by then-White House counsel Alberto Gonzales. In a letter to two Democratic Senators, he explained why, in his view, the committee should not allow a home state Senator to block committee consideration of a judicial nominee:

> We agree strongly with the bipartisan policy maintained by Senators Kennedy, Thurmond, Biden, and Hatch as Chairs of the Judiciary Committee. We respectfully agree that the tradition of consultation does not and should not entail a veto for home-state Senators, particularly a veto wielded for ideological or political purposes. Rather, the intention of the Constitution and the tradition of the Senate require, in our judgement, that the full Senate hold an up or down vote on each judicial nominee. If the objections of home-state Senators to a nominee are persuasive, those objections either will deter the President from submitting the nomination in the first instance or, alternatively, will convince a majority of the Senate that the nomination should be rejected. As Senator Kennedy stated in 1981, however, the Senate has not allowed and should not allow "individual Senators [to] ban, prohibit, or bar" consideration of a nominee [162].

The current chair of the Judiciary Committee, Senator Patrick J. Leahy (D-VT), however, has asserted, throughout the presidency of George W. Bush, that the committee — in keeping with the blue slip policy in effect during the period of the Clinton presidency when Republicans were in the Senate majority — should not act on a lower court nomination unless it has received positive blue slips from both home state Senators. In support of this position, Senator Leahy, in the first months of the Bush Administration, stated, as the committee's ranking Democratic member, that it had been "a longstanding practice of the committee for it to solicit and be guided by the views of home state Senators" and for it not to proceed "with action on a nominee without the return by both home state Senators of their blue slips." Such a policy, he said, "had the effect of encouraging the White House to consult with home state Senators in advance." [163] In a similar vein, in 2003, Senator Leahy objected to the holding of a committee hearing for a circuit court nominee who had not had two positive blue slips returned to the committee. He contrasted the blue slip policy then in effect with the policy applied during the Clinton Administration, which, he said, "operated as an absolute bar to the consideration of any nominee to any court unless both home state Senators had returned positive blue slips" [164].

CONSULTATION BETWEEN THE PRESIDENT AND HOME STATE SENATORS IN THE CURRENT ENVIRONMENT

Under the Judiciary Committee's current blue slip policy, the objection of a home state Senator to a judicial nomination, registered by failing to return a positive blue slip, would doom the nomination's chances for committee consideration (and hence, also for Senate consideration and confirmation). Given that policy, the onus is on the Administration, if it hopes to see its nominee confirmed, not only to consult with the home state Senator but also, through a process of consultation, to select a nominee who is acceptable to both the Administration and the home state Senator. If the White House and a home state Senator cannot agree, the President would appear to have at least four options — to nominate someone objectionable to the home state Senator (and who thus would have a reduced chance of being confirmed), to decline to nominate someone at all (leaving the appointment in question to be made in the next Congress, by the next President), to make a temporary recess appointment (which would not require confirmation by the Senate), or to re-enter consultations with the Senator (in the hope of finding a nominee acceptable to both sides).

Reaching agreement on the choice of nominee, recent experience suggests, might not always be possible. It especially might be difficult when a presidential administration and a home state Senator differ over the criteria to use in selecting judicial nominees or over the policy goals to be served by judicial appointments, or when there are sharp partisan differences between the President and the opposition party in the Senate over judicial appointments. In such circumstances, however, the consultative process might sometimes present an opportunity for the Administration and home state Senator to resolve their differences. The process, for instance, might be an opportunity for the Administration to address, and seek to ease, concerns a home state Senator might have about a judicial candidate. Alternately, during consultation with the Administration, the Senator's input might, in particular circumstances, increase the chances for the selection of a "compromise" nominee, or one less objectionable to the Senator than a candidate under earlier consideration by the Administration.

As noted earlier, various policy statements by chairs of the Senate Judiciary Committee have listed various specific consultative steps which, at the time, the chairs regarded as requisite elements in consultation between an administration and home state Senators concerning the selection of lower court nominees. Although not binding on the Administration then or now, such statements can be seen as helping to identify points during the consultative process when Senators and the Administration might make a point of contacting each other before a nominee is actually selected.

For any given Senator, the actual consultative process that takes place between the Senator (or his or her staff) and the Administration will be unique to the situation at hand. For the particular judicial candidate search in question, there will be such unique elements as the extent and nature of input that the Senator conveys, whether he or she recommends specific candidates (and if so, the comparative strengths of the Senator's candidates vis-à-vis others the Administration might be considering), the predisposition of the Administration to the Senator's input, and a host other political factors that the Administration might have to take into account (including its own policy preferences for judicial nominees).

A President, experience has shown, sometimes nominates a judicial candidate other than one favored by a home state Senator, often, by custom, doing so when the home state Senator is of the opposition party. Whether the President, when making such a choice, has shown due respect for the advisory part of the Senator's advice and consent role will be a personal question for the Senator to answer — but one also of likely interest to other Senators concerned about the nature of their advice and consent prerogatives as home state Senators. Of key relevance to the question will be the extent to which the Administration consulted with the Senator or the Senator's staff, and whether it did so with an apparent openness to the Senator's views.

REFERENCES

[1] See, for example, "Acrimony Reigns over Judicial Picks," in *CQ Almanac Plus, 2002*, vol. 58 (Washington: Congressional Quarterly Inc., 2003), pp. 13.12-13.13; "Judicial Nominee Battles Intensify," in *CQ Almanac Plus, 2003*, vol. 59 (Washington: Congressional Quarterly Inc., 2004), p. 13.19; "Acrimony over Judges Continues," in *CQ Almanac Plus, 2004*, vol. 60 (Washington: Congressional Quarterly Inc., 2005), pp. 12.15-12.16; "'Gang of 14' Averts Judicial Showdown," in *CQ Almanac Plus, 2005*, vol. 61 (Washington: Congressional Quarterly Inc., 2006), pp. 14.8-14.9; and Sheldon Goldman et al., "Picking Judges in a Time of Turmoil: W. Bush's Judiciary During the 109th Congress," *Judicature*, vol. 90, May-June 2007, pp. 252-283. (Hereafter cited as Goldman et al., "Picking Judges").

[2] See, in this vein, a discussion by judicial appointments scholars in 2005 of "the debate over the scope of consultation that the [George W.]Bush White

House has and should have with senators, presumably of any political stripe...." Sheldon Goldman et al., "W. Bush's Judiciary: The First Term Record," *Judicature*, vol. 88, May-June 2005, p. 249. (Hereafter cited as Goldman et al., "W. Bush's Judiciary: The First Term Record").

[3] This chapter, it should be noted, does not cover the role played by Senators in the selection of persons nominated by the President to be U.S. attorneys or U.S. marshals in the Senators' states. Also outside the scope of this chapterare the selection processes for nominees to district or circuit courts in jurisdictions not geographically connected to states (and thus not represented by Senators). Specifically, not examined herein are the selection processes for nominees to the U.S. District Court for the District of Columbia, the U.S. Court of Appeals for the District of Columbia Circuit, the U.S. District Court for the District of Puerto Rico, and the U.S. Court of Appeals for the Federal Circuit (a court which is headquartered in Washington, D.C., and has nationwide jurisdiction defined by subject matter).

[4] Subject to Senate confirmation, the President makes judicial appointments to the following federal courts — the Supreme Court of the United States, U.S. Circuit Courts of Appeals, U.S. District Courts (including the Territorial courts), U.S. Court of International Trade, U.S. Court of Federal Claims, U.S. Tax Court, U.S. Court of Appeals for Veterans Claims, and U.S. Court of Appeals for the Armed Forces. (Regarding the role played by Senators in the appointment of Supreme Court Justices, see CRS Report RL3 1989, *Supreme Court Appointment Process: Roles of the President, Judiciary Committee, and Senate*, by Denis Steven Rutkus.) The President also appoints, subject to Senate confirmation, judges to two local courts — the Superior Court of the District of Columbia and the District of Columbia Court of Appeals. Federal judges whom the President does not appoint include the following: bankruptcy judges (appointed by the U.S. Courts of Appeals); administrative law judges (appointed by federal executive agencies); magistrates (appointed by the U.S. District Courts); and trial and intermediate court judges in the Armed Forces (appointed by the Judge Advocate General in each military service).

[5] Article II, Section 2, Clause 2. In fuller part, Clause 2 provides that the President "shall nominate, and by and with the Advice and Consent of the Senate, shall appoint Ambassadors, other public Ministers and Consuls, Judges of the supreme Court, and all other Officers of the United States, whose Appointments are not herein otherwise provided for, and which shall be established by Law: but the Congress may by Law vest

the Appointment of such inferior Officers, as they think proper, in the President alone, in the Court of Law, or in the Heads of Departments."

[6] Specifically, Article II, Section 2, Clause 3 of the U.S. Constitution empowers the President "to fill up all Vacancies that may happen during the Recess of the Senate, by granting Commissions which shall expire at the End of their next Session." Since the first Administration of George Washington, Presidents have made more than 300 recess appointments to the federal judiciary, including 12 to the Supreme Court. See Henry B. Hogue, "The Law: Recess Appointments to Article III Courts," *Presidential Studies Quarterly*, vol. 32, Sept. 2004, pp. 656-673; and CRS Report RL3297 1, *Judicial Recess Appointments: A Legal Overview*, by T.J. Halstead.

[7] A Senate vote to confirm requires a simple majority of Senators voting, a quorum being present. See CRS Report RL3 1980, *Senate Consideration of Presidential Nominations*, by Elizabeth Rybicki (under heading "Consideration and Disposition"). This quorum requirement is derived from Article I, Section 5, Clause 1 of the U.S. Constitution, which states in part that "a Majority of each [House] shall constitute a Quorum to do Business...." Hence, the quorum for conducting business in a Senate of 100 Members is 51 Senators

[8] Writing in 1953, a scholar noted that the President had "wider discretion" in the selection of judges to such specialized courts as the Tax Court and the Customs Court [now the U.S. Court of International Trade], as well as to federal courts in the District of Columbia and the Territorial Courts, than he did in selecting U.S. district court nominees in each of the states, "for members of the Senate may not claim the right to dictate these appointments though they often press for the appointment of their candidates." Joseph P. Harris, *The Advice and Consent of the Senate* (Berkeley: University of California Press, 1953; reprint, New York: Greenwood Press, 1968), p. 314 (page citation here, and in subsequent footnotes, is to the reprint edition). (Hereafter cited as Harris, *Advice and Consent.*) Subsequently, in 1972, another scholar wrote: "In appointing judges to the District Court of the District of Columbia, the Court of Appeals for the District of Columbia, the United States Court of Customs and Patent Appeals, the United States Court of Claims, and the United States Customs Court, the power of the individual senator is further diminished in favor of the president's men. Since the selection for those posts can be made from any state in the union, any one senator's claim to an appointment cannot be very strong." Harold W. Chase, *Federal Judges; The Appointing Process* (Minneapolis: University

of Minnesota Press, 1972), p. 45. (Hereafter cited as Chase, *Federal Judges*).

[9] Courts within the U.S. courts of appeals system are divided geographically into 11 regional circuits, with each circuit court including at least three states. (There also is a twelfth, geographically based federal court of appeals, in the District of Columbia.) In the following pages, nominations to court of appeals judgeships are referred to as circuit court nominations, and the courts are referred to as circuit courts. A map showing the geographic boundaries of the 11 regional circuit courts, and all of the U.S. district courts, is available on the federal judiciary's website, at [http://www.uscourts.gov/images/CircuitMap.pdf], accessed on Feb. 15, 2008.

[10] Walter Kravitz, *Congressional Quarterly's American Congressional Dictionary*, 3d ed. (Washington: Congressional Quarterly Inc., 2001), p. 231.

[11] Chase, *Federal Judges*, p. 7.

[12] Harris, *Advice and Consent,* pp. 40-41. For more on Senate precedents and senatorial courtesy, see also Floyd M. Riddick and Alan S. Frumin, *Riddick's Senate Procedure*, 10 1st Cong., 2nd sess., S. Doc. 10 1-28 (Washington: GPO, 1992), pp. 95 1-952

[13] Ibid., p. 41

[14] Ibid, p. 314.

[15] Evan Haynes, *The Selection and Tenure of Judges* (Newark, NJ: National Conference of Judicial Councils, 1944), p. 23.

[16] Larry C. Berkson and Susan B. Carbon, *The United States Circuit Judge Nominating Commission: Its Members, Procedures and Candidates* (Chicago: American Judicature Society, 1980), p.12.

[17] Joseph W. Tydings, "Merit Selection for District Judges,"Judicature, vol. 61, Sept. 1977, p. 113. (Hereafter cited as Tydings, "Merit Selection.") By contrast, he noted (also at p. 113), "no single senator automatically controls" each circuit court of appeals judgeship, because each appellate court "generally covers several states."

[18] Ruth Marcus, "GOP Senators Feud with Administration over Naming Judges," *The Washington Post*, Nov. 23, 1989, p. A6. (Hereafter cited as Marcus, "GOP Senators Feud").

[19] Ibid.

[20] See Walter R. Mears, "A Battle of Wills over Picking Federal Judges," *Associated Press*, Aug. 16, 1990, accessed Feb. 5, 2008, at [www.lexisnexis.com].

[21] In some scholarly works, senatorial courtesy also has come to be synonymous with presidential deference to Senators over federal appointments in their states. See, for example, Michael J. Gerhardt, *The Federal Appointments Process; A Constitutional and Historical Analysis* (Durham, NC: Duke University Press, 2000), p. 143: "*Traditionally, the term senatorial courtesy has referred to the deference the president owes to the recommendations of senators from his own political party on the particular people whom he should nominate to federal offices in the senators' respective states.*" (Emphasis in original.)

[22] Occasionally, however, Presidents have selected district court nominees over the public opposition of home state Senators of the President's party, usually (but not always) with unhappy results for the Presidents and the nominees. In 1939, over the objections of Virginia's two Democratic Senators, President Franklin D. Roosevelt nominated Floyd H. Roberts to a judgeship on the U.S. District Court for the Western District of Virginia. The nomination ultimately was rejected by the Senate 72-9. See Harris, *Advice and Consent*, pp. 1-234. By contrast, in 1947 President Harry S Truman succeeded in having the nomination of Joe B. Dooley to the U.S. District Court for Northern Texas confirmed, over the objection of the junior Democratic Senator of Texas, W. Lee O'Daniel. (The Senator had been in disagreement with Texas's senior Senator, Tom Connally, also a Democrat, who had recommended the nominee.) The nomination was approved by the Senate Judiciary Committee by a 8-4 vote and confirmed by the Senate by a vote of 48-36. Sheldon Goldman, *Picking Federal Judges: Lower Court Selection from Roosevelt Through Reagan* (New Haven, CT: Yale University Press, 1997), p. 80. (Hereafter cited as Goldman, *Picking Federal Judges*.) Subsequently, however, President Truman was unsuccessful when he transmitted four other district court nominations to the Senate, all over the objections of home state Senators of his party. The nominations in question — one each to the judicial districts of Northern Georgia and Southern Iowa in 1950, and two to the judicial district of Northern Illinois in 1951 — were rejected by the Senate in voice votes. See again Harris, *Advice and Consent*, p. 221 (for the Georgia and Iowa district nominations) and pp. 321-323 (for the Illinois district nominations). More recently, in 1976, President Gerald R. Ford, a Republican, nominated William B. Poff to the U.S. District Court for the Western District of Virginia over the objection of a home state Senator of the President's party. The Senator invoked senatorial courtesy, and the Senate Judiciary Committee tabled the nomination. A month later, President Ford withdrew the nomination (after receiving a letter from the

nominee, who asked that his nomination be withdrawn because of the Senator's invocation of senatorial courtesy). Goldman, *Picking Federal Judges*, p. 210. In 1980, President Jimmy Carter, a Democrat, nominated James E. Sheffield to the U.S. District Court for the Eastern District of Virginia, over the objection of Senator Harry F. Byrd Jr. of Virginia. Although Senator Byrd, formerly a Democrat, had become an Independent, he remained a member of the Senate's Democratic caucus, and was treated as a Democrat by President Carter for judicial selection purposes. (When President Carter, earlier in his presidency, wrote a letter to Democratic Senators, requesting that they appoint merit commissions to select candidates for vacant district judgeships in their states, he included Senator Byrd on his list.) Although the Sheffield nomination received a hearing by the Senate Judiciary Committee, controversy arose over the nominee's personal finances, as well as over the Carter Administration's efforts to persuade Senator Byrd to add more names to the list of candidates he had recommended for vacant Virginia judgeships. The Sheffield nomination received no further action in the Senate and was returned to the President in December 1980 upon the final adjournment of the 96th Congress. See "Sen. Byrd Pledges To Oppose Carter on Judge Choice," *The Washington Post*, April 17, 1980, p. C2; Karlyn Barker, "Tax Inquiry Snarls Hearings on Carter Nominee to Bench," *The Washington Post*, Aug. 27, 1980, p. A1; Donald P. Baker and Glenn Frankel, "A Litany of Mistakes; White House Defeated, Embarrassed in Fight To Appoint Black Va. Judge; Fight for Black Judge Embarrasses Carter," *The Washington Post*, Sept. 21, 1980, p. A1; Goldman, *Picking Federal Judges*, pp. 262-264.

[23] Chase, *Federal Judges*, p.12. "It does not necessarily follow," Chase continued, "that because individual senators may well be in a position to exercise a veto power in the appointment of judges they must do the appointing. Close examination of the appointment process suggests otherwise." Ibid., p. 13.

[24] For instance, in an executive order signed on Nov. 8, 1978, President Jimmy Carter specified (thus signaling to home state Senators) that, among the standards he would use to determine a person's fitness to serve as a district judge was whether the person possessed a "demonstrated commitment to equal justice." Also, under the order, the Attorney General, before recommending a district court candidate to the President, would consider whether an "affirmative action" had "been made, in the case of each vacancy, to identify candidates, including women and members of minority groups."

U.S. President (Carter), "Standards and Guidelines for the Merit Selection of United States District Judges," Executive Order 12097, *Federal Register*, vol. 43, Nov. 13, 1978, p. 52455. (Executive order revoked by President Ronald Reagan on Feb. 25, 1986. See "Executive Orders Disposition Tables," at [http://www.archives .gov/federal-register/codification/executive-orders- 1 6.html], accessed Feb. 5, 2008.) During the presidency of Ronald Reagan, the Administration's evaluation of judicial candidates was, as a matter of policy, concerned not only with intellectual ability, legal experience, and judicial temperament, but also "with an individual's overall judicial philosophy and concept of the judicial role." Sheldon Goldman, "Reagan's Second Term Judicial Appointments: The Battle at Midway," *Judicature*, vol. 70, April-May 1987, p. 326. During the presidency of George W. Bush, a Department of Justice official involved in the process of evaluating candidates for lower court judgeships has spoken of the President's "mandate to us" — namely, "that the men and women who are nominated by him to be on the bench have his vison of the proper role of the judiciary. That is, a judiciary that will follow the law, not make the law, a judiciary that will interpret the constitution, not legislate from the bench." Sheldon Goldman et al., "W. Bush Remaking the Judiciary: Like Father Like Son?", *Judicature*, vol. 86, May-June 2003, p. 284. (Hereafter cited as Goldman et al., "W. Bush Remaking the Judiciary").

[25] A 1996 study noted that "during the administration of Democratic President Jimmy Carter, home state senators were asked for more than one name for each district court vacancy in their state. That practice and other presidential attempts to curb senatorial patronage over lower federal court judgeships continued under Republican Presidents Ronald Reagan and George [H. W.] Bush," although "with limited success." Miller Center Commission on the Selection of Federal Judges, *Improving the Process of Appointing Federal Judges: A Report of the Miller Center Commission on the Selection of Federal Judges* (Charlottesville, VA: Miller Center of Public Affairs, University of Virginia, 1996), p. 4.

[26] See Alan Neff, *The United States District Judge Nominating Commissions: Their Members, Procedures and Candidates* (Chicago: American Judicature Society, 1981), 203 p. (Hereafter cited as Neff, *Un ited States District Judge Nominating Commissions.*) See also Charles W. Hucker, "Report Card on Judicial Merit Selection," *Congressional Quarterly Weekly Report*, vol. 37, Feb. 3, 1979, pp. 189-191. President Carter's advocacy, one news report noted, included issuance of an executive order "urging senators to voluntarily forego their patronage prerogatives and

establish commissions for the selection of U.S. district court judges on the basis of merit." Alan Berlow, "Carter Order Raises Doubts Whether Judges Will Be Selected on Merit Basis," *Congressional Quarterly Weekly Report*, vol. 36, Nov. 18, 1978, p. 3313.

[27] The current use of outside nominating commissions by some Senators to evaluate and recommend judicial candidates is discussed in more detail later in this report, under the heading "Procedures Used to Identify and Evaluate Candidates."

[28] See CRS Report RL32013, *The History of the Blue Slip in the Senate Committee on the Judiciary, 1917-Present*, by Mitchel A. Sollenberger. (Hereafter cited as CRS Report RL32012, *History of the Blue Slip.*) See also Sarah A. Binder, "Where Do Institutions Come From? Exploring the Origins of the Senate Blue Slip," *Studies in American Political Development*, vol. 21, March 2007, pp. 1-15. (Hereafter cited as Binder, "Where Do (continued[28] (...continued) Institutions Come From?")

[29] CRS Report RL32013, *History of the Blue Slip*, p. 4.

[30] Ibid., p. 9.

[31] By contrast, prior to 1956, during the first four decades of the Judiciary Committee's blue slip policy, "no chair of the Judiciary Committee allowed any negative blue slips to automatically veto a nomination." Instead, judicial nominations prompting negative blue slips from home state Senators received committee hearings and even, in some cases, were reported by the committee to the full Senate. These episodes appeared to show that the committee's policy, during this time, "was that a negative blue slip was not intended to prevent committee action. Instead, a Senator's negative assessment of a nominee was meant to express to the committee his views on the nominee so that the chairman would be better prepared to deal with the review of the nomination. The end result was that Judiciary Committee chairmen did not traditionally view a negative blue slip as a sign to stop all action on judicial nominations." Ibid. p. 9.

[32] See, for example, in Brannon P. Denning, "The Judicial Confirmation Process and the Blue Slip," *Judicature*, vol. 85, March-April 2002, pp. 2 18-226, the following quote, at p. 222: "Just making known [to the administration] that the senator is opposed and would, if the person is nominated, withhold the blue slip, sends a powerful signal that trouble is in the offing. Then the administration must decide whether or not it wants to pick a fight. With judicial nominations, then, the Senate has created an effective procedure for ensuring that its 'advice' is sought by the president prior to the announcement of a nomination.... " See also Binder, "Where Do

Institutions Come From?", who, at p. 1, observed that the blue slip "allows home state senators to influence the course of nominations prospectively — encouraging presidents to heed the preferences of home state senators in selecting new federal judges."

[33] CRS Report RL32013, *History of the Blue Slip*, pp. 11-14, 24.

[34] Ibid., pp. 13, 22; Binder, "Where Do Institutions Come From?," p. 15, note 53.

[35] For example, Sen. Joseph R. Biden, Jr. (D-DE), Judiciary Committee chairman from 1987 to 1994, in a 1989 letter to President George H.W. Bush emphasized the importance of the President's Administration consulting "with both home state Senators prior to submitting the nomination to the Senate." If such "good faith consultation" did not take place, he said, "the Judiciary Committee will treat the return of a negative blue slip by a home state Senator as dispositive and the nominee will not be considered." Sen. Joseph R. Biden Jr., letter to President George H.W. Bush, The White House, June 6, 1989. Sen. Orrin G. Hatch (R-UT), the committee's chairman from 1995 to 2001 and again from 2003 to 2004, wrote in 1997 to the White House counsel to President William J. Clinton that "the Senate expects genuine, good faith consultation by the Administration with home state Senators before a judicial nomination is made, and the Administration's failure to consult in genuine good faith with both home state Senators itself is grounds for a Senator's return of a negative blue slip. Where the Administration has failed to provide good faith pre-nomination consultation, a negative blue slip is treated as dispositive, and precludes Committee consideration of a judicial nominee." Sen. Orrin G. Hatch, letter to Charles F.C. Ruff, counsel to the President, The White House, Apr. 16, 1997. Sen. Patrick J. Leahy (D-VT), the committee's chairman from 200 1-2002, was reported as having said, in an June 6, 2001, interview, that "unless he is satisfied that both senators from the home state of a nominee have been consulted by the Bush administration, a nomination will not move." Elizabeth A. Palmer, "Senate GOP Backs Down from Dispute over Handling of Nominees," *CQ Weekly*, vol. 59, June 9, 2001, p. 1360.

[36] CRS Report RL32013, *History of the Blue Slip*, p. 25.

[37] For instance, in his 1997 letter to the White House counsel to President William Clinton, Sen. Orrin G. Hatch (R-UT), chairman of the Judiciary Committee, listed five circumstances indicating "an absence of good faith consultation" by the White House with home state Senators. One of the five circumstances, he said, was the "failure to give serious consideration to individuals proposed by home state Senators as possible

nominees." Sen. Orrin G. Hatch, letter to Charles F.C. Ruff, counsel to the President, April 16, 1997. For a listing of all five "circumstances" in Sen. Hatch's letter, see CRS Report RL320 13, *History of Blue Slip*, pp. 15-16. Similarly, in an April 2001 letter to the White House counsel to President George W. Bush, the Democratic members of the Senate Judiciary Committee, including Sen. Patrick J. Leahy (D-VT) — who became committee chairman two months later when the Democrats became the majority party in the Senate — urged the Administration to undertake six specific "consultative procedures" prior to selecting a judicial nominee. One of the six procedures, the letter said, entailed the Administration giving "serious consideration to individuals proposed by home state Senators as possible nominees." Democratic Senators, Committee on the Judiciary, U.S. Senate, letter to Counsel to the President Alberto R. Gonzales, April 27, 2001. For a listing of all six consultative procedures in the Democratic Senators' letter, see CRS Report RL32013, *History of the Blue Slip,* pp. 19-20.

[38] See earlier section in this report under the heading "Senatorial Courtesy."

[39] Sheldon Goldman, "Judicial Selection," in Robert J. Janosik, ed., *Encyclopedia of the American Judicial System: Studies of the Principal Institutions and Processes of Law*, 3 vols. (New York, Scribner, 1987), vol. 2, p. 589. (Hereafter cited as Goldman, in *Encyclopedia of American Judicial System*.)

[40] Ibid., p. 590.

[41] For example, in 10 states during the Carter presidency (1977-1980), a scholar has noted, Senators "who were not in the president's party played a significant role in selection by establishing or co-cosponsoring nominating commissions." Neff, *United States District Judge Nominating Commissions,* p. 20. In a long-standing arrangement in New York, when that state had both a Republican and a Democratic Senator, the Senator of the President's party customarily proposed candidates for three out of every four vacancies in the federal district courts located in New York, with the other Senator proposing a candidate to fill the fourth judicial vacancy. For a fuller description of the arrangement in New York, see Federal Bar Council Committee on Second Circuit Courts, "Judicial Vacancies: The Processing of Judicial Candidates: Why It Takes So Long and How It Could Be Shortened," *Federal Rules Decisions*, v. 128, Jan. 1990, p. 145. More recently at the start of the presidency of George W. Bush, in 2001, Nevada's two Senators (one Republican and the other Democrat) announced an agreement in which the latter Senator would recommend candidates for one out of every four district court vacancies occurring in the state (an

arrangement described as based on the bipartisan arrangement, just discussed, that was in effect for many years in New York). Matthew Tully and Emily Pierce, "Senators Work Out Novel Agreements on Judiciary Posts," *CQ Daily Monitor*, June 13, 2001, p. 5. The same story reported that a "similar agreement" had been reached by the Senators from Illinois (one a Republican, the other a Democrat) for making judicial nominee recommendations.

[42] An administration might generally regard bipartisan cooperation between home state Senators on judicial nominations as politically beneficial, insofar as it paves the way for bipartisan support for these nominations in the Senate. Sometimes, however, an administration might regard cooperation as going too far — for instance, when the Senator of the other party is allowed to assume the role of recommending candidates for some of the state's judicial nominations and the Senator then makes recommendations of which the Administration disapproves. In such instances, an administration might feel it does not have to accept these recommendations or reach accommodations with the Senator on a mutually acceptable choice, as an administration typically would in its interactions with the home state Senator of the President's party.

[43] The ability of opposition party Senators to block lower court nominations from their state will be particularly enhanced if their party is in the Senate majority and if the chair of the Judiciary Committee or the Senate majority leader is prepared to support the Senators in opposition to a home state nomination.

[44] Indicative of this custom was a survey in early 1993, during the first months of Democrat William J. Clinton's presidency, of staff in Senate offices on methods used to select candidates for district judgeships. At that time, 18 states were represented by two Democratic Senators. Of these 18 states, 11 were identified in the survey as having both of their Senators jointly involved in the selection of judicial candidates, while in five other states one of the Senators was identified as the "chief sponsor" or as "taking the lead" in the selection process. (In the two other states, the Senators had yet to decide on what selection process they would use.) *Citizen's Handbook Supplement: A State-by-State Guide to Federal Judicial Selection* (Washington: Alliance for Justice, April 1993), 15 p. (Hereafter cited as *Citizen's Handbook Supplement.*) (Copy of pamphlet available from author).

[45] This endorsement, or commitment not to oppose, is essential to assure that the nomination will not later be blocked by the second Senator either in the

Senate Judiciary Committee (through non-return of a blue slip or return of a negative blue slip) or, in the event the nomination were reported by the committee, on the Senate floor (by invoking senatorial courtesy).

[46] Chase, *Federal Judges*, p. 37.

[47] *Citizen's Handbook Supplement*, pp. 3-15. The Secretary of Agriculture, identified by the survey as the chief sponsor for federal judicial candidates in Mississippi, was Mike Espy, who, prior to his appointment as Secretary of Agriculture, served as a Democratic Member of the U.S. House of Representatives for six years.

[48] R.G. Ratcliffe, "Lawmaker's Tip a Curve to Clinton; Brooks Recommends Other Judge for Post," *The Houston Chronicle*, Nov. 18, 1993, p. A29.

[49] In January 1995, however, under a new dean, the state's Democratic House Members shared among themselves the recommending role — creating four panels, for each of the state's four judicial districts, to recommend district court candidates to the President. See Steve McGonigle, "Gonzalez Parcels Out Responsibility for Making Federal Judicial Selections; Representatives to Recommend Candidates for their Regions," *The Dallas Morning News*, Dec. 18, 1994, p. 10A; William E. Clayton Jr., "Jurist Nominees To Be Picked in New Process; Texas Federal Judgeships Are First Test, *The Houston Chronicle*, Jan. 16, 1995, p. A5.

[50] Jonathan Ringel, "GOP Senators Ready to Enter the Judges Game," *Legal Times*, vol. 24, Jan. 22, 2001, p. 6.

[51] Ibid., p. 8.

[52] Of course, if the Senators objected to a candidate under consideration, their views might often be expected to carry weight with the Administration, in light of the formidable opposition they could mount against home state nominations later in the Senate Judiciary Committee or on the Senate floor.

[53] Neff, *United States District Judge Nominating Commissions*, p. 20.

[54] "Department of Justice; Memorandum on Judicial Selection Procedures, 3/2/198 1," *United States Law Week*, vol. 49, no. 37, 1981, p. 2604. For another source for full text of the memorandum, see "The Attorney General's Memorandum on Judicial Selection Procedures," *Judicature*, vol. 64, April 1981, p. 428.

[55] Joel B. Grossman, *Lawyers and Judges: The ABA and the Politics of Judicial Selection* (New York: John Wiley and Sons, Inc., 1965), p. 30.

[56] The commission charter excluded officers of the state's political parties from membership as commissioners. This provision, a scholar observed, "could be read as attempting to oust Florida's Republican officials from participation in selection during the Republican administration in office at

that time." Neff, *United States District Judge Nominating Commissions*, p. 21.

[57] "It is significant," Neff wrote, "that the commission reported to its sponsoring senators rather than directly to the President." Ibid.

[58] Ibid., p. 23. Neff did not identify which of the three vacancies was not filled by a nominee recommended by the commission or provide any details explaining the commission's noninvolvement in filling that vacancy.

[59] Ibid., pp. 23-24.

[60] Ibid., p. 24.

[61] Nina Totenberg, "Will Judges Be Chosen Rationally?" *Judicature*, vol. 60, Aug.-Sept. 1976, p. 95.

[62] Carl Tobias, "Federal Judicial Selection in a Time of Divided Government," *Emory Law Journal*, vol. 47, Spring 1998, p. 543.

[63] Ibid. Providing a similar perspective, a former assistant attorney general, in a 2002 symposium, noted that, in the Clinton Administration, "we did try to make arrangements and accommodations with Republican senators. It became a matter of necessity when we reached the point in a number of quarters of the country where we were looking at states and circuits with lots of Republican senators, some of whom absolutely refused to consider any person put forward by President Clinton at the district or circuit court level." Eleanor D. Acheson, former assistant attorney general, Office of Policy Development, quoted in "Selecting Federal Judges: The Role and Responsibilities of the Executive Branch," *Judicature*, vol. 86, July-Aug. 2002, p. 17.

[64] See Sen. Dianne Feinstein, "Senators Boxer and Feinstein Announce Bipartisan Judicial Nomination Panel," news release, May 22, 2001, accessed Feb. 5, 2008, at [http://feinstein.senate.gov/releases01/judicial_nomination _panel. html]; Sen. Bob Graham, "White House Commits to Honor Florida Nominating System; Graham Says Judiciary Needs to Maintain Independence," news release, March 12, 2003 (copy available from author); Katherine Pfleger, "Senators, White House Might Be Close to Resolution on Federal Judicial Nominee," Associated Press, March 18, 2002, accessed Feb. 5, 2008, at [www.lexisnexis.com]; "Murray, Cantwell to Form Panel," *The Seattle Times*, March 19, 2002, p. B3; Sen. Herb Kohl, "Kohl, Feingold Announce Activation of Wisconsin Federal Nominating Commission," news release, June 25, 2003 (copy available from author); and Eric J. Frommer, "White House Nominates Wisconsin State Judge for Federal Judgeship," Associated Press, Nov. 14, 2003, accessed Feb. 5, 2008, at [www.lexisnexis.com]. As of January 2005, it should be noted, Florida ceased to be represented by two opposition party Senators, following that

state's election of a Republican to the Senate in November 2004. Thereafter, as a result, the primary role for selecting members of Florida's judicial nominating commission, as well as for reviewing and forwarding the commission's candidate recommendations to the White House, was assumed by a Senator of the President's party.

[65] Also, in at least one of the states, Wisconsin, the Senators retained the prerogative to block from being forwarded to the President any commission recommendation of which they might disapprove. See David Callender, "Sykes Is 7th Circuit Finalist; Bush to Make Pick for Appeals Court," *The Capital Times and Washington State Journal*, Aug. 5, 2003, p. 3A.

[66] In recent floor remarks during Senate consideration of a district court nomination, one of Illinois's two Democratic Senators noted that the nominee had been recommended by the leader of that state's Republican House delegation, "with the understanding he faced a veto" if either of the Senators objected. Sen. Richard J. Durbin, "Nomination of Robert M. Dow, Jr., To Be United States District Judge for the Northern District of Illinois," remarks in the Senate, *Congressional Record*, daily edition, vol. 153, Nov. 13, 2007, p. S 14238. The state's other Senator stated that the nomination had "continued the bipartisan approach to filling judgeships in the Federal district courts — an approach that has served Illinois well." Sen. Barack Obama, "Nomination of Robert M. Dow, Jr., To Be United States District Judge for the Northern District of Illinois," remarks in the Senate, *Congressional Record*, daily edition, vol. 153, Nov. 13, 2007, p. S 14239.

[67] Harris, *Advice and Consent*, p. 314.

[68] Chase, *Federal Judges*, p. 43.

[69] Tydings, "Merit Selection," p. 113.

[70] See Goldman, *Picking Federal Judges*, pp. 238-24 1. Goldman recounted that President Carter created the commission through Executive Order 11972, and that the commission "consisted of thirteen eleven-member panels appointed by the president (one for each judicial circuit, with the exception of the large Fifth and Ninth circuits which were split geographically with eastern and western Fifth Circuit panels and northern and southern Ninth Circuit panels)." Ibid., p. 238. See also W. Gary Fowler, "Judicial Selection under Reagan and Carter: A Comparison of Their Initial Recommendation Procedures," *Judicature*, vol. 67, Dec.-Jan.1984, pp. 267-268.

[71] In disbanding the commission, President Reagan "ordered a return to the pre-Carter method of selection, with senators and others recommending people to the Justice Department." Sheldon Goldman, "Reagan's Judicial

Appointments at Mid-Term: Shaping the Bench in His Own Image," *Judicature,* vol. 66, March 1983, p. 342.

[72] Goldman, *Picking Federal Judges,* p. 291.

[73] Alliance for Justice Judicial Selection Project, *Justice in the Making: A Citizen's Handbook for Choosing Federal Judges* (Washington: Alliance for Justice, 1993), p. 9. (Copy available from author).

[74] "Clinton Nominee Kent Markus: Judicial Delays Are Hurting the Country," nationaljournal.com, June 20, 2001, "Insider Interview," accessed on Feb. 5, 2008, at [http://nationalj ournal.com/]. Markus, who had served in the Department of Justice as a counselor to Attorney General Janet Reno, was nominated by President Clinton to the U.S. Court of Appeals for the Sixth Circuit on Feb. 9, 2000. His nomination, however, received no action in the Senate and was returned to the President on Dec. 15, 2000, at the end of the 106th Congress.

[75] Goldman et al., "W. Bush Remaking the Judiciary," p. 285.

[76] For mentions of a few instances in which Senators succeeded in having President Bush nominate someone recommended by them to circuit court judgeships, see Mitchel A. Sollenberger, "The Law: The President 'Shall Nominate': Exclusive or Shared Constitutional Power?," *Presidential Studies Quarterly,* vol. 36, Dec. 2006, p. 725.

[77] As discussed earlier, there is also a twelfth geographically based federal court of appeals — the U.S. Court of Appeals for the District of Columbia — which, like the other 11 geographically based circuit courts, considers appeals of federal trial court cases decided within the circuit. A thirteenth federal court of appeals, the U.S. Court of Appeals for the Federal Circuit, is headquartered in Washington, D.C., but unlike the other 12 circuit courts, has nationwide jurisdiction defined by subject matter.

[78] Elliot E. Slotnick, "A Historical Perspective on Federal Judicial Selection," *Judicature,* vol. 86, July-Aug. 2002, pp. 14-15.

[79] The Senators might point to other considerations as well to justify filling the court vacancy with a representative of their state. They might, for instance, advance the argument that the various states in the circuit should be proportionally represented, with each having a certain minimal number of judges on the court, to insure adequate representation based on each state's population or the proportion of the court's overall caseload originating from the state.

[80] A CRS report updated on Sept. 4, 2007, found that, from the presidency of Lyndon B. Johnson (1963-1969) to the update of that report, 86% of appointments to the circuit courts had been of nominees who, at the time of

their appointment, were residents of the same state as the vacating judges' state of residence at the time of appointment. CRS Report RS225 10, *"State Representation" in Appointments to Federal Courts of Appeals*, by R. Sam Garrett and Kevin M. Scott.

[81] A federal statute that has been in effect since 1997 provides that every state must be represented by at least one judge on the circuit court of appeals that geographically encompasses it. Specifically, it provides that "[i]n each circuit (other than the Federal judicial circuit) there shall be at least one circuit judge in regular active service appointed from the residents of each state in that circuit." 28 U.S.C. §44(c); 111 Stat. 2493; P.L. 105- 119, sec. 307.

[82] Goldman, in *Encyclopedia of American Judicial System*, p. 589.

[83] Chase, *Federal Judges*, pp. 43-44.

[84] See CRS Report RL32013, *History of the Blue Slip*, pp. 13, 22; Binder, "Where Do Institutions Come From?," p. 15, note 53; and Seth Stern, "Saad Nomination Advances Despite Senate 'Blue Slips," *Congressional Quarterly Weekly,* vol. 62, June 18, 2004, p. 1479.

[85] For the President, however, a consideration against nominating someone from a state other than that of the vacating judge will be the likelihood of controversy arising over the change in "state representation." In recent episodes in the Senate, involving a circuit court nominee whose state of residence was different from that of the vacating judge (or, in one instance, different from that of the vacating judge at the time that judge was nominated), the Senators representing the state of the vacating judge publicly objected on state representation grounds, and the nominations failed to be confirmed. See "Background" section of CRS Report RS225 10, *"State Representation" in Appointments.* See also Spencer S. Hsu, "Senators Delay Vote on Va. Bench Nominee; Sarbanes, Mikulski Want a Md. Appointee," *The Washington Post*, July 10, 2004, p. B 1; Sen. Dianne Feinstein, "Statement by Senator Dianne Feinstein on the Nomination of Randy Smith to the 9th Circuit Court of Appeals," news release, March 1, 2006, accessed Feb. 5, 2008, at [http://feinstein.senate.gov/]; "Most Say Boise Lawyer Who Is Up for Seat on 9th Circuit Has Little Chance of Being Approved by Democratic Congress," *The Idaho Statesman*, Dec. 13, 2006, accessed Dec. 13, 2006, at [http://www.idahostatesman.com]. See also remarks by Sen. Patrick J. Leahy discussing the failure of a Virginian to be confirmed to a circuit judgeship vacated by a Marylander and the success of an Idahoan in being confirmed to a circuit judgeship vacated by an Idahoan (following controversy, however, over his earlier unsuccessful nomination

to a circuit judgeship which California's Senators maintained was a "California seat"). Specifically, see Sen. Leahy' s remarks in "Nomination of Sandra Segal Ikuta To Be United States Circuit Judge for the Ninth Circuit ,"*Congressional Record*, daily edition, vol. 152, June 19, 2006, pp. S6053-S6054, and in "Norman Randy Smith To Be United States Circuit Judge for the Ninth Circuit," *Congressional Record*, daily edition, vol. 153, Feb. 15, 2007, p. S1986 (each statement discussing both the Virginia-Maryland and Idaho-California controversies).

[86] In March 2003, the federal judiciary's governing body, the Judicial Conference of the United States, adopted a committee recommendation, in which it "strongly urge[d] all judges to notify the President and the Administrative Office of the United States Courts as far in advance as possible of a change in status, preferably 12 months before the contemplated date of change in status." Prior to that, retiring judges and those taking senior status had been encouraged by the Conference to provide "substantial (i.e., six-month or one-year) advance notice of that action." U.S. Judicial Conference of the United States, *Report of the Proceedings of the Judicial Conference of the United States*, March 18, 2003, pp. 20-21, accessed Feb. 5, 2008, at [http://www.uscourts.gov/judconfindex.html].

[87] The federal judiciary's website is located at [http://www.uscourts.gov/].

[88] Within the website, a list of current district and circuit court vacancies can be accessed, at [http://www.uscourts.gov/judicialvac.html], as can a list of future court vacancies (including, for each judgeship in question, the date that the vacancy will take effect).

[89] The current use by some Senators of outside judicial nominating commissions to evaluate and recommend judicial candidates is discussed in more detail later in this report, under the heading "Procedures Used To Identify and Evaluate Candidates."

[90] Robert A. Carp and Ronald Stidham, *Judicial Process in America*, 3d ed. (Washington: CQ Press, 1996), p. 240. (Hereafter cited as Carp and Stidham, *Judicial Process*) Merit, the authors continue, "may mean no more than an association with a prestigious law firm, publication of a few law review articles, or respect among fellow attorneys; a potential judge need not necessarily be an outstanding legal scholar. Nevertheless, one of the unwritten codes is that a judicial appointment is different from run-of-the-mill patronage," with tradition creating "an expectation that the would-be judge have some reputation for professional competence." Ibid., pp. 240-241.

[91] For detailed information on the process by which the ABA committee investigates and evaluates a judicial nominee, see, on the ABA's website, the background booklet entitled *American Bar Association Standing Committee on the Federal Judiciary: What It Is and How It Works*, accessed Feb. 5, 2008, at [http://www.abanet.org/scfedjud/].

[92] Carp and Stidham, *Judicial Process*, p. 241.

[93] Ibid.

[94] Ibid., p. 242.

[95] In recent years, Senators have expressed different views on whether it is appropriate to evaluate judicial nominees by their ideology, judicial philosophy, or views on specific issues. A notable instance of this was a June 26, 2001, hearing held by a Senate Judiciary subcommittee on the question,"Judicial Nominations 2001: Should Ideology Matter?" For the complete record of that hearing, see U.S. Congress, Senate Committee on the Judiciary, Subcommittee on Administrative Oversight and the Courts, *The Judicial Nomination and Confirmation Process*, hearings, 107th Cong., 1st sess., June 26 and Sept. 4, 2001 (Washington: GPO, 2002), pp. 1-109.

[96] Senate financial management regulations, it should be noted, anticipate that some Senators will use advisory panels or groups to assist them in selecting judicial candidates. The regulations provide, in part, that individuals "who are not Senate employees selected by Senators to serve on a panel or other body making recommendations for nominees to Federal judgeships, service academies, U.S. Attorneys or U.S. Marshals may be reimbursed for transportation, per diem, and for certain other expenses incurred in performing duties as a member of such panel or other body." U.S. Congress, Senate Committee on Rules and Administration, *United States Senate Handbook* (Washington: United States Senate, Nov. 2006), p. IV-43.

[97] The speech was one made by many Senators during 40 hours of continuous Senate debate concerned with the judicial appointment process and with whether to close debate on three controversial circuit court nominations. The debate, which began in the evening of Wednesday, Nov. 12, 2003, concluded on the morning of Friday, Nov. 14, 2003, when the Senate voted against motions to close debate on the circuit court nominations of Priscilla Richman Owen of Texas, Carolyn B. Kuhl of California, and Janice R. Brown, also of California. For the entirety of the 40-hour debate, see *Congressional Record*, daily edition, vol. 149, Nov. 12, 2003, pp. S14528-S 14785.

[98] Sen. Richard G. Lugar, "Executive Session," remarks in the Senate, *Congressional Record,* daily edition, vol. 149, Nov. 12, 2003, p. S14677.

[99] Ibid.

[100] In taking this different approach, the Senator said he "appreciated that those vacancies ... were going to come in to the particular milieu about which we are now talking," i.e., an atmosphere in the Senate Judiciary Committee of heightened conflict over judicial nominations. Ibid.

[101] Ibid.

[102] For instance, in announcing the creation of such a commission in 2001, a Senator declared, "It is my hope that this Committee can bring forward the best and most qualified candidates for the federal bench and provide a bipartisan balance that can lead to speedy approval by the Senate." Sen. Dianne Feinstein, "Senators Boxer and Feinstein Announce Bipartisan Judicial Nomination Panel," news release, May 22, 2001, accessed Dec. 3, 2007, at [http://feinstein.senate.gov/releases01/judicial_nomination_ panel.html].

[103] For thumbnail descriptions of the structure and operations of nominating commissions currently used in the federal judicial selection process in certain states, see: [http://www.judicialselection.us/federal_judicial_ selection/ federal_judicial_nominating_ commissions.cfm?state=FDsee], accessed Feb. 5, 2008. For comprehensive state-by-state information on the structure and operations of nominating commissions used by U.S. Senators in the lower court selection process during the presidency of Jimmy Carter, see Neff, *United States District Judge Nominating Commissions.* A sound rationale for nominating commissions, a recent study concluded, is that they "can be forums of genuine, constructive consultation in the initial phase of nominee selection" and help Senators and the President "strain out fringe candidates with more political clout than potential judicial ability." Russell Wheeler, "Prevent Federal Court Nomination Battles: De-Escalating the Conflict over the Judiciary," Brookings Institution Position Paper, Nov. 20, 2007, p. 12, accessed Feb. 5, 2008, at [http://www.brookings.edu/]. Hereafter cited as Wheeler, "Prevent Federal Court Nomination Battles").

[104] Goldman, *Picking Federal Judges*, p. 244, observing that before 1977 Senators "from only two states (Florida in 1974 and Kentucky in 1976) had commissions."

[105] Ibid.

[106] Ibid., p. 290.

[107] A March 1981 Department of Justice memorandum by Attorney General William French Smith encouraged Senators to utilize "screening mechanisms" — which it said included "advisory groups or commissions" — to "ensure that highly qualified candidates are recommended." "Department of Justice; Memorandum on Judicial Selection Procedures, 3/2/198 1," *United States Law Week*, vol. 49, no. 37, 1981, p. 2604. See also

Stuart Taylor Jr., "Smith Issues Rules for Naming Judges," *The New York Times*, March 7, 1981, sec. 1, p. 11.

[108] Wheeler, "Prevent Federal Court Nomination Battles," pp. 13-14.

[109] When both Senators are of the same political party as the President, four members are appointed by each Senator; when one Senator is of the same political party as the President, five members are appointed by that Senator, with three members appointed by the other Senator; and when both Senators are of the opposite political party as the President, two members are appointed by each senator, with four members of the commission appointed "by the most senior elected official of the President's party." In all three situations just noted, two more members are appointed by the state bar of Wisconsin. In the case of district judge or U.S. attorney appointments, the eleventh member of the commission is appointed by the dean of the University of Wisconsin Law School, or the dean's designee, for consideration of vacancies in the Western District of Wisconsin, or by the dean of the Marquette University Law School, or the dean's designee, for vacancies in the Eastern District of Wisconsin. In the case of circuit court appointments, the commission's eleventh and twelfth members are the deans of both law schools, or their designees.

[110] "Wisconsin Federal Nominating Commission Charter," 5 p. (Copy obtained from the offices of Senators Herb Kohl and Russell D. Feingold).

[111] In some past instances, Senators have reportedly considered themselves bound to accept, and pass along to the President, the recommendations of their nominating commissions. A study of judicial selection during the presidency of Jimmy Carter, when senatorial use of nominating commissions was widespread, found that the commissions could be divided into two groups — "based on whether the commissions submitted their lists of candidates directly to the executive branch without alteration by their sponsors, or to their sponsors, who reserved the right to reduce the lists and submit smaller lists of selected candidates to the executive branch. In 17 states, senators chose to take their commissions' lists and select one or more candidates from their lists for each vacancy." Neff, *United States District Judge Nominating Commissions*, p. 65.

[112] A Department of Justice official involved in the judicial selection process during the first two years of George W. Bush's presidency explained, in a Jan. 6, 2003, interview with scholars, that the "outreach to senators, the liaisons for senators, are done by the White House Counsel's office.... The White House Counsel's Office handles the contact and consultations to all home state senators, even on circuit courts, and even if the person is from

the opposite party." Goldman et al., "W. Bush Remaking the Judiciary," p. 287. The same scholars, after interviewing Bush Administration officials two years later, reiterated their earlier impression about the consultative role played by the White House: "If there is one domain in the selection process that remains an exclusive preserve of the White House Counsel's Office, as we found two years ago, that area involves consultation and negotiation with senators about specific nominees or potential nominees." Goldman et al., "W. Bush's Judiciary: The First Term Record," p 247.

[113] If FBI and other forms and questionnaires already have been filled out, these will be reviewed by Administration vetters for any points that might need to be raised or cleared up when a candidate is interviewed. Vetters also might make telephone contact with individuals named in the questionnaires (such as the chief judges of the federal district and appeals courts in which the candidates practiced law) to elicit their impressions of the candidates.

[114] From 1952, during the last months of the Truman presidency, to the end of the Clinton presidency in 2001, the ABA's Standing Committee on Federal Judiciary played a quasi- official advisory role to each Administration in the lower court selection process, confidentially evaluating the professional qualifications of candidates for lower court judgeships, prior to their nomination. During this process, each Administration informed the ABA committee of persons under final consideration for nomination to district or circuit court judgeships, with the President awaiting the committee's evaluations of the candidates before deciding whether to nominate. See Archived CRS Report 96-446, *The American Bar Association's Standing Committee on Federal Judiciary: A Historical Overview,* by Denis Steven Rutkus. (Copy available from author.) In 2001, however, President George W. Bush ended this process, excluding the ABA committee from any further role in the pre- nomination judicial selection process. Since then, the committee has performed an evaluation of judicial candidates only after their nominations have been made by the President. Evaluations are sent to the Senate Judiciary Committee, which typically awaits receipt of the ABA evaluations before it holds confirmation hearings on the nominations in question.

[115] However, as noted above, the ABA committee does not perform this role for the current Bush Administration (which, unlike previous recent administrations, does not inform the ABA committee of judicial candidates it is considering or seek the committee's evaluation of these candidates before making nomination decisions).

[116] Subsequently, during a particular presidency, a Senator might consider it necessary to have additional contact with the Administration to confirm or further clarify the nature of the Senator's recommending role. This situation might arise, for example, if the Senator believes that the Administration is not fully conforming to earlier agreed-upon procedures regarding the Senator's role in the judicial selection process, if new Administration officials assume responsibility for judicial candidate selection or liaison with Senators on judicial selection matters, or if a new Member is elected to the state's other Senate seat.

[117] President Ronald Reagan's Administration appears to have been the first to institute a regular requirement that a home state Senator provide the names of at least three candidates for a vacant judgeship. This practice was continued by the Administration of George H.W. Bush, observed part of the time by the Clinton Administration, and re-instituted as a systematic practice by the Administration of George W. Bush. Such Administration requirements, however, have not always prevented Senators from expressing strong preferences for one candidate or from securing for that candidate an "inside track" in the Administration's selection process. For instance, during the Reagan presidency, an attorney working on judicial selections in the White House counsel's office noted that "some of our fiercest battles were with same-party Republican senators on district judges, where President Reagan sought to institute a very controversial rule. He insisted on receiving three names from Republican senators for district court nominees. We tried to enforce that rigorously. We had some senators who would say, 'If President Reagan wants three names, I'll give him three names, Smith, Smith, and Smith.' Ultimately, Judge Smith got appointed." Alan Charles Raul, associate counsel to President Ronald Reagan, quoted in, "Selecting Federal Judges; The Role and Responsibilities of the Executive Branch, *Judicature*, vol. 86, July-Aug. 2002, p. 20. For district court appointments during the presidency of George H.W. Bush, a scholar noted, "the Justice Department asks Republican senators to submit three names for Department consideration. There has been some resistance on the part of some senators, but the Administration is not sympathetic to senators who submit one name and insist that person be named. However, the Justice Department will consider one candidate at a time provided that if the person proposed is not satisfactory to Justice, the senator will submit another name until a suitable candidate is found." Sheldon Goldman, "The Bush Imprint on the Judiciary: Carrying on a Tradition," *Judicature*, vol. 74, April-May 1991, p. 297. During most of the Clinton presidency, the Justice Department

"evaluated one person at a time for each district court vacancy ... although the proclivity was relaxed somewhat during the last two years in contentious settings where [Assistant Attorney General Eleanor D.] Acheson noted, 'we knew the whole thing was going to take a whole lot longer. We found ourselves on more than one occasion looking at two or three people simultaneously and making a decision about whom to go with.' With appeals court positions, it remained more common to evaluate multiple candidates for specific slots...." Sheldon Goldman, Elliot Slotnick, et al., "Clinton's Judges; Summing Up the Legacy," *Judicature*, vol. 84, March-April 2001, p. 231. (Hereafter cited as Goldman, "Clinton's Judges.") For the Administration of President George W. Bush, the standard practice has been to require that home state Senators recommending candidates for district judgeships provide "multiple names." Nov. 21, 2003, telephone interview with attorney Sheila Joy, Office of Legal Policy, Department of Justice.

[118] In this vein, political scientists in a 2005 article examining the lower court selection process of the Administration of President George W. Bush noted, "Historically, identification of potential district court nominees has largely been the role of home state presidential party senators, or in their absence, other prominent persons from the president's party. The White House's role in designating nominees has increased dramatically, particularly in recent administrations, at the court of appeals level." Goldman et al., "W. Bush's Judiciary: The First Term Record," p. 246. Similarly, in a 2001 article reviewing the lower court selection process of the Administration of President Bill Clinton, the same political scientists noted that the names of district court candidates "were typically directly submitted by Democratic senators, or when there were no Democratic senators from the states of the vacancies, by Democratic House members or Democratic state officials. Where appeals court vacancies were to be filled, names typically came from the White House Counsel's office." Goldman, "Clinton's Judges," pp. 229-230.

[119] The Administration of President George W. Bush has asserted on various occasions that it is very open to judicial candidate recommendations from Senators of both parties as well as to their views about other candidates under Administration consideration. At the conclusion of President Bush's first term, for instance, a White House counsel told scholars, "We always consult with home state senators, Democrats or Republicans, to find out if there are candidates that they would like for us to consider. We are also interested in receiving their feedback on candidates were are considering. The consultation has been extensive and consistently so." Dabney Friedrich,

associate White House counsel, quoted in Goldman et al., "W. Bush's Judiciary: The First Term Record," p. 247.

[120] See, for example, table entitled "Senate Judiciary Committee Blue-Slip Policy by Committee Chairman (1956-2003)," in Archived CRS Report RL32012, History of the Blue Slip, p. 26. See also, in same report, pp. 13, 22, which discuss two instances, one in 1985 and the other in 2003, in which the Judiciary Committee considered judicial nominations that had received negative blue slips from both home state Senators.

[121] Of course, if a member of the Judiciary Committee, the Senator himself or herself may engage in this filibuster, either alone or (ideally, from the Senator's standpoint) with support from other members of the committee.

[122] U.S. Congress, Senate Committee on the Judiciary, Rules of Procedure, accessed Feb. 5, 2008, at [http://www.judiciary.senate.gov/committee_rules.cfm].

[123] Sen. Patrick J. Leahy, "Nomination of Miguel A. Estrada, of Virginia, To Be United States Circuit Judge for the District of Columbia Circuit," remarks in the Senate, *Congressional Record,* vol. 149, March 13, 2003, p. 6185.

[124] Sen. Orrin G. Hatch, "Nomination of Miguel A. Estrada, of Virginia, To Be United States Circuit Judge for the District of Columbia Circuit," letter to Senate Democratic leader introduced into the *Record* during remarks in the Senate, *Congressional Record*, vol. 149, March 3, 2003, p. 4954.

[125] The Senator initially may place the hold with the party leader anonymously. However, if, in response to a motion, the party leader or the leader's designee objects explicitly on behalf of the Senator, the leader, under new Senate rules, would apparently identify the Senator. For an analysis of the process by which Senators use holds to block or delay Senate floor consideration of, or action on, a measure or matter, see CRS Report RL34255, *Senate Policy on "Holds": Action in the 110th Congress*, by Walter Oleszek.

[126] A filibuster-minded Senator would be one prepared to use extended debate and other delaying actions to prevent a vote from occurring.

[127] For analysis of Senate procedure and rules that govern efforts by Senators to end floor debate on nominations, see CRS Report RL3 1948, *Evolution of the Senate's Role in the Nomination and Confirmation Process: A Brief History*, by Betsy Palmer (under heading "Filibuster"); and CRS Report RL32843, *"Entrenchment" of Senate Procedure and the "Nuclear Option" for Change: Possible Proceedings and Their Implications*, by Richard S. Beth.

[128] "It is up to the majority leader to decide whether, or for how long, he will honor a colleague's hold. Scheduling the business of the Senate is the

fundamental prerogative of the majority leader, and it is done in consultation with the minority leader." CRS Report 98- 712, *"Holds" in the Senate*, by Walter J. Oleszek.

[129] If an initial cloture motion is not agreed to, supporters of the nomination are not precluded from filing additional cloture motions to limit debate and force a vote on the nomination.

[130] See more detailed discussion of these letters in above report section on "Blue Slip Policy of Senate Judiciary Committee."

[131] Alberto R. Gonzales, counsel to the President, to Sen. Patrick J. Leahy and other Democratic members of Senate Judiciary Committee, May 2, 2001. (Copy available from author.) Gonzales wrote to the Democratic Senators that "we generally agree with your specific suggestions for keeping home state Senators informed and seeking their advice." He added that in "all cases, you may be certain that we will work hard to ensure that home state Senators will have a suitable opportunity to express their views concerning possible nominees well in advance of nomination."

[132] Sen. Orrin G. Hatch, "Statement of Sen. Orrin Hatch," news release, April 17, 1997. (Copy available from author).

[133] Sen. Orrin G. Hatch, "Nomination of Miguel A. Estrada, of Virginia, To Be United States Circuit Judge for the District of Columbia Circuit," *Congressional Record*, vol. 149, March 3, 2003, p. 4933.

[134] In this vein, the ranking Democratic member on the Senate Judiciary Committee, at a June 17, 2004, executive business meeting of the committee, noted that a controversial nominee to the U.S. Court of Appeals for the Sixth Circuit about to be voted on by the committee was opposed by Michigan's two Democratic Senators (who each returned a negative blue slip to the committee). Both of these Senators had "attempted to work with the White House to offer their advice, but their input was rejected." Statement of Sen. Patrick J. Leahy, "Senate Judiciary Committee, Executive Business Meeting, The Saad Nomination," June 17, 2004. (Copy available from author.) Similarly, in a 2005 letter to the Senate Republican majority leader, the Senate Democratic leader maintained that "[o]ver the last four years President Bush too often failed to seek the advice of the Senate before making unwise nominations, and Democrats lacked any means short of a filibuster to carry out our duty under the Advise and Consent Clause of the Constitution." Sen. Harry Reid, Senate Democratic leader, letter to Sen. William Frist, Senate majority leader, May 10, 2005. (Copy available from author.)

[135] See, for instance, the remarks of Sen. Orrin G. Hatch (R-UT), then-chair of the Judiciary Committee, during Senate floor debate in 2003 on a circuit court nomination opposed by the majority of Senate Democrats, during which Sen. Hatch said: "I think some of our colleagues on the other side want to choose these judges, and we are finding that continuously in their arguments, that the administration does not 'consult' with them. If consultation means the administration has to take whatever judges the Democrats desire, that is not consultation. Consultation is letting them know what is on the mind of the President, and the administration discussing it with them, seeing if they have any real objections to the choices of the President, asking them to weigh in and give the administration whatever information they can, and then making the choice and going from there. That is consultation." Sen. Orrin G. Hatch, "Nomination of Miguel A. Estrada, of Virginia, To Be United States Circuit Judge, for the District of Columbia Circuit," Congressional Record, vol. 149, Feb. 12, 2003, p. 3544.

[136] Available on the website of the U.S. Department of Justice's Office of Legal Policy are lists showing, for each circuit and district court nomination in the 107th and 108th Congress, whether the home state Senators returned a blue slip and whether the blue slip was "positive" or "negative." (Comparable blue slip information is not available on the website for the 109th and 110th Congresses.) See [http://www.usdoj .gov/olp/blueslips/htm], accessed on Feb. 5, 2008. During the 108th Congress, the website shows, that "negative" blue slips were returned to the Judiciary Committee for the circuit court nominations of Richard A. Griffin, David W. McKeague, Susan B. Neilson, and Henry S. Saad (all of Michigan) and that one home state Senator declined to return a blue slip for the circuit court nomination of Carolyn B. Kuhl of California (with the other Senator having "reserved judgement"). Notwithstanding the absence of positive blue slips from their home state Senators, the five nominations all were considered and reported by the Senate Judiciary Committee. See Appendix 3 in CRS Report RL3 1868, *U.S. Circuit and District Court Nominations by President George W. Bush During the 107th-109th Congresses,* by Denis Steven Rutkus, Kevin M. Scott, and Maureen Bearden. (Hereafter cited as CRS Report RL3 1868, Nominations During the 107th-109th Congress.)

[137] In the case of four of the nominations, motions were made by Senate Republicans to close debate, but these motions proved unsuccessful. The Senate (as discussed above) can close debate by passing a cloture motion, which requires a super-majority of three-fifths of the Senate, or 60

Members, voting in favor. During the 108th Congress, there were 10 circuit nominations on which the Senate, on one or more occasions, voted not to close debate, including the nominations of Carolyn B. Kuhl, Richard A. Griffin, David W. McKeague, and Henry S. Saad. The number of votes cast to close debate on these four nominations, in each case, fell short of 60. No floor vote of any kind, procedural or on whether to confirm, was cast by the Senate during the 108th Congress on the fifth nomination cited in the previous footnote, Susan B. Neilson. See Appendix 3 in CRS Report RL3 1868, *Nominations During the 107th-109th Congress.*

[138] Of the five aforementioned nominees, the three who received Senate confirmation in the 109th Congress were Richard A. Griffin, David W. McKeague, and Susan B. Neilson. See Appendix 1 in CRS Report RL3 1868, *Nominations During the 107th-109th Congresses.*

[139] See, for example, Sen. Debbie Stabenow, "Judicial Nominees," *Congressional Record*, vol. 149, July 16, 2003, p. 18212.

[140] See, for example, Sen. Bill Frist, "Stalled Nominations for the Sixth Circuit," *Congressional Record*, vol. 149, July 16, 2003, pp. 18207-18211.

[141] See, for example, Carl Hulse, "Filibuster Fight Nears Showdown,"*The New York Times*, May 8, 2005, pp. 1,19; Charles Babington, "Clash Over Judicial Filibusters Nears Boiling Point," *The Washington Post*, May 9, 2005, p. A2 1; and Bill Sammon and Charles Hurt, "Bush Raps Judicial Filibuster," *The Washington Times*, May 10, 2005, p. A12.

[142] Senate Republican leaders announced that their move to change Senate precedents to bar filibusters against judicial nominations would occur in conjunction with their efforts to close floor debate on the nomination of Priscilla Owen to be a U.S. circuit court of appeals judge. (An earlier nomination of Owen to the same judgeship, during the 108th Congress, had been successfully filibustered four times by Senate Democrats.) Keith Perine and Daphne Retter, "Judicial Showdown Starts with Owen," *CQ Today*, vol. 41, May 18, 2005, pp. 1,32.

[143] Charles Babington and Shailagh Murray, "A Last-Minute Deal on Judicial Nominations," *The Washington Post*, May 24, 2005, pp. A1, A4. See also CRS Report RS22208, *The 'Memorandum of Understanding': A Senate Compromise on Judicial Filibusters*, by Walter J. Oleszek; and CRS Report RL3 3094, *Congress and the Courts: Current Policy Issues*, by Walter J. Oleszek (under headings "The Bipartisan Agreement: A Memorandum of Understanding" and "Diverse Definitions of 'Extraordinary Circumstances'").

[144] Other controversial nominees received no further Senate action during the rest of the 109th Congress, and four of them were not re-nominated in the 110th Congress. See David G. Savage and Henry Weinstein, "4 White Flags Fly in Courts Fight; With the Senate in the Hands of Democrats, the Most Controversial of Bush's Judicial Nominees Are Withdrawn," *Los Angeles Times*, Jan. 10, 2007, p. A12.

[145] Seth Stern, "Deconstructing the Senate's Bipartisan Deal on Judicial Nominations," *CQ Today*, vol. 41, May 25, 2005, p. 31. The full text of the memorandum of understanding can be found in the *Congressional Record*, daily edition, vol. 151, May 24, 2005, pp. S5830- S583 1.

[146] Blue slip information for the 107th Congress posted on the U.S. Department of Justice website has listed five circuit court nominations and one district court nomination for which one or both home state Senators returned a negative blue slip or declined to return a positive blue slip. These specifically were the circuit court nominations of Terrence W. Boyle of North Carolina, Carolyn B. Kuhl of California, and David W. McKeague, Susan B. Neilson, and Henry W. Saad, all of Michigan, and the district court nomination of James C. Dever III of North Carolina. See [http:i/www.usdoj .gov/olp/blueslips/htm], accessed Feb. 5, 2008. In the absence of positive blue slips from both home state Senators, none of these five nominations was considered by the Judiciary Committee during the 107th Congress. See Appendices 2 and 4 in CRS Report RL31868, *Nominations During the 107th-109th Congresses*. The five were among 12 circuit court nominees and 15 district court nominees failing to be confirmed who did not receive a hearing during the Congress, while 17 other circuit court and 83 other district court nominees during the Congress did receive Senate confirmation. See Ibid., under the headings "President Bush's Circuit Court Nominations During Particular Congresses," and "President Bush's District Court Nominations During Particular Congresses." For analysis of the kind of opposition that President George W. Bush's lower court nominations encountered in the Senate during the 107th Congress, including use of the Judiciary Committee's blue slip procedure to prevent nominations from receiving committee consideration, see Jonathan Groner, "A Major Shift in the Battle for the Bench," *Legal Times*, vol. 25, Nov. 11, 2005, p. 8.

[147] See "Senators Can Veto Judicial Picks," *Grand Rapids Press*, Jan. 5, 2007, p. B6, reporting that "U.S. Sen. Patrick Leahy, D-Vt., who chairs the Senate Judiciary Committee, said this week both senators from a state, regardless of party affiliation, will have to concur with a nomination before his committee will consider it." See also Keith Perine, "As Judicial Battles

Loom, Leahy Revives Senate 'Blue Slip' Tradition," *CQ Today*, Jan. 3, 2007, accessed Feb. 5, 2008, at [www.cq.com].

[148] See, for instance, the opening statements of Sen. Patrick J. Leahy, chairman of the Senate Judiciary Committee, at committee hearings held on judicial nominations on July 19, 2007, at [www.leahy.senate.gov/press/200707/071907c.html] and on Dec. 18, 2007, at [www.leahy.senate.gov/press/200712/121907f.html], both accessed Feb. 5, 2008, as well as the Senate floor statement of Sen. Leahy on March 3, 2008, at "Judicial Nominations," *Congressional Record*, daily edition, vol. 154, March 3, 2008, pp. S 1460-S 1462.

[149] On March 3, 2008, in a Senate floor statement, the chairman of the Judiciary Committee noted that of "the 11 circuit nominations that have been pending before the Senate this year, 8 have not had the support of home State Senators." Sen. Patrick J. Leahy, "Judicial Nominations," *Congressional Record*, daily edition, vol. 154, March 3, 2008, p. S1461. See also Keith Perine, "No Easing of Bush's Stance on Judicial Nominations," *CQ Weekly*, vol. 65, Nov. 5, 2007, pp. 3315-3316. (Hereafter cited as Perine, "No Easing of Bush's Stance.")

[150] Sen. John Warner (R-VA) was quoted as having told the White House that "I steadfastly remain committed to the recommendations stated in my joint letter with Senator Webb." Jerry Markon, "Bush's Picks for Court Spur Criticism by Warner, Webb," *The Washington Post*, Sept. 7, 2007, p. B5. Sen. Jim Webb (D-VA) declared that "despite our good faith, bipartisan effort to accommodate the President, the recommendations that Senator Warner and I made have been ignored. The White House talks about the spirit of bipartisanship, lamenting congressional obstructionism. The White House cannot expect to complain about the confirmation of federal judges when they proceed to act in this manner." Sen. Jim Webb, "Webb Responds to White House's Nomination of Duncan Getchell," news release, Sept. 6, 2007, accessed Feb. 5, 2008, at [www.webb.senate.gov/].

[151] Peter Hardin, "Webb Has Pair of Fights on his Hands; He May Block Judge Pick and Will Push Again for More Time Off for Troops,"*Richmond Times Dispatch*, Sept. 13, 2007, p. B2.

[152] Manu Raju, "Judicial Nominee Withdraws amid Democratic Criticism," *TheHill.com*, Jan. 18, 2008, accessed Jan. 24, 2008, at [www.thehill.com]. The nominee, Duncan Getchell of Virginia, had been nominated by President Bush to a judgeship on the U.S. Court of Appeals for the Fourth Circuit. In a letter sent to the White House, Getchell said that "recent press reports indicate ... that the Senate Democratic leadership will not allow a hearing [on the

nomination] to go forward...." Ibid. During the 110th Congress, opposition by home state Senators also has blocked at least two U.S. district court nominations from being considered by the Senate Judiciary Committee (in one case influencing President George W. Bush to withdraw the nomination). See Jay Jochnowitz, "Donohue Won't Get Federal Judgeship; Ex-Lieutenant Governor's Quest formally Ended by White House Action," *The Times Union* [Albany, NY], Sept. 7, 2007, p. A3 (reporting on President Bush's withdrawal, on Sept. 6, 2007, of the nomination of Mary O. Donohue to the U.S. District Court for the Northern District of New York); Erica Werner, "Boxer Blocking Former Rep. Rogan Nomination to Federal Judiciary," *Associated Press*, Nov. 30, 2007, accessed on Feb. 5, 2008, at [www.lexisnexis.com] (regarding nomination of former Rep. James E. Rogan to the U.S. District Court for the Central District of California); David G. Savage, "Rogan May Be Denied Seat on Federal Bench," *Los Angeles Times*, Dec. 4, 2007, p. A14.

[153] See, for example, in Goldman et al., "W. Bush Remaking the Judiciary," p. 287, quoting Brett Kavanaugh, associate White House counsel, early in the Bush presidency, as follows: "We consult with the home state senators on both district court and courts of appeals and run by them, before an FBI background check, names of people who are under consideration to get their reaction ahead of time, and that helps avoid problems down the road. We maintain consultation logs, and I think there's been extensive consultation." See also the previously cited remarks, later in the Bush presidency, of White House counsel Dabney Friedrich, quoted in Goldman et al, "W. Bush's Judiciary: The First Term Record," p. 247.

[154] Elana Schor and Manu Raju, "Dems Grapple with Appeals Nominee, High Court's Future," *The Hill*, vol. 14, July 19, 2007, p. 4. The nomination in question was that of Shalom Stone of New Jersey to the U.S. Court of Appeals for the Third Circuit, which another news account reported "was made without input from the state's [New Jersey's] two Democratic Senators. Lisa Brennan, "N.J. Republican Lawyer Nominated to Fill Alito Seat on 3rd Circuit," *New Jersey Law Journal*, July 19, 2007, accessed Feb. 5, 2008, at [http://www.law.com].

[155] See earlier section of this report under the heading "Lesser Role for Senators When Recommending Circuit Court Candidates."

[156] The article also reported that "[s]ome conservatives privately say that the Republican senators are overstepping their responsibility, which traditionally gives them a much larger role in district courts than in the

appellate courts." Robert Barnes and Michael Abramowitz, "Conservatives Worry about Court Vacancies," *The Washington Post*, June 10, 2007, p. A4.

[157] At the start of the 110th Congress, an aide to Sen. Patrick J. Leahy, chairman of the Judiciary Committee, said that Sen. Leahy would abide by the same blue slip policy as he had when he previously had been chairman (during the 107th Congress). Under this policy, it was explained, both Senators from a state, regardless of party affiliation, would have to return a positive blue slip on a judicial nomination before it could be considered by the Judiciary Committee. Sarah Kellogg, "Michigan Senators Get More Say over Judges," *Mlive.com*, Jan. 5, 2007, accessed Feb. 23, 2007, at [www.mlive.com].

[158] A news story in November 2007, for instance, cited Senators from five states — California, Michigan, New Jersey, Rhode Island, and Virginia — who had openly faulted the Bush Administration for not having consulted them about potential circuit court nominees from their states. Perine, "No Easing of Bush's Stance," p. 3315.

[159] Ibid., for example, commenting that President Bush's "reluctance to consult with Democrats makes it likely that few, if any nominees from a state represented by a Democratic senator are going to receive a confirmation vote."

[160] Carrie Budoff Brown, "Bush Stirs Sparks on Judges," *The Politico,* Oct. 2, 2007, accessed Feb. 5, 2008, at [www.politico.com], quoting White House spokeswoman Emily Lawrimore.

[161] Manu Raju, "Republicans Seek Quicker Action on Judges from the White House," *The Hill*, vol. 14, Oct. 4, 2007, p. 3, quoting White House spokeswoman Emily Lawrimore.

[162] Alberto R. Gonzales, counsel to the President, letter to Sen. Carl Levin and Sen. Debbie A. Stabenow, April 2, 2003, printed in "Stalled Nominations for the Sixth Circuit," *Congressional Record*, vol. 149, July 16, 2003, p. 18210.

[163] Opening statement of Sen. Patrick Leahy, ranking Democratic member, Senate Judiciary Committee, Committee Business Meeting, May 3, 2001, accessed May 3, 2001, at [www.senate.gov/~judiciary/pjl050301e.htm]. (Copy available from author.)

[164] Statement by Sen. Leahy at an April 1, 2003, hearing on judicial nominations, in U.S. Congress, Senate Committee on the Judiciary, *Confirmation Hearings on Federal Appointments*, hearings, part 2, 108th Cong., 1st sess., Feb. 5, 12, March 12, 27, and April 1, 2003 (Washington: GPO, 2004), p. 997.

In: Court Nominations
Editor: Peter C. Kesterhoff, pp. 87-153
ISBN 978-1-60692-556-0

Chapter 2

NOMINATION AND CONFIRMATION OF LOWER FEDERAL COURT JUDGES IN PRESIDENTIAL ELECTION YEARS*

Denis Steven Rutkus and Kevin M. Scott

ABSTRACT

This chapter seeks to shed light on whether Senate processing of lower court nominations, particularly to the courts of appeals, has tended over recent decades to slow down in presidential election years. The chapter begins by reviewing recent debate, and historical events dating back to 1980, concerning whether the Senate and its Judiciary Committee customarily observe a practice referred to as the "Thurmond rule." Next, the chapter provides narratives on each presidential election year from 1980 to 2004, reviewing Senate and committee actions taken on court of appeals and district court nominations in each of the years. The chapter then compares these years quantitatively, examining the number and percent of nominations processed and the last dates of committee and Senate action taken. Findings include the following:

- Senators of both parties at different times have spoken of their expectations of a drop-off in processing of judicial nominations occurring earlier in presidential election years than in other years. However, there is no written Senate or Judiciary Committee rule —

---

* Excerpted from CRS Report RL34615, August 13, 2008.

nor was any bipartisan agreement reached during the 1980-2004 period — concerning judicial nominations in presidential election years.

- The Senate has, on average, confirmed fewer court of appeals nominees in presidential election years than in any other year of a presidential term between 1977 and 2007.
- In the presidential election years from 1980 to 2004, there was no consistently observed date after which the Judiciary Committee or Senate ceased processing lower court nominations; however, in the three most recent completed presidential election years, the Senate confirmed its last court of appeals nominee in July or earlier, while in the four preceding presidential election years, the Senate confirmed its final court of appeals nominee in October or later.
- On average, fewer court of appeals nominations received hearings, were reported, and were confirmed in the three most recent completed presidential election years (1996, 2000, and 2004) than in the four preceding presidential election years (1980, 1984, 1988, and 1992).
- From 1980 to 2004, the Senate confirmed, on average, more nominations (and a greater percentage of pending nominations) in years when the Senate majority was of the President's party than years in which partisan control of the presidency and the Senate was divided.

The chapter also outlines relevant considerations for Senators in deciding whether to seek to speed or slow the judicial confirmation process in a presidential election year. These considerations include the public policy views of the incumbent President (and his successor), patronage considerations for Senators of both political parties, the appearance of a partisan judicial confirmation process, and whether a slowdown might greatly affect the judicial vacancy rate.

INTRODUCTION

A continuing point of contention in the second session of the 110th Congress has been the pace at which the Senate should consider judicial nominations, particularly those to the courts of appeals, in a presidential election year. Some Senators, along party lines, have differed as to whether, thus far in the 110th Congress, a sufficient number of court of appeals nominees have been confirmed, or are on track to be confirmed. [1] As of July 31, 2008, the Senate had confirmed 10 court of appeals nominations in the 110th Congress, with 4 of those confirmations coming in the second session [2].

President Bush has repeatedly claimed that the Senate has failed to hold hearings, report, and provide confirmation votes for his court of appeals nominees at a pace that he views as acceptable, [3] and several Senators have argued that previous Presidents fared better as their terms came to an end. [4] Other Senators, however, in defense of the Senate's recent performance in considering judicial nominations, have asserted that the Senate's consideration of nominees to the courts of appeals traditionally slows in presidential election years, and that the Senate, in the 110th Congress, has more than kept pace with the judicial confirmation performance of the Senate in other recent Congresses [5].

The ranking minority member of the Senate Judiciary Committee, Senator Arlen Specter of Pennsylvania, has faulted the Senate majority for declining to allow committee consideration of several court of appeals nominees who, he maintains, are highly qualified and deserve to be confirmed. "The reason they have not been approved," Senator Specter contended, "is that there is an interest in holding open these vacancies in the event there is a President of the other party to fill them with the Democrats." [6] Senator Patrick J. Leahy of Vermont, chairman of the Judiciary Committee (to which circuit court of appeals and district court nominations are referred), has rejected minority criticisms of the committee's handling of President Bush's judicial nominations. "I have always said," Senator Leahy stated on the Senate floor, "that we would treat this President's nominees more fairly than Republicans treated President Clinton's. And we have." [7]

This chapter seeks to inform the current debate by analyzing how the Senate processed court of appeals and district court nominations in presidential election years dating back to 1980. In so doing, the chapter addresses the question of whether the Senate would be in keeping with past experience if, at some point in the current session of this Congress, it deliberately slowed down, or stopped altogether, its consideration of pending lower court nominations in anticipation of the November 4, 2008, presidential election. It also seeks, among other things, to determine whether Members of the Senate have had a shared understanding or expectation that there will be a decline in Senate action on judicial nominations in presidential election years, at what point in presidential election years such declines in Senate activity on lower court nominations have tended to occur, and whether a smaller number of lower court nominations are typically processed in a presidential election year than in other years of a presidential term.

The chapter begins its inquiry with an overview of recent Senate debate on whether the Senate and its Judiciary Committee customarily observe a practice referred to by some as the "Thurmond rule." [8] Next, to provide historical perspective, the chapter provides separate narratives on each presidential election year from 1980 to 2004, reviewing the actions taken on lower court nominations in each of these years. The chapter then compares each of these presidential election years quantitatively, examining in each year the number and percent of judicial nominations processed as well as the last dates of committee and Senate action taken on the nominations.

Thereafter, the chapter compares the number of judicial nominations processed by the Judiciary Committee and the Senate in each of the presidential election years from 1980 to 2004 with the other years of the presidential terms in question. A final section reviews a range of reasons for Senators to oppose, or to favor, a slowdown in processing judicial nominations in presidential election years. It concludes by noting possible options for the Senate, during the remainder of the 110th Congress, that, if undertaken, might alleviate partisan controversy concerning the processing of judicial nominations in a presidential election year. The chapter, in most sections, focuses primarily on Senate consideration of court of appeals nominations, and to a lesser extent on district court nominations, reflecting the fact that, in the 110th and other recent Congresses, controversies over the judicial confirmation process usually, if not always, have involved court of appeals nominations.

Various findings can be drawn from the chapter's aforementioned sections, among them the following:

- Senators of both parties, some closely associated with the judicial confirmation process, have, at different times, spoken of their expectations of a drop-off in Senate processing of lower court nominations occurring earlier in presidential election years than in other years. Usually, if not always, they have done so when they were not members of the President's political party.
- There is no written Senate or Judiciary Committee rule concerning judicial nominations in a presidential election year. Nor, during the 1980-2004 period, was an apparent consensus or bipartisan agreement ever reached in the Senate regarding how many judicial nominations should be processed in a presidential election year or how late in the year they should be processed.
- In the presidential election years from 1980 to 2004, there was no consistently observed date, or point in time, after which the Senate Judiciary Committee or the Senate ceased processing lower court nominations.

- The last seven presidential election years have varied considerably in terms of number of lower court nominations that received hearings, were reported, and were confirmed by the Senate.
- The 1996 presidential election year and subsequent presidential election years (2000 and 2004) have seen fewer court of appeals nominees processed, on average, than the presidential election years from 1980 to 1992.
- Fewer judicial nominations tended to be processed when the presidency and the Senate were controlled by different political parties than when they were under unified partisan control.
- Since 1980, fewer nominees to the courts of appeals, on average, have been reported by the Judiciary Committee and confirmed by the Senate in presidential election years than in other years of a presidential term.
- Of the four years of a presidential term, the presidential election year, on average, has been the second-least productive in terms of number of district court nominations processed by the Senate (the first year of the term being the least productive).

WHETHER THE SENATE CUSTOMARILY OBSERVES THE "THURMOND RULE"

Senators have expressed differing views as to whether a drop-off in Senate processing of lower federal court nominations occurs, or should occur, in presidential election years. Some have asserted that, in these years, the Senate Judiciary Committee and the Senate customarily slow down the processing of judicial nominations at earlier points, and confirm fewer nominations, than in other years. Others Senators, however, have rejected the notion that such slowdowns are customary or appropriate, pointing to past presidential election years in which the Judiciary Committee and Senate processed relatively large numbers of judicial nominations, some relatively late in the year.

Recent Debate over Thurmond Rule

Thus far in the 110th Congress, the debate in the Senate has revolved largely around the question whether the Senate and its Judiciary Committee customarily observe a practice referred to by some as the "Thurmond rule," named after the late Senator, and former Judiciary Committee chairman, Strom Thurmond of South Carolina. Those who claim the Thurmond rule exists allege that its origins can be traced to events that occurred in 1980, when Senator Edward M. Kennedy of Massachusetts chaired the Judiciary Committee and Senator Thurmond was the ranking minority member on the committee. Adherents of a Thurmond rule have sometimes differed as to precisely when in the year it takes effect; nevertheless, almost all Senators who have cited it have described it as an established practice according to which, at some point in a presidential election year, the Judiciary Committee and the Senate no longer act on judicial nominations — with exceptions sometimes made for nominees who have bipartisan support from Senate committee and party leaders.

December 2006, just before assuming the chairmanship of the committee, Senator Leahy told a law school audience

> The Thurmond Rule, in memory of Strom Thurmond — he put this in when the Republicans were in the minority — which said in a presidential election year after Spring no judges would go through except by the consent of both the Republican and Democratic leader.... I want to be bi-partisan. We will institute the Thurmond Rule. [9]

Subsequently, in a March 3, 2008, Senate floor statement, Senator Leahy referred to the "history of the Thurmond Rule, by which Republicans, then [in 1980] in the minority, insisted that judicial vacancies in the last year of a President's term remain vacant in order to be filled with the nominations of the next President." [10] Again, four days later, in another floor statement, Senator Leahy recalled that

> ...when President Reagan was running for President and Senator Thurmond, then in the Republican minority as ranking member of the Judiciary Committee, instituted a policy to stall President Carter's nominations. That policy, known as the "Thurmond Rule," was put in when the Republicans were in the minority. It is a rule that we still follow, and it will take effect very soon here. [11]

Subsequently, at a June 12, 2008, meeting of the Judiciary Committee, Senator Leahy indicated that the Thurmond rule he had enunciated earlier was now in effect:

> We are now way past the time of a Thurmond rule named after Senator Thurmond when he was in the minority, and I'm trying to respect that. We are still putting judges through. But I must note this point — further judges will be

> moved only by a consent of the two leaders of the Senate and the two leaders of the committee. [12]

Senator Harry Reid, the Senate majority leader, has expressed agreement with Senator Leahy about the existence of a Thurmond rule. In April 10, 2008, floor remarks, Senator Reid said, “In a Presidential election year, it is always very tough for judges. That is the way it has been for a long time, and that is why we have the Thurmond rule and other such rules.” [13] In similar floor remarks five days later,

> Senator Reid stated, “you know, there is a Thurmond doctrine that says: After June, we will have to take a real close look at judges in a Presidential election year.” [14]

Various minority Senators, however, have disputed the assertion by some majority Senators that there is an established Judiciary Committee or Senate practice known as the Thurmond rule. In an April 1, 2008, floor statement, Senator Orrin G. Hatch, a former chairman of the Judiciary Committee (1995-200 1 and 2003-2005), declared, “We have already heard about the so-called Thurmond rule, supposedly justifying grinding the confirmation process to a halt in this Presidential election year. The Thurmond rule neither is a rule nor can it be attributed to the late Senator Strom Thurmond....” [15] Expressing similar sentiments, Senator Jeff Sessions, in April 16, 2008, floor remarks, stated,

> I would say there has been talk about invoking the so-called Thurmond Rule. The Thurmond Rule could sort of be, if you want it to be, an excuse for slow-walking nominees and not approving the nominees who ought to be approved just because there is a Presidential election on the horizon. Majority Leader Harry Reid mentioned last night that the so called rule would be invoked in June. Senator Leahy has mentioned before he would invoke it in the second half of this year. Let me say this about the Thurmond Rule. It is a myth. It does not exist. There is no reason for stopping the confirmation of judicial nominees in the second half of a year in which there is a Presidential election. [16]

A similar view was expressed earlier, at the start of the 110th Congress in January 2007, by Senator Specter, ranking minority member on the Judiciary Committee (who served as committee chair in the 109th Congress). In a Senate floor statement, Senator Specter alluded to “what has been called the ‘Thurmond Rule.’” Some, he said, “have suggested that this so-called rule holds that the Senate should dramatically curtail confirmations after the spring of a presidential election year. Review of the historical record suggests that this rule is more myth than reality" [17].

More recently, in a July 17, 2008 floor statement Senator Specter rejected the idea of applying a Thurmond rule to judicial nominations, no matter which party was in control of the Senate or of the White House. "There is no Thurmond rule for Democrats when Republicans are in control and there is a Democratic President, and there is no Thurmond rule when the situation is reversed," Senator Specter said [18].

Events Cited as Origin of Thurmond Rule

The debate over whether there is, or has ever been, such a "rule" appears to arise from different meanings attached to events involving Senator Thurmond in 1980. At that year's Republican Party national convention, held in Detroit on July 14-17, Senator Thurmond reportedly said that, at his suggestion, the party's presidential nominee, Ronald Reagan, had agreed to urge Senate Republicans to block all presidential nominations by President Jimmy Carter until after the November 4 elections. [19] One account, without directly quoting Senator Thurmond, reported him as having said that by withholding their consent, Senators could "prevent appointments that would continue beyond Jimmy Carter's term, should he be defeated in the general election." [20] At this time, Senator Thurmond was the ranking minority member on the Judiciary Committee, to which all circuit and district court nominations were referred. The blocking of appointments urged by Senator Thurmond presumably extended to these judicial nominations.

In the weeks immediately thereafter, however, the Judiciary Committee processed district and circuit court nominations, although not all that were referred to the committee. This processing occurred without Senator Thurmond, during this time or during the rest of the year, repeating his earlier call for a blocking of President Carter's appointments. As described below, in a more detailed narrative of judicial nominations activity in the Senate during 1980, the Judiciary Committee continued to hold hearings on and report judicial nominations during August and September, although the committee reported only one circuit court nomination during this period. The Senate, in turn, in September confirmed 12 judicial nominations (11 district court, 1 circuit court). Following the November 4 presidential election, in which the Republican challenger, Ronald Reagan, defeated Democratic incumbent Jimmy Carter, the Judiciary Committee and Senate acted on one more judicial nomination. Without opposition from

Senator Thurmond or other minority committee members, the Judiciary Committee voted 12-0 to report President Carter's nomination of Stephen G. Breyer to the U.S. Court of Appeals for the First Circuit, [21] a nomination that the Senate subsequently confirmed, by a vote of 80-10, in December, a week before the Senate adjourned sine die. [22]

Earlier, in mid-September 1980, the news media had reported conflict between the Democratic majority and Republican minority in the Senate Judiciary Committee over the pace at which judicial nominations were being processed. A press account of the committee's September 10 meeting reported that Senator Thurmond' s move to block a vote on 13 judicial nominations was perceived by "some Democrats ... as a Republican plot to delay all judgeship nominations in the hopes that Ronald Reagan will be elected president and can fill the posts with good Republicans." [23] However, a week later, on September 17, the committee approved motions, to which no objections were heard, to report 10 of the judicial nominations (all district court nominations) to the Senate. Six other judicial nominations that were also on the committee's agenda on September 17 were not reported. Following the votes to report, Senator Thurmond stated that he intended to exercise his privilege, under the committee's rules, of "carrying over" to a later committee meeting a vote on three other judicial nominees who had "just had a hearing." Senator Thurmond prefaced that statement with the following remarks:

> Now, Mr. Chairman, I want to say at this juncture, let me make the point, that the Minority has tried to be more than fair in considering all of the nominees that have appeared before this committee. I would remind you it is just about six weeks before the election, and I want to say that for a year and a half before the last election, there was no action taken on judges when we had a Republican President. But, anyway, last week it was necessary for me to lay over all 13 judicial nominees because our investigation had not been entirely completed on some of them. Today I will again exercise the privilege and request that the three that have just had a hearing ... be held over" [24].

For more than 15 years after the 1980 events just described, debates over judicial nominations in the Senate took place without Senators ever referring to a Thurmond rule by name. At various points in that time period, however, majority Senators recalled the 1980 events, critically characterizing Senator Thurmond' s role in 1980 as aimed at "shutting down" the judicial confirmation process [25].

The first actual public mentions by Senators of the Thurmond rule as such appear to have been made in 1997. At a February 12, 1997 press conference, Senator Leahy alluded to a Thurmond rule while noting the lack of progress on President Clinton's nominations to the courts of appeals during 1996, a presidential election year. [26] The phrase "Thurmond rule" first appeared in the Congressional Record two months later, in a floor statement by Senator Leahy, expressing frustration with the pace of Senate consideration of judicial nominations at the beginning of President Clinton's second term. [27]

Emergence of Thurmond Rule as an Issue

The Thurmond rule first emerged as a major point of contention between Senate Democrats and Republicans in 2004. In a Senate floor statement in July 2004, Senator Leahy, then the ranking minority member on the Judiciary Committee, maintained that the majority in the Senate was, at that point, "intent on violating the 'Thurmond Rule' and the spirit of cooperation reached earlier this year" on processing President George W. Bush's judicial nominations. The "Thurmond rule," Senator Leahy said,

> ... dates back at least to July 1980 when the Reagan campaign urged Senate Republicans to block President Carter's judicial nominees. Over time, Senator Thurmond and Republican leaders refined their use and practices under the rule to prevent the consideration of lifetime judicial appointments in the last year of a Presidency unless [unless the nominees under consideration were] consensus nominees." [28]

At about the same time, however, Senator Hatch, then chairman of the Judiciary Committee, rejected the notion that a Thurmond rule existed. In Senate floor remarks, he stated,

> We have heard from the other side about the mythical 'Thurmond rule' and all kinds of other suggestions that judges should not be confirmed from here on, this late in a Presidential election year. I remember way back when, cases where we confirmed judges, Democratic nominees, Carter nominees, even after President Reagan had won the election. In fact, one of them [Stephen Breyer] is sitting on the Supreme Court of the United States of America. [29]

Senator Hatch had also dismissed the Thurmond rule a month earlier. During a Judiciary Committee business meeting, Senator Hatch referred to the "so-called Thurmond Rule," while expressing hope that the committee would report several of President Bush's circuit court nominations. [30]

Amid this debate in 2004, an analysis of the Thurmond rule by a Capitol Hill newspaper referred to it as a "new concept [that] has crept into the back-and-forth between Republicans and Democrats — or at least a long-dormant one [that] has been dusted off.... " The article, based on contacts made with some Senators and senior Senate staff, reported that "even some of the most skillful senators aren't quite sure whether the Thurmond Rule is really a rule at all. Some call it a 'precedent.' Others term it a 'general understanding.' Some have never even heard of it." [31] Sources for the article cited different points in time at which, according to their view of the rule, the Senate would stop processing judicial nominations: on July 1, or at the beginning of the first national political party convention that summer, or during the last few months of a President's term in office.

One of the Senators interviewed for the article was Senator Kennedy, a longtime member of the Judiciary Committee and former chairman (1979-1981). The article reported that Senator Kennedy said that, at the point the Thurmond rule went into effect during a presidential election year, "'for all intents and purposes, we'd leave it,' meaning not confirm any more judges. 'That having been said,' he added, 'there has always been sort of an effort to try and work through some sort of accommodation at different times.'" [32]

The article (without identifying any Republican Senator by name) reported that Republicans, as well Democrats, "acknowledge there is a Thurmond Rule, or at least a precedent dating back to the days when Thurmond chaired the Judiciary Committee." [33] However, the article also indicated that, in 2004, with Republican President George W. Bush then in office, invocation of a Thurmond rule to slow down processing of judicial nominations would be more to the advantage of Senate Democrats than to Senate Republicans. "By invoking the Thurmond Rule," the article said, "Democrats may be able to attach legitimacy to their ongoing campaign against some [of] President Bush's controversial nominees in a chamber that reveres history and precedent." [34]

Slowdowns Cited as Traditional, without Reference to Thurmond Rule

Sometimes, in recent decades, Senators, without referring to a Thurmond rule for support, have maintained that it is traditional Senate practice to slow down, or stop altogether, the processing of judicial nominations in presidential election years. For example, in a Senate floor statement in September 1980, Senator Mark Hatfield of Oregon, spoke (although he did so disapprovingly) of "what may have been a tradition in this body in years past of holding up nominations per se in an election year." [35]

Subsequently, in March 2000, during Senate floor consideration of two Clinton court of appeals nominations, Senator Robert C. Smith of New Hampshire, a member of the Senate's Republican majority, questioned a contention allegedly made in floor remarks by two Democratic Senators — specifically, "that there does not seem to be much of a history of blocking nominees and that it is not good for the constitutional process." [36] Senator Smith indicated he had a contrary view:

> There is thinking among some that we should not start down this path of blocking a judicial nominee whom we do not think is a good nominee for the court because it may come back to haunt us at some point when and if a Republican should be elected to the Presidency.
>
> Let me say, with all due respect to my colleagues, I am not starting down any new path. The tradition of the Senate is one of blocking judicial nominees in the final year of an administration. [37]

Other Senators, also without referring to a Thurmond rule, have characterized Senate practice in a presidential election year not as one of blocking judicial nominations but of slowing down the confirmation process. In July 2000, for instance, the chairman of the Senate Judiciary Committee, Senator Hatch disagreed with assertions of some minority Senators that the Senate in 2000 had not confirmed a sufficient number of court of appeals nominations. Senator Hatch maintained that the Senate's record in considering circuit nominees up to that point in the session compared favorably with the record of the Senate in prior presidential election years. He added, however, that in "presidential election years, the confirmation of appellate court nominees historically has slowed." [38] A few weeks later, Senator Hatch was reported as saying (without, however, being quoted directly) that "in every election year, a point is reached when the Senate simply ceases anyway to move judicial nominees, deciding to leave filling vacancies up to the next president." [39]

Senate Processing of Nominations in Presidential Election Years, 1980-2004

To some degree, debate concerning judicial nominations during presidential election years dates back to 1948. [40] In that presidential election year, a scholar noted, "with Republicans anticipating the recapture of the White House, confirmations ground to a virtual halt: only two lifetime federal district court nominees and one appeals court nominee were confirmed." [41] Commentators have also called attention to perceived slowdowns in the consideration of judicial nominees in 1960 [42] and 1976. [43] In 1960, the Senate confirmed two court of appeals and nine district court nominees while returning the nominations of four district court nominees when the Senate adjourned sine die on September 1, 1960. [44] In 1976, the Senate confirmed five court of appeals nominees (the last on September 17, 1976) and 26 district court nominees (the last on September 23, 1976) and returned two court of appeals and eight district court nominees upon adjourning sine die on October 1, 1976. [45]

Although 1948, 1960, and 1976 are occasionally held up as examples of the Senate slowing consideration of judicial nominees in presidential election years, events that took place in 1980 appear to be the earliest points of reference for current debate on this subject. Accordingly, the following narratives of Senate consideration of judicial nominees in specific presidential election years start with 1980 and end with 2004.

1980

In a retrospective look at the second session of the 96th Congress, the 1980 Congressional Quarterly Almanac reported that Senate Republicans, "hoping to keep as many appointments as possible open for President-elect Reagan, managed to defer action on many presidential nominees at the end of the second session of the Ninety- sixth Congress." These, the Almanac said, included "17 prospective federal judges ... left unconfirmed by the Senate." [46] From a different perspective, however, the Senate, and its Judiciary Committee, could be viewed as having approved the bulk of President Carter's lower court nominations pending in the second session. In the course of doing so, the committee processed some lower court nominations in late September, shortly before the Senate recessed for the month of October in anticipation of the presidential election on November 4. It also acted on one court of appeals nomination as late as December, after the Senate reconvened for a "lame duck" session.

The Senate convened for the start of the second session of the Ninety-sixth Congress on January 3, 1980, and adjourned sine die on December 16, 1980. At the start of the session, 16 district court nominations and 4 circuit court nominations were pending (having been carried over from the first session). Subsequently, during the second session, the Senate received 51 more district court and 10 more circuit court nominations. Of the 67 district court nominations pending during the second session, the Senate confirmed 53 while returning 12 at the end of the session.47 Of the 14 circuit court nominations pending during the second session, the Senate confirmed 10 and, at session's end, returned 4.

During the second session, the Judiciary Committee continued to hold hearings or report district and circuit nominations during the months of June,48 July, August and September. Committee actions on lower court nominations occurring in closest proximity to presidential election day (November 4) were hearings on September 22 (on one district court nomination) and 23 (on two district court nominations) and committee votes to report on September 17 (on 10 district court nominations) and 24 (on one district court nomination). The last committee actions on circuit court nominations prior to the presidential election were an August 25 vote to report one nomination and a September 15 hearing on another nomination. The last votes by the full Senate on lower court nominations prior to the November 4 elections were votes on September 11 to confirm one circuit court nomination, on September 26 to confirm one district court nomination, and September 29 to confirm 10 district court nominations. On October 2, the Senate recessed until November 12.

Earlier in the session, news media reports had raised the possibility of Senate Republicans blocking some or all lower court nominations then pending in the Senate. During the Republican Party convention in July, news accounts reported that Senator Thurmond had asked the party's presidential nominee, Ronald Reagan, to ask Republican members of the Senate to block all presidential nominations to federal posts until after the November 4 election. Reagan, according to one account quoting Senator Thurmond, "said he would be glad to do that." [49] In the weeks immediately thereafter, however, the Senate Judiciary Committee, without concerted opposition from Republican committee members, voted to report favorably a district court nomination (on July 30) and a circuit court nomination (on August 25), and both of these nominations, soon thereafter, were confirmed by the Senate by unanimous consent (the district nomination on August 19, the circuit nomination on September 11).

In mid-September, a press account reported that a "campaign" by Senate Republicans was underway to impede confirmation of 13 of President Carter's lower court nominations as well as of pending nominations to a wide range of appointive positions in the executive branch. [50] The purpose, the press account said, was to reserve these appointments for presidential candidate Ronald Reagan, in the event he were to win the November election. The account was published a few days after a September 10 Judiciary Committee meeting at which 13 lower court nominations (1 circuit, 12 district) had been placed on the agenda for a vote by the committee's chairman, Senator Kennedy. The committee's ranking minority member, Senator Thurmond, asserted that minority committee members had not had sufficient time to complete an investigation of 6 of the 13 nominees. As a result, he said, he insisted, in keeping with committee procedure that allowed any member the right to delay a vote until the next committee meeting, that the committee's vote on all 13 nominations be postponed. [51]

A press account of the committee's September 10 meeting reported that Senator Thurmond's move to block a vote on the 13 judicial nominations was perceived by "some Democrats ... as a Republican plot to delay all judgeship nominations in the hopes that Ronald Reagan will be elected president and can fill the posts with good Republicans." [52] A week later, however, the committee on September 17 approved motions, to which no objections were heard, to report 10 of the judicial nominations (all district court nominations) to the Senate. Six other judicial nominations that also were on the committee's agenda on September 17 were not reported. These included three nominations (one circuit court, two district court), which were before the committee in executive session for the first time. Senator Thurmond, on behalf of the minority, asked that these three nominations be held over until the next meeting of the committee [53].

The other three nominations not reported (one circuit court, two district court) on September 17 were among the 13 nominations carried over from the September 10 meeting. Senator Thurmond stated that, regarding these three nominees, the committee's minority members had "some questions of substance" that would "have to be discussed," but added that he did "not mean to imply that any questions cannot be resolved or that all of these gentlemen will not be outstanding federal judges. We are, however, at this time prepared to fully and extensively discuss these candidates if you wish to go into detail." [54] In reply, the chairman of the committee, Senator Kennedy, stated that it was his preference to proceed with the other legislative matters on the committee's agenda, with the "hope to be able to work with the Minority to see if we cannot gain their approval [on the judicial nominations] at a subsequent time." [55]

All 10 district court nominations approved by the Judiciary Committee on September 17 were considered and confirmed en bloc by the Senate on September 29. In floor remarks on September 29, Senator Mark Hatfield of Oregon noted that, a few months earlier, he was one of the three Senators appointed by the Senate minority leader to a committee within the Republican Conference tasked with screening the qualifications of President Carter's nominations ("not just judicial appointments but all nominations" [56]). The three-member committee, he said, had "gone over all the nominations that have been sent up here for many posts besides the judiciary." [57] In anticipation of the Senate confirming the 10 judicial nominations, Senator Hatfield stated,

> I think today is again strong evidence that we want to try to minimize what may have been a tradition in this body in years past of holding up nominations per se in an election year because our commitment is that all the functions of Government must perform to their utmost capacity and efficiency. If there is a failure to confirm, it is going to impinge upon that ability to perform in a judicial district or in an administrative post. We are not going to try to frustrate that ability because we want to facilitate that highest performance of duties and responsibilities of government [58]

The final weeks of the second session, following the November 4 election, witnessed an unusually late consideration by the Senate Judiciary Committee and the Senate of a circuit court nomination. The nomination was transmitted to the Senate by a "lame-duck" President, who had just lost his bid for reelection, and was the only lower court nomination made by President Carter in the second session after September. The nominee was Stephen G. Breyer of Massachusetts, then the chief majority counsel for the Senate Judiciary Committee. The nomination (to the First Circuit Court of Appeals) was received in the Senate on November 13, received a Judiciary Committee hearing on November 17, was reported by the committee on December 2, and was confirmed by the Senate on December 9, just one week before the Senate adjourned sine die on December 16. Although its expedited treatment generated some controversy, the Breyer nomination enjoyed the wholehearted support of the committee's ranking minority member, Senator Thurmond, as well as of other minority members of the committee, which approved the nomination by a 12-0 vote. The nomination ultimately was confirmed by the Senate by a vote of 80- 10. [59]

1984

During this year, the lower court appointment process was marked by a notable statutory event — the creation of new circuit and district court judgeships in early July — and by President Ronald Reagan, in August and September, sending nominations to the Senate to fill these new positions. In August, September, and October, committee hearings were held and committee and Senate votes were cast on lower court nominations (including nominations to the new judgeships) before the Senate adjourned sine die in October.

The Senate convened for the start of the second session of the Ninety-eighth Congress on January 23, 1984, and adjourned sine die on October 12, 1984. At the start of the session, no circuit or district court nominations were pending as the Senate, at the end of the first session of the Congress, had returned the one district court nomination and two circuit court nominations then pending. [60] Subsequently, during the second session, the Senate received 14 circuit court nominations (one resubmission and 13 new nominations) and 46 district court nominations (one resubmission and 45 new nominations). Of the 14 circuit nominations pending during the second session, the Senate confirmed 10, while returning 3 to the President at session's end. [61] Of the 46 district court nominations pending during the second session, the Senate confirmed 33 while returning 13 to the President.

On June 29, 1984, the Senate and House adjourned until July 23. (During the adjournment, the Republican Party held its National Convention, on July 14-17.) Up to the June 29 adjournment, the Senate, during the second session, had received 5 circuit court nominations, confirming 4, and had received 26 district court nominations, confirming 21. The month of June was marked by hearings, committee votes, and Senate votes on both circuit and district court nominations. [62]

On June 29, before adjourning, the Senate and House both approved the conference report on H.R. 5174, the Bankruptcy Amendments and Federal Judgeship Act of 1984. The act, which President Reagan signed into law on July 10, authorized, among other things, the creation of 24 new circuit court judgeships and 61 new district court judgeships. [63] The act, however, provided that no more than 11 of the circuit court judgeships, and no more than 29 of the district court judgeships, could be filled prior to January 21, 1985 — the day immediately after the inauguration of the President elected in November 1984. A July 29, 1984 news report stated that, in "passing the judgeship bill, Democrats and Republicans agreed that only a portion of the new appointments would be made before next January's presidential inauguration — a compromise to allow for the possibility of a change in administration in November." [64]

On August 1, the Senate received six circuit court nominations, all to new positions, with President Reagan described by one news report as "acting quickly to fill some of the judgeships created last month by Congress." [65] Subsequently, between September 6 and October 5, the Senate received 3 more circuit and 20 more district court nominations from the President. During the remainder of August, the Judiciary Committee held two days of hearings on circuit court nominations and on another day voted to report four district court nominations. In September the committee held hearings on four days (on two occasions, for both circuit and district court nominations, once for only circuit nominations, and once for only district nominations). The Judiciary Committee on four occasions — August 9, September 20, September 28, and October 3 — voted to report out circuit nominations, district nominations, or both. The Senate voted to confirm a circuit court nomination on August 9, a district court nomination on September 2, three district court nominations on September 17, six district and five circuit court nominations on October 4, and two circuit court nominations on October 11. The last two confirmations occurred one day before the Senate adjourned sine die on October 12.

Among the 3 circuit court nominations and 13 district court nominations returned to the President at the end of the Congress were 1 circuit nomination and 4 district nominations received by the Senate on October 5, less than a week before adjournment.

1988

During this year, debate arose over the pace with which judicial nominations were being processed in the Senate Judiciary Committee and the Senate as a whole. Some committee minority members claimed the majority was deliberately slowing the confirmation process. Committee majority members defended the committee's performance, saying it was acting briskly on noncontroversial nominees, while taking more time to examine nominees with potential problems. Amid the debate, the Judiciary Committee and the full Senate processed lower court nominations as late as October — with 17 unconfirmed judicial nominations, however, returned to the President at the Senate's final adjournment.

The Senate convened for the start of the second session of the 100th Congress on January 25, 1988 and adjourned sine die on October 14, 1988. During the previous three Congresses, the lower court appointment process had operated with Republican control of the Senate and the White House. In the 100th Congress, however, President Reagan sent his judicial nominations to the Senate, and its Judiciary Committee, with the Democrats in the majority.

At the start of the second session, 9 circuit and 19 district court nominations were pending, all having been carried over from the first session. [66] Subsequently, during the second session, the Senate received 7 more circuit and 26 more district court nominations. Of the 16 circuit court nominations pending during the second session, the Senate confirmed 7, while returning 7 at session's end. (The other two unconfirmed circuit nominations were withdrawn by the President during the session.) Of the 45 district court nominations pending during the second session, the Senate confirmed 33, while returning 9 to the President. The other three unconfirmed district court nominations were withdrawn by the President during the session.

By June 1, 1988, during the second session, the Senate had confirmed 5 circuit and 19 district court nominations, while 6 other circuit nominations and 17 other district court nominations were pending. Earlier in the session, according to one news account, Senators of the majority party had "promised to move quickly on all Reagan nominees, despite the temptation to stall during an election year." [67] By June, however, a partisan debate had arisen in the Judiciary Committee over the pace with which judicial nominations were being processed within the committee. The committee's ranking member, Senator Thurmond, reportedly characterized that pace as "agonizingly slow." [68] Another minority committee member, Senator Orrin G. Hatch, also referring to the processing of judicial nominations, was quoted in the press as saying, "This last year has been absolutely excruciating." [69] In response to these criticisms, a majority member of the committee, Senator Patrick J. Leahy, it was reported, asserted that delays by the Department of Justice in providing information had "severely retarded the processing of" some judicial candidates, and suggested that the committee, when under Republican leadership, might have abdicated its constitutional responsibilities by "rubber-stamping nominees." [70]

Senator Leahy's assertions, it was reported, were contained in a 10-page letter responding to complaints that Senator Thurmond had made the previous month about the committee's processing of judicial nominations. The letter concluded with what the news report said was an "implicit attack" on Senator Thurmond' s handling of nominations as committee chairman when Republicans controlled the Senate. [71] While nominees for judgeships, Senator Leahy's letter said,

> ... may well have gained the impression, from examining some of the past practices of this committee, that ... the advice and consent process was a simple formality in which the Senate rubber-stamped the president's choice ... it is not in any sense "unfair" to them that the committee now approaches its constitutional responsibilities with greater seriousness and deliberation. [72]

In response, Senator Thurmond stated, "I very much appreciate Sen. Leahy compiling responses to my questions, although the reply, which took three weeks to compile, forced the cancellation of one nomination hearing." The "lengthy reply" by Senator Leahy, Senator Thurmond added, "much like the other tactics employed by Democrats on the committee, seems to do little more than ensure some judicial nominees will not get an up or down vote as promised last year" by the committee's chair, Senator Biden. [73]

Against this backdrop, the Judiciary Committee held hearings or voted on lower court nominations during June, July, August, and October (but not in

September), meeting for these purposes two to four times a month. [74] Committee actions on lower court nominations occurring in closest proximity to presidential election day (November 8), were hearings on October 4 (on one circuit court and three district court nominations) and committee votes to report on October 5 (two circuit court and nine district court nominations). [75] On one day each in July, August, and October (but not in June or September), the Senate voted to confirm district court nominations (seven in all), without, however, confirming any circuit court nominations. Then, in its last vote on lower court nominations during the second session, the Senate on October 14 confirmed two circuit and nine district court nominations. [76] Almost six months had passed since the Senate's last previous confirmation of a circuit court nomination, on April 19.

In early October, just before the Judiciary Committee voted to report the above- noted 11 lower court nominations to the Senate, a press story reported that a compromise had been reached between Democrats and Republicans on the Judiciary Committee. The compromise, it was reported, would "allow about a dozen stalled judicial nominations to come up for confirmation votes," [77] with the committee clearing about half of the 22 judicial nominees before the committee and blocking further action on the other half. The news report quoted the committee's chairman, Senator Biden, as saying that the judicial nominees who would not be allowed to proceed had either "clear, substantive problems" with qualifications or backgrounds or were in "intractable situations" with Senators from the nominees' home states [78]

1992

The second session of the 102nd Congress is particularly notable in the context of judicial nominations for two things: first, the Senate confirmed more nominees, 11, to the courts of appeals that year than in any other presidential election year in United States history; second, at its sine die adjournment, the Senate also returned more court of appeals nominations to the President, 10, than at the end of any other Congress until the 106th Congress (1999-2000).

The Senate convened for the start of the second session of the 102nd Congress on January 3, 1992, and adjourned sine die on October 8, 1992. At the start of the session, there were 7 circuit court and 36 district court nominees pending; during the session, the President nominated an additional 11 individuals to the circuit courts and 59 individuals to the district courts. All told, there were 21 circuit court and 95 district court nominees pending at some point during the second session of the 102nd Congress. Of those nominees, 11 circuit court nominees and 53 district court nominees were confirmed during that session; 10 circuit and 42 district court nominees were returned to the President at the end of the 102nd Congress.

During the second session of the 102nd Congress, the Senate held hearings on district court nominees every month from January to September; court of appeals nominees received hearings in every month from February to September. The Judiciary Committee held its last judicial nominations hearing for the year, for one court of appeals and five district court nominees, on September 24. The Judiciary Committee reported at least one district court nominee every month between February and October. The committee reported at least one circuit court nominee in February, April, May, June, August, September, and October, reporting three circuit nominees in May, and two each in June and August. At its last business meeting of the year, on October 2, 1992, the Judiciary Committee reported five district court and one circuit court nominee, all of whom were confirmed on October 8, the day the Senate adjourned sine die. One circuit court nominee, Timothy K. Lewis, was nominated on September 17, 1992, and confirmed by the Senate 21 days later, on October 8, 1992.

During most of the second session of the 102nd Congress, the pace of Senate consideration of judicial nominations did not generate much controversy in the Senate Judiciary Committee, on the floor of the Senate, or subsequently on the campaign trail. This prompted one campaign observer to note that "about 100 of 828 federal judgeships are waiting to be filled, but three debates yielded not a single comment about how George Bush, Bill Clinton or Ross Perot would use such appointments to affect a generation of justice." [79] While the Senate was in its traditional August recess, news reports quoted Judiciary Committee staffers as saying that the pace of confirmations generated "very little criticism from either the Justice Department or the White House." [80] Soon afterwards, however, a news account reported that Democrats, who had the Senate majority, began, upon their return from the August recess, "to delay confirming some of President Bush's nominees for major judgeships to preserve the vacancies for Gov. Bill Clinton if he is elected President" [81].

As the presidential election neared, two significant clashes over judicial nominations occurred in the Senate. The first involved the confirmation of Edward Carnes of Alabama to the Eleventh Circuit Court of Appeals. News reports indicate that the controversy over the Carnes nomination spread to other nominations; when "four anonymous senators" placed holds on the Carnes nomination in late June, the nomination of Sonia Sotomayor to a district judgeship in New York was "delayed more than three weeks by Senate Republicans, apparently in retaliation for the attempt to block Carnes." [82] Sotomayor, whose nomination was reported by the Senate Judiciary Committee on June 11, was confirmed by the full Senate by unanimous consent on August 11. The Senate voted 66-30 to invoke cloture on the Carnes nomination, and 62-36 to confirm Carnes on September 9. The second controversy involved Frank Keating of Oklahoma, who had been nominated to the Tenth Circuit Court of Appeals. The Judiciary Committee held a hearing on the Keating nomination on July 22, at which time several witnesses criticized his record as general counsel at the Department of Housing and Urban Development (HUD). According to news reports, the Judiciary Committee chairman, Senator Joseph Biden, "expressed more concern over inconsistencies in Keating' s record handling housing discrimination complaints than in what he was alleged to have said in meetings with housing advocates. [83] The Judiciary Committee did not vote on the Keating nomination, and it was returned to the President at the end of the 102nd Congress.

Against this backdrop, the Senators in attendance at the Judiciary Committee's September 12 business meeting sparred over the pace of judicial confirmations, with majority Senators faulting the Bush Administration for failing to submit nominees in a timely manner. Senator Joseph Biden, chairman of the Judiciary Committee, used the Tenth Circuit to illustrate his complaint:

> ...the one we are talking about, Mr. Keating here — there was a vacancy for a total of 15 months before this committee was in a position to act on Mr. Keating because the Administration, A, hadn't even come up with Mr. Keating's name for 11 months, and after they came up with his name they held him up for four more months in an investigation. So it is 15 months before the Committee could even act on Mr. Keating and then he became a controversial nominee, rightly or wrongly. [84]

Minority Senators claimed that the Judiciary Committee was not processing the nominations it did have, as the following exchange between Senator Howard Metzenbaum, Democrat of Ohio, and Senator Thurmond, suggests:

> SENATOR METZENBAUM. Mr. Chairman, it is with some difficulty that I address myself to this point, but my good friend from South Carolina was the leader in shutting down entirely the question of judicial nominees in 1980.
>
> SENATOR THURMOND. Seventeen judges, but before this Committee now are over 50. [85]

At the September 17 meeting, the Judiciary Committee reported three district court and one circuit court nominee; it reported one more district court nominee on September 23 and five more district court and one circuit court nominee on October 2. All 11 of these nominations were confirmed before the Senate adjourned sine die on October 8, 1992.

1996

From the standpoint of Senate processing of circuit court nominations, 1996 is notable among the presidential election years in the 1980-2004 period in several respects:

- In 1996, fewer circuit court nominations were confirmed (two), than in any other year from 1980 to 2004.
- The two confirmations occurred on January 2, 1996, the last day of the first session of the 104th Congress, the latest first session confirmations of lower court nominations in the 1980-2004 period.
- During the second session of the 104th Congress, which began and ended in 1996, no circuit court nominations were confirmed, making this the only session of a Congress in the 1980-2004 period in which the Senate did not confirm a circuit court nominee.
- The Senate Judiciary Committee's last vote to report a circuit court nomination to the Senate in 1996 occurred on June 27, the earliest date in a second session of Congress for the committee's last report of a circuit nomination in the 1980-2004 period.

Of the 38 district court nominations pending in 1996, during the second session of the 104th Congress, 17 were confirmed, 1 was withdrawn by the President, and 20 were returned to the President at the final adjournment of the Congress.

The Senate convened for the start of the second session of the 104th Congress on January 3, 1996 and adjourned sine die on October 3, 1996. At the start of the session, five circuit court nominations were pending, having been carried over from the first session. [86] Subsequently, during the second session, the Senate received four more circuit court nominations. Of the nine circuit court nominations pending during the second session, none was confirmed: one was withdrawn by the President (in May), and the other eight were returned at the end of the session. This, as already mentioned, was the only session of a Congress in the 1980-2004 time period in which the Senate did not confirm a circuit court nominee [87].

During the second session, the Judiciary Committee held one hearing or voted to report on one circuit court nomination each month from February through July. The committee's last meeting on which it voted favorably on a circuit court nomination was, as mentioned above, on June 27. Subsequently, the committee held its last hearing on a circuit court nomination on July 31. In all, the committee, during the second session, voted to report three circuit nominations to the Senate (on April 25, May 20, and June 27), and one other circuit nomination, reported earlier in the first session, was also pending throughout the second session. While all four nominations, pursuant to Senate rules, were (after being reported) placed on the Senate's Executive Calendar, none was scheduled for Senate floor consideration. These four circuit nominations, and the four other circuit nominations pending in the Senate which had not been reported by the Judiciary Committee, were returned to the President upon the Senate's sine die adjournment on October 3.

For the first six months of 1996, the pattern of Senate processing of district court nominations closely resembled that for circuit court nominations during the same period. On January 2, the last day of the first session of the 104th Congress, the Senate confirmed one district court nomination. The next day, at the start of the second session of the Congress, 21 district nominations were pending. Over the next six months, the Senate Judiciary Committee met on eight different occasions to hold hearings on or report out 19 district court nominations. However, during the same period, no district court nominations received Senate confirmation. The absence of Senate confirmations of lower court judges prompted one press report on June 20 to note that "the Senate has confirmed only three judges this year, compared with more than 50 last year." [88] Another press report commented that for "the first six months of this year, political and parochial fighting among senators had prevented confirmation of a single federal judge." [89]

In July and August, the situation changed. Following reports of an agreement between the new Senate majority leader and the Senate minority leader to begin steadily processing judicial nominations, [90] the Senate on 12 different days, starting on July 10 and ending on August 2, confirmed 17 district court (but, as already discussed , no circuit court) nominations. After the August recess, however, no more district court nominations were confirmed. The last actions in the Senate on lower court nominations for the year occurred at the committee level, with the Judiciary Committee reporting a district court nomination on September 19 and holding a hearing on another district court nomination on September 24.

At the Senate's sine die adjournment on October 3, 20 district court nominations were returned to the President, including 3 which had been reported by the Judiciary Committee. A press account on the Senate's adjournment noted that the1 7 judicial confirmations during the second session of the Congress (all of district court nominees) were "fewer than [had] been approved in any election year going back to 1976." The Senate, the account added, was "still at odds over a backlog of Clinton administration judicial nominees that has irked Democrats for months." [91]

2000

The Senate convened for the start of the second session of the 106th Congress on January 24, 2000, and adjourned sine die on December 15, 2000. At the start of the session, 17 circuit court and 18 district court nominations were pending, all having been carried over from the first session. Subsequently, during the second session, the Senate received 9 more circuit and 38 more district court nominations. Of the 26 circuit nominations pending during the second session, the Senate confirmed 8, while returning 17 to the President at the end of the session. [92] Of the 56 district court nominations pending during the second session, the Senate confirmed 31, while returning 24 at session's end. [93]

During 2000, the Judiciary Committee held hearings on, or voted to report, lower court nominations each month from February to July. The committee held its last such hearing, on four district court nominations, on July 25, and cast its last vote on July 27 (voting to report favorably the four district court nominations on which hearings were held two days earlier). The committee, for the year, held its last hearing on a circuit court nomination on June 16, and cast its last vote on a circuit nomination on July 20 (the same nomination on which the June16 hearing was held.)

At its July 20 meeting, the Judiciary Committee's chairman and its ranking minority member disagreed on whether the committee, until that point, had acted on a sufficient number of judicial nominations, and on whether more needed to be done. The committee's Republican chairman, Senator Orrin G. Hatch of Utah, detailed the volume of committee and Senate activity on judicial nominations up to that point in the session. This activity, he maintained, compared favorably with that recorded in the Senate in the most recent prior presidential election years:

> The Federal judiciary is at virtually full employment because the Senate has appropriately carried out its advice and consent duties. So far this year, the

> Judiciary Committee has held 7 hearings for 30 judicial nominees. In addition, we intend to hold a hearing next week for several more nominees. So far this year, we have confirmed 30 nominees, including 7 nominees for the U.S. courts of appeals. Today, we have on the agenda four additional district court nominees and one additional circuit court nominee.
>
> With seven court of appeals nominees already confirmed this year, and [an] additional appeals court nominee likely to be voted out of this committee, it is clear that the Senate and the Judiciary Committee have acted fairly with regard to appeals court nominees. In presidential election years, the confirmation of appellate court nominees historically has slowed. [94]

Referring to the three previous presidential election years, Senator Hatch noted that the Senate had confirmed seven circuit court nominees in 1988, 11 circuit nominees in 1992, and, in Senator Hatch's word, "zero" circuit nominees in 1996. "In all likelihood, our action with respect to Judge Rawlinson [the circuit nominee to be approved by the committee later that day] will mean that no less than eight appeals court nominees will be confirmed in this election year. As history shows, we are right on track with regard to circuit nominees." [95]

A different perspective on the committee's activity was put forward by its ranking minority member, Senator Patrick J. Leahy of Vermont. The Senator questioned the notion, which he maintained was subscribed to by Senator Hatch, that "it is getting too late to do much of anything more on judges...." [96] Senator Leahy pointed to the year 1992, the end of Republican George H. W. Bush's presidency, when the Senate majority party was Democratic, as a better standard for the current Judiciary Committee to follow in acting on judicial nominations.

> That year [1992], we confirmed 11 court of appeals nominees. Sixty-six nominees were confirmed overall. We held hearings that year in July; we held two in August. We had a hearing in September. Even though the Thurmond rule would normally cut if off, to help out a Republican President the Democrats held hearings in September. We had a lot more hearings than you have been willing to do here.
>
> In fact, we had a hearing on September 24th — we were right up against the election, and that included a court of appeals nominee, and then we went ahead and confirmed them all. We were confirming them right up almost to the last week we were in session. [97]

On July 21, the Senate confirmed the circuit court nomination, as well as four district court nominations, approved by the Judiciary Committee the day before. Subsequently, before the end of the end of the Congress in December, the Senate voted on lower court nominations on only one more occasion, on October 3, when it confirmed four district court nominations. [98]

After the committee and Senate votes in July, the prospects for further Senate activity on judicial nominations were put in doubt in early August, as the result of a recess appointment that President Clinton made to the Department of Justice. On August 3, the President appointed Bill Lann Lee to be assistant attorney general for the Department of Justice's Civil Rights Division. [99] In doing so, the President was exercising his constitutional authority, during a congressional recess, to make temporary "recess appointments" to positions that otherwise would require Senate confirmation. Lee's nomination, however, it was reported, "was among five vigorously opposed by a group of [Senate] Republicans who indicated they might retaliate against recess appointments by blocking all judicial nominees for the rest of Clinton's term, which ends Jan. 20." [100] In another news story, Senator Hatch, chairman of the Judiciary Committee, was (without being quoted directly) reported as saying that the recess appointment of Lee might "doom all other judiciary nominees" for the rest of the Clinton presidency. [101] The story added,

> Hatch noted that in every election year, a point is reached when the Senate simply ceases anyway to move judicial nominees, deciding to leave filling vacancies up to the next president. On Thursday, Hatch said the new recess appointment "upsets party leaders, who are fed up with this." So, he said, the point of moving none except the most essential of nominees may now have been reached. [102]

After the Senate's return from its August recess, majority Senator James Inhofe of Oklahoma put a hold on all judicial nominations for the rest of the session. Senator Inhofe said his hold was in response to recess appointments made by President Clinton during the Senate's August recess (including the recess appointment of Bill Lann Lee). [103] Soon thereafter, however, the hold was lifted on four of the nominations, specifically the four district court nominations that the Judiciary Committee reported to the Senate on July 27, [104] and on October 3 the Senate confirmed the four nominees (three by voice vote en bloc and the fourth by a 95-0 roll call vote).

The Senate recessed on November 2, shortly before the national elections on November 8. The Senate reconvened on November 14, with 17 circuit court and 24 nominations pending in the Judiciary Committee. During the remainder of the 106th Congress, which adjourned on December 15, there was no further Judiciary Committee or Senate floor activity on judicial nominations.

2004

The 2004 presidential election year was characterized by repeated exchange between the President and the Senate over the topic of judicial nominations. President Bush and leaders of the Republican majority in the Senate blamed Senate Democrats for preventing confirmation votes on several nominees whose nominations had been reported by the Senate Judiciary Committee. [105] Minority Senators responded that President Bush's nominees were too politically extreme to merit Senate confirmation. [106] In 2004, President Bush made two recess appointments to the courts of appeals. Also in 2004, the Senate failed to invoke cloture on the nominations of four individuals to the courts of appeals; one cloture vote occurred on July 20, and the other three votes on July 22. These votes came on the heels of the Senate not invoking cloture on six other court of appeals nominees during the first session of the 108th Congress in 2003.

The Senate convened for the start of the second session of the 108th Congress on January 20, 2004 and adjourned sine die on December 8. At the start of the second session, there were 18 pending circuit court nominations (including the nomination of Claude Allen of Virginia, which had been returned at the end of the first session but was resubmitted on January 20) and 27 pending district court nominations. During the second session, the President submitted two additional nominations to the courts of appeals (as well as nominations to make permanent the recess appointments of Charles W. Pickering, Sr. of Mississippi and William H. Pryor, Jr. of Alabama) and 12 additional nominations to the district courts. Of the 20 circuit court nominations pending at some point during the second session of the 108th Congress, the Senate confirmed 5, and 15 were returned to the President at the end of the session. Of the 39 district court nominations pending at some point during the second session of the 108th Congress, the Senate confirmed 30, 8 were returned at the end of the session, and one nomination was withdrawn by the President.

On January 16, 2004, President Bush recess-appointed Charles W. Pickering Sr. to a seat on the Fifth Circuit Court of Appeals. Because the recess appointment was made before the second session started, it lapsed when the Senate adjourned sine die on December 8. On February 20, President Bush recess-appointed William H. Pryor, Jr., to the Eleventh Circuit, a recess appointment that would expire at the end of the first session of the 109th Congress without Senate confirmation. Neither Pickering nor Pryor was confirmed in the 108th Congress, though Pryor was confirmed in 2005, in the first session of the 109th Congress.

The recess appointments of Pryor and Pickering prompted Minority Leader Tom Daschle to threaten to block all judicial nominees, saying "we will not be able to move on the confirmation of judges until we are given the assurance that they will not recess-appoint future judges, especially judges who have been rejected by the Senate." [107] One majority Senator responded by asserting that the recess appointments were necessary; he maintained that "the only reason the President had to use the power that is very clearly conferred upon him in the U.S. Constitution is because of this unprecedented obstruction by the Democratic minority in the Senate, which denied these two highly qualified nominees, Charles Pickering, now Judge Pickering of the Fifth Circuit Court of Appeals, and Judge Bill Pryor, an up-or-down vote." [108]

The standoff over the recess appointments and the prospect of additional recess appointments meant that, while the Senate Judiciary Committee held hearings on appeals nominees in each month from January to April, with seven appeals nominees receiving hearings between January 22 and April 27, and seven court of appeals nominees being reported between March 4 and April 29, the Senate did not confirm any court of appeals nominees until May 20. At that time, news reports indicated that minority Senators had agreed to allow the confirmation of 25 judicial nominees — 20 to the district courts and 5 to the courts of appeals — as long as President Bush promised not to make any additional recess appointments to the federal judiciary in 2004. [109] The Senate confirmed two nominees to the courts of appeals on May 20, three more on June 28, and no other court of appeals nominees were confirmed in the second session of the 108th Congress. The Senate did, as noted above, fail to invoke cloture on four additional court of appeals nominees during 2004; those votes occurred in July (one on July 20; three on July 22). In addition to the hearings on court of appeals nominees held before May, the Senate Judiciary Committee also held hearings on June 16 (for two nominees to the courts of appeals), September 8, and November 16. The Judiciary Committee voted to report appeals nominees on June 17, July 20 (two nominees), and October 4.

Nominations to the district courts appear to not have been subjected to the same delay as court of appeals nominees in the disagreement over President Bush's recess appointments. The Judiciary Committee, by May 1, had held hearings on 14 nominees and reported 20 nominees (10 of whom were reported on March 4, 2004). The full Senate confirmed one district judge each in January and February, two in March, one more in May, and 18 in June. Thereafter, the Senate confirmed one district judge in July, three in September, and three in November, after the presidential election. Eight district court nominees, two of whom had received hearings (and none of whom were reported to the full Senate) were returned to the President upon the sine die adjournment of the 108th Congress on December 8.

Comparative Analysis of Presidential Election Years

In the preceding section, the pace of Senate consideration of judicial nominations was discussed in narrative form for each presidential election year during the 1980-2004 period. The narratives, however, did not compare those years with one another, with regard to the number of nominees considered and the final dates of action. To arrive at comparisons of this sort, the following sections examine data on various aspects of the judicial confirmation process in the Senate, using tables to illustrate the findings. Specifically, the data presented below indicate:

- A decline in number of nominations processed in most recent presidential election years: The processing of court of appeals nominations, in terms of average number of hearings held, nominations reported, and nominees confirmed, was lower in the 1996, 2000, and 2004 presidential election years than in the 1980, 1984, 1988, and 1992 presidential election years.
- More nominees confirmed in years of unified partisan control: In presidential election years from 1980 to 2004, more court of appeals nominees (and a greater percentage of pending court of appeals nominees) were confirmed, on average, in years where the Senate majority and the President were of the same political party than when not.
- Nominations confirmed at earlier points in most recent presidential election years: In 1980, 1984, 1988, and 1992, the Senate confirmed its last court of appeals nominee of the session in October or later. In 1996, 2000, and 2004, the last court of appeals nominee confirmed in presidential election years happened in July or earlier.

Number and Percent of Judicial Nominations Processed in Presidential Election Years

Table 1 presents data on the number of nominations pending, receiving hearings, reported, and confirmed in each presidential election year between 1980 and 2004. These data indicate, among other things, a sharp decrease in the average number of court of appeals nominees confirmed by the Senate in recent presidential election years. Specifically, the average number of court of appeals nominees confirmed in the three most recently completed presidential election years (1996, 2000, and 2004) was less than half of the corresponding average for the four presidential elections before that time (1980, 1984, 1988, and 1992). On average, the Senate confirmed 9.5 court of appeals nominees in the presidential election years from 1980 to 1992. In 1980, 1984, 1988, and 1992, there were 65 total nominations to the courts of appeals pending; the Senate confirmed 38 nominees, or 58.5%, in those presidential election years. The average has fallen to 4.3 confirmed court of appeals nominees over the last three presidential election years. In 1996, 2000, and 2004, there were a total of 55 nominations to the courts of appeals pending; the Senate confirmed 13 nominees, or 23.6%, in those presidential election years.

Another trend in Table 1 can be illustrated by comparing years of unified and divided partisan control of the presidency and the Senate. Those averages are presented in Table 2.

Table 1. Nominations to the U.S. Courts of Appeals in Presidential Election Years, 1980-July 31, 2008

Year	New	Previously Pending [a]	Total	Received Hearings	Reported	Confirmed	% Confirmed
1980	10	4	14	12	10	10	71.4%
1984	13	1	14	12	11	10	71.4%
1988	7	9	16	7	9	7	43.8%
1992	14	7	21	12	11	11	52.4%
1996b	4	5	9	4	3	0	0.0%
2000	9	17	26	5	3	8	30.8%
2004	2	18	20	11	11	5	25.0%
2008c	4	14	18	4	4	4	—

Source: CRS Judicial Nominations Database, based on data from the Journal of the Executive Proceedings of the Senate, various years. In cases where a nominee was nominated more than once in a given year, more than one hearing was held on a nominee in a given year, or where a nominee was reported more than once in a given year, only the first nomination/hearing/report is included in Table 1.

Notes: a Includes nominations held over from the previous session of a Congress and those returned at the end of the previous session of Congress but resubmitted by the President during the session of Congress that coincided with the presidential election year. b The data are for the second session of the 104th Congress, which began on January 3, 1996. The Senate confirmed two nominees to courts of appeals on January 2, 1996, at the end of the first session of the 104th Congress. c Through July 31, 2008. 2008 data are not included in historical average calculations.

Table 2. Average Number of Court of Appeals Nominations Acted on in Presidential Election Years of Divided and Unified Party Control of Senate and Presidency, 1980-2004

Party Control	Total Nominations	Nominations Receiving Hearings	Nominations Reported	Nominations Confirmed	% Confirmed
Unified[a]	16.0	11.7	10.7	8.3	52.1%
Divided[b]	18.0	7.0	6.5	6.5	36.1%

Source: CRS Judicial Nominations Database, based on data from the Journal of the Executive Proceedings of the Senate, various years. In cases where a nominee was nominated more than once in a given year, more than one hearing was held on a nominee in a given year, or where a nominee was reported more than once in a given year, only the first nomination/hearing/report is included in Table 2. Cell entries are arithmetical means.

[a]Includes 1980, 1984, and 2004.

[b]Includes 1988, 1992, 1996, and 2000.

The data presented in Table 2 indicate that the Senate has, in presidential election years, confirmed fewer court of appeals nominees when controlled by a party opposite that of the President. In presidential election years where there was unified partisan control of the Senate and the presidency (1980, 1984, 2004), the Senate confirmed an average of 8.3 nominees to the courts of appeals. In those years, the Senate confirmed 25 of 48, or 52.1%, of pending nominees. In presidential election years where there was divided partisan control of the Senate and the presidency (1988, 1992, 1996, 2000), the Senate confirmed an average of 6.5 nominees to the courts of appeals. In those years, the Senate confirmed 26 of 72, or 36.1%, of pending nominees.

Last Dates of Committee or Senate Action on Nominations in Presidential Election Years

As the narratives above demonstrated, the dates on which the Senate Judiciary Committee and the full Senate last considered court of appeals nominees have varied widely since 1980. Table 3 presents, for each presidential election year between 1980 and 2004, the last dates on which the Senate received a court of appeals nomination, the Judiciary Committee held a hearing or reported such a nomination, or the Senate voted on confirmation of such a nomination.

Table 3. Last Dates of Court of Appeals Nominations, Hearings, Committee Reports, and Confirmations, Presidential Election Years 1980-2004

Cong.	Party[a] Pres.	Sen. Maj.	Year	Last Nomination	Last Hearing	Last Report	Last Confirmation	Adjourn Sine Die
96th	D	D	1980	11/13/1980	11/17/1980	12/2/1980	12/16/1980	12/16/1980
98th	R	R	1984	10/5/1984	9/26/1984	9/28/1984	10/4/1984	10/12/1984
100th	R	D	1988	9/16/1988	10/4/1988	10/5/1988	10/14/1988	10/22/1988
102nd	R	D	1992	9/17/1992	9/24/1992	10/2/1992	10/8/1992	10/9/1992
104th	D	R	1996	4/18/1996	7/31/1996	6/27/1996	— b	10/4/1996
106th	D	R	2000	10/26/2000	6/16/2000	7/20/2000	7/21/2000	12/15/2000
108th	R	R	2004	5/10/2004	11/16/2004	10/4/2004	6/24/2004c	12/8/2004

Source: CRS Judicial Nominations Database.

[a.] D=Democratic; R=Republican.

[b.] The Senate confirmed two court of appeals nominees on January 2, 1996, the final day of the first session of the 104th Congress.

[c.] The Senate failed to invoke cloture on one court of appeals nominee on July 20, 2004, and three court of appeals nominees on July 22, 2004.

The data in Table 3 offer insight into the Senate's ability to move nominees forward in presidential election years, particularly after July of presidential election years. [110] In most presidential election years since 1980, the Senate Judiciary Committee, as Table 3 shows, has continued its consideration of court of appeals nominees past July. In 1980, 1984, 1988, 1992, and 2004, the Senate Judiciary Committee held hearings for at least one court of appeals nominee after July 31 and reported at least one nominee after that date as well. In 1996 and 2004, however, the Judiciary Committee did not act on court of appeals nominees after July 31. In 1996, the Judiciary Committee's last hearing for a court of appeals nominee was on July 31; its last report of a court of appeals nominee was on June 27. In 2000, the last hearing date for a court of appeals nominee was June 16; its last report of a court of appeals nominee was on July 20.

The full Senate has also confirmed its final court of appeals nominee earlier in the last three presidential election years than in the previous four presidential election years. A relatively early end to confirmations of court of appeals nominees occurred in 2004, even though the Senate and the presidency were under the control of the same party. In 1980, Judge Stephen Breyer was confirmed to the First Circuit on December 16; in 1984, 1988, and 1992, the Senate confirmed court of appeals nominees in October of each year, in each case within several days of the Senate's adjournment sine die. In the past three presidential election years, however, the Senate has not confirmed court of appeals nominees after July. In 1996, the Senate confirmed no court of appeals nominees in the second session of the 104th Congress; its last confirmations were on January 2, 1996, the final day of the first session. In 2000, the last confirmation of a court of appeals nominee occurred on July 21. In 2004, the last confirmation occurred on June 24; although four nominees were considered in late July, the Senate rejected attempts to invoke cloture on those nominees. [111]

PRESIDENTIAL ELECTION YEARS COMPARED WITH OTHER YEARS OF A PRESIDENTIAL TERM

This section presents, for each of the four years of a presidential term, data on the number of vacancies to be filled, nominations pending, nominations receiving hearings, reports of nominations, and Senate confirmations. These data may help illustrate if, and to what degree, presidential election years represent declines in Senate consideration of nominees relative to other years of the presidential term. The following findings can be derived from the data below:

- Court of appeals nominees: In presidential election years between 1977 and 2007, the Senate, on average, held hearings on fewer court of appeals nominees than in the second and third years of the presidential terms and, on average, reported and confirmed fewer nominations than in any other year of the presidential terms.
- District court nominees: In presidential election years between 1977 and 2007, the Senate, on average, held hearings on fewer district court nominees and reported and confirmed fewer nominations than in the second and the third years (but not the first year) of the presidential terms.
- Days in session: The Senate has, on average, been in session fewer days in presidential election years between 1977 and 2007 than in other years of a presidential term (with this possibly a factor in the Senate's generally reduced consideration of judicial nominees in presidential election years relative to other years of a presidential term).

Senate Consideration of Court of Appeals Nominees

For nominees to the circuit courts of appeals, presidential election years (the fourth year of each term) have, on average, seen fewer hearings held than any year except the first year of a presidential term, and have had fewer nominees reported and confirmed than any other year in a President's term. Table 4 reports the average number of nominees pending, and the number of nominees who received a hearing, were reported by the Senate Judiciary Committee, and were confirmed by the Senate in each year of a four-year presidential term between 1977 and 2007 [112].

Specifically, the data shown in Table 4 indicate that, on average, the Senate has had an average of 17.1 nominees pending at some point during presidential election years.

Table 4. Average Number of Court of Appeals Vacancies, Nominations Pending, Hearings, Committee Reports, and Confirmed Nominees to the Courts of Appeals by Year of Presidential Term, 1977-2007

Year of Presidential Term	Vacancies[a]	Nominations			
		Pending	Receiving Hearings	Reported	Confirmed
First	15.9	14.9	8.1	9.0	8.5
Second	15.1	16.4	12.4	11.4	11.3
Third	18.5	21.3	13.8	13.4	11.8
Fourth	14.8	17.1	9.0	8.3	7.3

Source: Court of appeals vacancies data (1981-2007) derived from vacancies list of Administrative Office of the U.S. Courts, [http://www.uscourts.gov/judicialvac.html]. Vacancy data for 1977-1980 derived from Lower Federal Court Confirmation Database, available at [http://www.binghamton.edu/ cdp/lfccd.htm]. All other data derived from CRS Judicial Nominations Database, based on data from the Journal of the Executive Proceedings of the Senate, various years. In cases where a nominee was nominated more than once in a given year, more than one hearing was held on a nominee in a given year, or where a nominee was reported more than once in a given year, only the first nomination/hearing/report is included in Table 4. Cell entries are arithmetical means.

[a] Number of vacancies as of January 1 of each year.

On average, 9.0 of those nominees received hearings in presidential election years, 8.3 were reported to the full Senate by the Judiciary Committee, and 7.3

were confirmed by the Senate in presidential election years.113 The average number of confirmed nominees in presidential election years, 7.3, is 62% of the average number confirmed in the third year of a presidential term (11.8). Put differently, between 1977 and 2007, the Senate has confirmed, on average, 38% fewer court of appeals nominees in presidential election years than in the year preceding presidential elections.

The decline observed in presidential election years appears to be confined to presidential, rather than all, national elections. In the second year of presidential terms between 1977 and 2007, during which there are elections for all Members of the House of Representatives and one-third of Senators, the Senate held, on average, 12.4 hearings for court of appeals nominees, reported an average of 11.4, and confirmed an average of 11.3 nominees to the courts of appeals. In terms of number of nominees receiving hearings, number of nominations reported, and number of confirmations, the second year of each presidential term has been, on average, the second most productive of each four-year presidential term between 1977 and 2007. The most productive year of each term was the third year.

Senate Consideration of District Court Nominees

As the data in Table 5 indicate, many of the same patterns as those observed in court of appeals nominees, though with less pronounced year-to-year variation, occurred in Senate consideration of district court nominees. On average, the Senate held hearings on 38.3 district court nominees, reported 36.3 district court nominees, and confirmed 35.7 district court nominees in presidential election years between 1977 and 2007. While these averages are lower than those in either the second or third years of each presidential term, the Senate processed more district court nominees in presidential election years than in the first years of presidential terms between 1977 and 2007.

This pattern differs from that of court of appeals nominees, of whom the Senate generally processed more nominees in the first year of a presidential term than in the fourth year of a presidential term. [114] Between 1977 and 2007, the Senate, in presidential election years, confirmed 77% of the number of district court judges confirmed in the third year of a presidential term. Put differently, the decline in the number of nominees confirmed from the third to the fourth year of a presidential term was 23%. This decline is smaller than the comparable decline for court of appeals nominees (for which there was a 38% decline in number of confirmed nominees from the third to fourth years of presidential terms).

Table 5. Average Number of District Court Nominations Pending, Hearings, Committee Reports, and Confirmed by Year of Presidential Term, 1977-2007

Year of Presidential Term	Vacancies[a]	Nominations			
		Pending	Receiving Hearings	Reported	Confirmed
First	48.8	38.0	27.9	28.5	26.8
Second	47.4	53.6	44.6	44.0	43.6
Third	59.6	66.5	46.6	47.0	46.1
Fourth	47.0	55.1	38.3	36.3	35.7

Source: District court vacancies data (1981-2007) derived from vacancies list of Administrative Office of the U.S. Courts, [http://www.uscourts.gov/judicialvac.html]. Vacancy data for 1977-1980 derived from Lower Federal Court Confirmation Database, available at [http://www.binghamton.edu/ cdp/lfccd.htm]. All other data derived from CRS Judicial Nominations Database, based on data from the Journal of the Executive Proceedings of the Senate, various years. In cases where a nominee was nominated more than once in a given year, more than one hearing was held on a nominee in a given year, or where a nominee was reported more than once in a given year, only the first nomination/hearing/report is included in Table 5. Cell entries are arithmetical means.

[a.]Number of vacancies as of January 1 each year.

Possible Explanations for the Differences Between Presidential Election Years and Other Years

Various factors might come into play to influence a decline in Senate processing of judicial nominations in presidential election years. Two institutional factors especially might have a bearing in this regard. One is the lesser amount of Senate time that typically is available for consideration of judicial nominations in presidential election years relative to other years. A second is the possible inclination on the part of Senators whose party is not in control of the White House to seek, during presidential election years, to slow down the number of judicial nominations confirmed during the year. This slowdown would preserve available judicial vacancies for the candidate they support in the upcoming presidential election.

Table 6 provides the average number of days in session for each year of a presidential term between 1977 and 2007.

Table 6. Average Number of Days Senate Was in Session, by Year of Presidential Term, 1977-2007

Year of Presidential Term	Average Number of Days Senate Was in Session
First	161
Second	145
Third	172
Fourth	138

Source: CRS analysis of Senate Calendar of Business, various editions. Though presidential terms and dates of congressional sessions do not perfectly match, the "first year" of a presidential term is equated with the first session of the overlapping odd-numbered Congress, the "second year of a presidential term is equated with the second session of the overlapping odd-numbered Congress, and so on.

As the data in Table 6 indicate, the Senate has, on average, been in session for fewer days in presidential election years than the other years of a presidential term. In those years, the Senate typically recesses for presidential nominating conventions (or the conventions are held during the customary congressional August recess) and Congress typically adjourns earlier in presidential election years than in those years (the first and third years of a presidential term) when there are no national elections. In the second and fourth years of a presidential term, the Senate typically adjourns for a period of time (or adjourns sine die) in October to allow for campaigning in anticipation of the November elections. In 1984, 1988, 1992, and 1996 election years, the Senate adjourned sine die in October. In 1980 and 2004, the Senate adjourned in October for the elections and returned following the presidential election for lame-duck sessions. In 2000, the Senate remained in session until November 2 and returned on December 5 for a lame-duck session. [115]

Another possible source of the judicial nominee slowdown in presidential election years might be a desire on the part of some Senators to preserve available vacancies on the courts of appeals (and, to some degree, on the district courts) for the candidate they support in the upcoming presidential election. The use of this tactic may be more common in years when the Senate majority is controlled by a party other than the President's. As noted earlier, debate has occasionally referenced presidential election years before 1980 as years in which the Senate slowed its consideration of judicial nominations in presidential election years. In the three years mentioned — 1948, 1960, and 1976 — different political parties controlled the Senate majority and the presidency.

While these examples suggest that one party's Senators may seek to hold open judicial vacancies for their party's presidential candidates, the historical record for other election years is not always clear in indicating that such a tactic has been employed. In 1988 and 1992, when the Democrats had a majority in the Senate and were considering nominations made by Republican Presidents, the Senate returned, respectively, two and ten court of appeals nominations to the President at the end of each session. Yet the Senate in these two years also confirmed 7 and 11 nominations to the courts of appeals, respectively. The 11 court of appeals nominations confirmed in 1992 are the most ever confirmed by the Senate in a presidential election year. In both of these years, there were differences of opinion, along party lines, as to whether the Democratic majority in the Senate was seeking to slow down the judicial confirmation process.

Slowdowns, it should be noted, also may occur in presidential election years when the President's party has a majority in the Senate. The year 1980, as discussed above, was marked by controversy over whether, as some Senate Democrats alleged, the Republican minority in the Senate was seeking to block confirmation of President Carter's lower court nominations. In 2004, with a Republican majority in the Senate and a Republican President, but with Senate Democrats unified in opposition to several of the President's court of appeals nominees, the Senate confirmed only five of 19 pending nominations (26.3%) to the courts of appeals, the second-lowest confirmation percentage for any presidential election year in the 1980-2004 period.

While Senators not of the President's party may, if they are so inclined, seek to slow consideration of judicial nominations in a presidential election year, Senators of the same party as the President, may, in turn, seek to speed up Senate consideration of pending judicial nominations, as any presidential election may bring about a change in the party of the President or in the Senate majority, or both.

Whether to Oppose or Favor a Slowdown in Senate Processing of Judicial Nominations

In a presidential election year, should the Senate act on fewer lower court nominations than it does in other years, or stop processing them earlier? In addressing this question, Senators might wish to take various considerations into account. One is that, in a presidential election year, the number of lower court nominations confirmed by the Senate will affect the number of opportunities to make nominations that will be available later for the person elected President in November. Another consideration is that the extent to which judicial nominations are confirmed during the year will affect the federal judiciary's vacancy rate, i.e., whether the percent of unfilled federal judgeship positions increases, decreases, or stays about the same.

The following paragraphs first review a range of considerations that might support taking a position against a slowdown in, and an earlier end to, processing of judicial nominations in a presidential election year; then discussed are considerations that might support taking a position in favor of slowing down the judicial confirmation process.

Reasons for Opposing a Slowdown

For some Senators, one or more of the following considerations might be regarded as sufficient reason to oppose a slowdown in Senate processing of judicial nominations in a presidential election year.

Acting on Nominations Seen as Inherent in Senate's Advice and Consent Role. Some Senators might be inclined to regard their "advice and consent" responsibility under the Appointments Clause of the Constitution as obligating them to consider a President's judicial nominations whenever possible. From this point of view, it would not be responsible for Senators, because of the arrival of a presidential election year, to deliberately avoid voting on judicial nominations, or to not consider judicial nominations, despite the availability of time to do this in the Senate's schedule. According to such an argument, the imminent arrival of a presidential election, which might or might not bring about a change in presidential administration, does not provide sufficient justification for the Senate to set aside its role in the confirmation process. The Senate should still, according to this argument, conduct its business according to its normal patterns.

Policy Concerns for Senators Generally Supportive of a President's Judicial Nominations. Some Senators, if they have generally been supportive of the President's judicial nominations in the past, might in be favor of processing as many lower court nominations as possible, and as late in a presidential election year as possible. These Senators, from a public policy standpoint, might regard the incumbent President's judicial nominees as more suitable for appointment than the kind of judicial nominees whom they anticipate the other major party's presidential candidate might select, if he or she were elected in November. Hence, from their standpoint, it would be preferable to fill as many vacant judgeships as possible with the President's nominees, rather than leave open the possibility of the judgeships being filled later by the other party's presidential candidate. This concern might be particularly pronounced at the end of a two-term presidency, as there may be uncertainty as to what criteria a new President, of either party, might use to select judicial nominees.

Patronage Concerns for Senators of the President's Party. Senators of the President's party might also consider patronage as an incentive to fill judgeships in a presidential election year. By custom, Senators who are of the President's party usually play a much more influential role in the selection of judicial nominees from their home states than Senators of the opposition party. To the extent that home state Senators of the President's party play a decisive role in the selection of judicial nominees (which, historically, has typically been the case in the selection of district court nominees), the judicial positions affected are often regarded as a form of senatorial patronage. When judicial vacancies present such patronage opportunities to Senators in a presidential election year, the opportunities may encourage Senators to oppose a slowdown in judicial confirmations in their state. Instead, they are likely to want the vacant judgeships to be filled with nominees whom they played a major role in selecting.

A Slowdown in Processing Nominations Increases the Judicial Vacancy Rate. Another consideration which might incline a Senator to oppose a decline in the processing of judicial nominations is that the slowdown would increase the federal judiciary's vacancy rate. The vacancy rate, which affects the ability of the judiciary to conduct its business, is directly affected by an increase or decrease in the rate of Senate consideration of judicial nominees. A growth in the vacancy rate could impair the ability of the judiciary to hear and decide cases in a timely manner.

The impact of slowing or stopping Senate consideration of judicial nominations in a presidential election year can be magnified if the election leads to a change in presidential administration. New Presidents often take several months after their inauguration to begin making judicial nominations. President Clinton made his first nominations to the lower federal courts on August 6, 1993, nearly seven months after taking office; the first confirmation occurred on September 30, 1993, nearly one year after the last confirmations of President George H.W. Bush's nominees, on October 8, 1992. [116] In the interim, the number of vacancies on the lower federal courts (district courts and courts of appeals) rose to 127 (15.6%) from 101 (12.4%), out of 811 permanent authorized judgeships. [117] President George W. Bush made his first nominations to the federal courts on May 9, 2001, nearly four months after taking office; the first confirmation occurred on July 20, 2001, more than nine months after the last district court nominee of President Clinton was confirmed and almost one year after the last court of appeals nominee of President Clinton was confirmed by the Senate. [118] From October 2000 to July 2001, the number of vacancies on the lower federal courts (district courts and courts of appeals) rose to 109 (13.1%) from 63 (7.6%) of 830 permanent authorized judgeships. [119]

A Slowdown Makes the Judicial Confirmation Process Appear More Partisan. A slowdown in the judicial confirmation process during a presidential election year, it can be argued, might make the process appear more partisan in nature if its underlying motivation is clearly to reserve judicial nomination opportunities for the presidential candidate of a party other than the President's. Also, a slowdown in such cases arguably increases the degree to which judicial appointments are regarded as political appointments.

Another related consideration is the possibility that partisan conflict in the Senate over a slowdown in processing judicial nominations in a presidential election year might serve to carry acrimony and contentiousness between the two political parties into the next presidency. In recent years, some Senators have stated the view that much of the contentiousness of the contemporary judicial confirmation process is the result of each political party having a sense of grievance against the other. From the Reagan through the Clinton presidencies, Senators of the President's party, it has been asserted, felt aggrieved when Senators of the other party blocked judicial nominations from being confirmed in the final years of each presidency. [120] This sense of grievance, it has further been asserted, inclined them to feel justified, when the other party won the presidency, to oppose the new President's judicial nominations, as they felt the other party had when it did not control the White House. [121] To the extent that a Senator would be concerned about such political grievances in the Senate carrying over from one presidency into the next, this would be another consideration against a slowdown in judicial appointments during a presidential election year.

A Slowdown in Presidential Election Years Is Not a Strictly Observed Practice. While the data presented above indicate that, on average, the Senate confirms fewer court of appeals nominees in presidential election years, it has not always been the case that, relative to other years, fewer lower court nominations are processed in presidential election years. In President Reagan's first term (1981- 1984), President George H.W. Bush's term (1989-1992), and President Clinton's second term (1997-2000), the fourth year of the term was the second-most productive year of the term (as measured by number of court of appeals nominees confirmed). Nor, the above research found, did the last confirmations of judicial nominations in the presidential election years from 1980 to 2004 always take place at a relatively early date — such as by early June or by July 4. In three of the years (1984, 1988, and 1992) the Senate confirmed court of appeals nominations as late as October, and in a fourth year (2000) as late as mid-December. The Senate during these years, in other words, found time even late in the second session of the Congress for nominations to be considered and confirmed. In sum, there is not a uniformly observed Senate practice to slow down, or end earlier, Senate confirmation of lower court nominations (including those to court of appeals judgeships) during presidential election years. These facts would be another consideration that a Senator might cite in opposition to slowing down the processing of judicial nominations in such years.

Reasons for Favoring a Slowdown

For some Senators, however, other considerations might be reason to favor, or not oppose, a slowdown in Senate processing of judicial nominations in a presidential election year. Some of the considerations, discussed below, relate only to Senators whose party does not control the White House — and would rest on a hope for change of party control of the presidency as a result of the election. Other considerations, having less to do with change in presidential administration (or of the party in control of the White House) might be of consequence to some Senators regardless of their party.

Desire to Reserve Judicial Appointments for Election Winner. A consideration for some Senators might be a personal belief that, as a general principle, opportunities to make judicial appointments arising after a certain point in a presidential election year should be reserved for the person elected President in November. [122] After a certain time in a presidential election year, these Senators might believe the President would no longer have a mandate to fill vacant judgeships, and that the Senate would no longer have a responsibility to confirm the President's judicial nominations. Rather, after that point, the responsibility of the Senate to give its attention to judicial nominations could temporarily be put "on hold," in anticipation of the presidential election. Thereafter, judicial nominations would be seen as having less legitimacy to the extent that they were regarded as among the last acts of a departing administration. Senators holding to this view, of course, might differ as to the precise point in a presidential election year after which judicial appointments should be reserved for the next President-elect.

Policy Concerns about a President's Judicial Nominations. In recent decades, the judicial confirmation process in the Senate periodically has been marked by conflict, with support for and opposition to the President's judicial nominees generally forming along party lines. Often in these conflicts, opposition to judicial nominees has largely been based on Senators' reservations about the policy or ideological orientations of nominees under consideration. In situations such as these, some Senators might be reluctant to confirm judicial nominees believed to have views of the Constitution, or of the role of the courts, incompatible with their own views. Senators especially might be reluctant to confirm nominees in a presidential election year if they believed that their party's presidential candidate, if elected, were likely to make judicial nominee selections more compatible with their policy preferences. Senators with these concerns, in anticipation of the presidential election, also might consider it desirable, at some point in the election year, to stop confirming judicial nominees in order to minimize the extent to which the federal judiciary would be filled with appointees of the President at the time of his leaving office.

Patronage Considerations of Opposition Party Senators. As discussed above, Senators of the President's party customarily play a primary role in recommending candidates for the President to nominate to federal district court judgeships in their states. They also play a lesser, but often significant, role in recommending candidates for federal court of appeals judgeships associated with their states. [123] Such appointments are often regarded as a form of senatorial patronage, given the role of home state Senators in nominee selection. Patronage of this sort, however, typically is available only to Senators of the same party as the President, and it reverts to opposition party Senators only after their party has regained the White House. For opposition party Senators, the possibility of gaining such patronage — provided their party's candidate is elected President — could be a consideration in favor of an election-year slowdown in Senate processing of judicial nominations in their states.

If Judicial Vacancy Rate Is Relatively Low. As discussed above, a Senate slowdown in the processing of judicial nominations could increase the federal judiciary's vacancy rate. This would occur, for instance, if, during a slowdown period, the number of judges leaving the bench were not matched by the number of judicial nominees confirmed by the Senate. To the extent that judicial vacancies impair the ability of the judiciary to hear and decide cases in a timely manner, a slowdown in Senate activity to fill judicial vacancies, it could be argued, contributes to that impairment. A counter-argument, however, is that a temporary slowdown in Senate processing of judicial nominations will not be harmful if it occurs at a time when the existing judicial vacancy rate is relatively low. In this vein, the chairman of the Senate Judiciary Committee in 2000 viewed the vacancy rate of federal lower court judgeships at that time as virtually synonymous with "full employment" in the federal judiciary. [124] (At the time, the combined vacancy rate for the courts of appeals and district courts was 7.1%.)

[125] From such a perspective, concerns about increasing the judicial vacancy rate would not rule out a Senate slowdown in processing judicial nominations as long as the rate were at an acceptably low level.

Other judicial vacancy considerations also might be relevant to a decision by a Senator in favor of a slowdown in the processing of judicial nominations in a presidential election year. One would be whether the Senate, in the years and months immediately preceding a contemplated slowdown, had significantly reduced the judicial vacancy rate. If so, that record would put a temporary slowdown in a broader context, showing it to be a brief period in a longer time frame in which Senate confirmations of judicial nominees had significantly reduced the judicial vacancy rate. Another consideration is a comparison of the judicial vacancy rate at the time of a contemplated slowdown with vacancy rates existing at corresponding times in earlier Congresses. A Senator arguably might be more inclined to favor a slowdown if the existing judicial vacancy rate were comparable to or less than those of earlier Congresses when the judicial vacancy rates then in place were not viewed as problematic.

Competing Priorities and Limited Time in a Presidential Election Year. Advising and consenting to a President's judicial nominations, it has been argued, is among the Senate's most important constitutional responsibilities. [126] Yet the Senate, of course, also exercises many other important responsibilities. All of these, including judicial nominations, compete for time that typically is more limited in a presidential election year than in other years. In a presidential election year, the Senate customarily is in session fewer days, a circumstance caused in part by being in recess during the political parties' national conventions and during a campaign period of several weeks immediately prior to the November elections. If it reconvenes for a brief "lame duck" session after the November elections, the unfinished business before the Senate usually does not include the consideration of judicial nominations. In short, the limited time available to the Senate, and the range of official responsibilities and issues that compete for the Senate's time, might be a consideration for some Senators in favor of devoting less time to the consideration of judicial nominations in a presidential election year than in other years.

Number of Judicial Nominations Processed Prior to a Slowdown. In deciding whether to favor, or not oppose, a judicial nominations slowdown at some point in a presidential election year, some Senators might be concerned with the number of judicial nominations the Senate had considered prior to that point. Some Senators might not oppose a slowdown in the processing of judicial nominations if they felt that the Senate, already at that point in the Congress, had processed enough judicial nominations. For guidance on that question, they might, for example, compare the number of judicial nominations confirmed thus far in the Congress with numbers confirmed in other recent Congresses. If the number compared favorably with those of other recent Congresses, it might be a consideration for some Senators not to oppose a slowdown. [127]

CONCLUDING OBSERVATIONS

In the 110th Congress, Senators have differed as to whether a sufficient number of judicial nominations, particularly nominations to the courts of appeals, have been confirmed or are on track to be confirmed before the end of the second session of the Congress. As of July 31, 2008, the Senate had confirmed 10 court of appeals nominations in the 110th Congress, with four of those nominations confirmed in the second session. [128] Some Senate Democrats have asserted that, in a presidential election year, the Senate customarily slows the processing of judicial nominations at an earlier point than in other years. In support of such an assertion, some have cited what has been called the "Thurmond rule," a precedent they maintain dates back to events in 1980 and which they say has, since 1980, shaped how the Senate and the Senate Judiciary Committee have processed judicial nominations in presidential election years. Conversely, some Senate Republicans have rejected the existence of a Thurmond rule in the Senate and the interpretations of events in 1980 that are the basis for Democrats invoking the rule.

In addressing the above issue, it is important to keep in mind that there is no written Senate or Senate Judiciary Committee rule concerning judicial nominations in a presidential election year. No bipartisan agreement has ever been reached, or any Judiciary Committee or Senate vote taken, regarding a Thurmond rule or the practices for which it is said to stand. On the other hand, it is also important to note that Senators of both parties have, on different occasions over the past few decades, characterized Senate processing of judicial nominations as slower during presidential election years. Usually, if not always, Senators making these characterizations have done so when they were of the opposite party to the President's. In addition, the data analyzed above, for the 1980-2004 period, demonstrate that Senate consideration of court of appeals nominees in the most recent presidential election years has resulted in fewer confirmations, and earlier final dates of Judiciary Committee and Senate action, than in the earlier presidential election years.

In a preceding section, this chapter provided chronological narratives of Senate Judiciary Committee and Senate actions taken on court of appeals and district court nominations in each presidential election year from 1980 to 2004. In most of these presidential election years, a fairly similar dynamic appeared to take place in the Judiciary Committee and in the Senate over the issue of whether to slow down the judicial confirmation process: Senators of the President's party supported processing as many judicial nominations as possible in the year, and as late in the year as possible, and they looked for examples of earlier presidential election years when relatively large numbers of nominations were processed or when nominations were processed relatively late in the year. On the other hand, Senators of the opposition party cited other presidential election years when relatively few nominations were processed, or when the processing of nominations stopped relatively early in the year, to put a slowdown in the current Congress in a more favorable perspective. Examples of presidential election years, in other words, could be found helpful to either party, with or without reference to the Thurmond rule. The impression that such a dynamic has often infused the judicial confirmation process prompted one Senator recently to comment in a floor statement, "We ought to try to move, I suggest, away from positions where we articulate a view when it suits our purpose and then articulate a different view later." [129]

The debate over the pace of Senate confirmations also regularly takes on a pattern of Senators of the President's party (and the President himself) blaming opposition party Senators for obstructing nominees viewed as qualified and deserving of Senate confirmation. In this debate, opposition party Senators often contend that the President's choices are controversial nominees selected to further the President's policy agenda and are not the best qualified nominations the President could make.

One component of the debate over Senate consideration of judicial nominations in a presidential election year (and of Senate consideration of judicial nominations more generally) is whether or not the increasing controversy over judicial nominations constitutes a policy "problem" for the Senate. Observers and scholars have pointed to the involvement of interest groups and the increasingly partisan nature of judicial nominations as a reason for concern, not only for the Senate, but for the ability of the judiciary to fulfill its role adjudicating controversies between litigants. [130] One indicator of this controversy is the increasing time-to-confirmation for those nominees who secure Senate confirmation. [131] At the same time, however, the vacancy rate for the federal judiciary has actually fallen over the course of the current presidential administration. On January 4, 2001, of 849 judgeships on the Article III lower courts (district courts, courts of appeals, and Court of International Trade), 80, or

9.4%, were vacant; on August 1, 2008, of 871 judgeships, 41, or 4.7%, were vacant [132].

Despite the falling vacancy rate, the current controversy over judicial nominations might still give the Senate a cause for concern. Because the Senate meets for fewer days in election years than in non-election years, the Senate may be concerned that the controversy over judicial nominations occupies an inordinate amount of the Senate's time. The Senate may also be concerned that acrimony over the judicial nomination process might spill over into other issues the Senate is considering and into the next Congress. Such acerbity might lead potential federal judgeship nominees to view the confirmation process as too time-consuming and unpleasant, thus discouraging qualified individuals from allowing themselves to be considered.

Should the Senate seek to confirm judicial nominees more promptly and later in presidential election years, one obstacle to overcome (or avoid) would be partisan conflict over the nominees. To that end, some Senators in the 110th Congress have indicated that the Senate is more likely to move forward late in presidential election years with what they view as "consensus" nominees. Some Senators have suggested that a nominee could be considered as a consensus choice if he or she has the support of both home state Senators. [133] Others, however, have stressed that, in addition to having the support of home state Senators, it is necessary, in order to be confirmed, that a nominee not be "controversial" — but rather have the support of the leaders of both parties in the Senate as well as of the chairman and the ranking minority member of the Judiciary Committee [134].

While there may be disagreement as to which nominees are "consensus" nominees, the support of both home-state Senators (particularly if the Senators are of the opposition party) is an important indicator of the President's willingness to work with individual Senators when making nominations. [135] Also, those nominations which have the support of both home-state Senators arguably would be much more likely to be considered by the Judiciary Committee and the full Senate in a presidential election year than if they lacked such support. [136] However, as already suggested, such support might not be sufficient to allow the nomination to be considered in committee or on the Senate floor, if the nomination lacks the bipartisan support of both the chair and ranking minority member of the Judiciary Committee and of both the Senate majority and the Senate minority leader.

Two other considerations may ultimately serve to limit the number of judicial nominations that can be considered after a certain point in presidential election years. First, as noted above, legislative time is more limited in a presidential election year. As noted in Table 6 above, the Senate has, over at least the last 30 years, been in session for fewer days in presidential election years than the other years of a President's term, in part due to the time taken for the national conventions and campaigning in advance of the elections. Judicial nominations, therefore, compete with other legislative priorities for the attention of the Senators, the Judiciary Committee, and the full Senate.

Second, the confirmation process, with all its steps, can be time-consuming. If nominations are made relatively late in the year, there might not be time for the Senate to proceed through the steps necessary to hold confirmation votes on nominees.137 Nominations typically require a background check by the Federal Bureau of Investigation, completion of a Judiciary Committee questionnaire by the nominee, and American Bar Association review. All of these steps typically, if not always, occur before a nominee receives a hearing by the Judiciary Committee — which then may report the nomination to the Senate, where the majority leader may schedule it for floor consideration.138 For some nominations, the time requirements of the pre-hearing process might not leave enough time for the Senate to consider the nominee on the floor prior to the November election. Thus, some judicial vacancies might have to wait to be filled by whoever is elected President in November.

References

[1] See, for instance, the contrasting views on this question in the floor remarks of the Senate minority leader on June 5, 2008, and of the chairman of the Senate Judiciary Committee on June 10, 2008. Sen. Mitch McConnell, "Judicial Nominations," Congressional Record, daily edition, vol. 154 (June 5, 2008), p. S5128; and Sen. Patrick J. Leahy, "Nomination of Mark Steven Davis to be United States District Judge for the Eastern District of Virginia," Congressional Record, daily edition, vol. 154 (June 10, 2008), pp. S5413-S5416.

[2] For periodically updated information on the number of pending and confirmed nominees to the U.S. courts of appeals and the district courts, see CRS Report RL33953, Nominations to Article III Lower Courts by President George W. Bush During the 110th Congress, by Denis Steven Rutkus, Kevin M. Scott, and Maureen Bearden.

[3] U.S. President (G.W. Bush), "Remarks on Nominations Awaiting Senate Confirmation," Weekly Compilation of Presidential Documents, vol. 44 (Feb. 7, 2008), pp. 160-162; U.S. President (G.W. Bush), "President's

Radio Address," Weekly Compilation of Presidential Documents, vol. 44 (Feb. 9, 2008), pp. 176-177; and U.S. President (G.W. Bush), "Remarks at the Federalist Society's 25th Annual Gala Dinner," Weekly Compilation of Presidential Documents, vol. 43 (Nov. 15, 2007), pp. 1507-1510.

[4] Sen. Arlen Specter, "Justice Delayed," Wall Street Journal, Feb. 1, 2008, p. A14; Sen. Orrin G. Hatch, "The Confirmation Process," remarks in the Senate, Congressional Record, daily edition, vol. 154 (Apr. 1, 2008), pp. S2263-S2265; and Sen. Mitch McConnell, "Nominations," remarks in the Senate, Congressional Record, daily edition, vol. 154 (July 17, 2008), pp. S6909-S6910

[5] Sen. Patrick J. Leahy, "Judicial Nominations," remarks in the Senate, Congressional Record, daily edition, vol. 154 (Mar. 3, 2008), pp. S1460-S 1462; and Sen. Harry Reid, "Confirmation of Judges," remarks in the Senate, Congressional Record, daily edition, vol. 154 (Apr. 10, 2008), pp. S2829-S2830.

[6] Sen. Arlen Specter, "Confirmation Process," remarks in the Senate, Congressional Record, daily edition, vol. 154 (July 17, 2008), pp. S6897.

[7] Sen. Patrick J. Leahy, "Nomination of Glenn T. Suddaby to be United States District Judge," remarks in the Senate, Congressional Record, daily edition, vol. 154 (July 22, 2008), p. S7084. On an earlier occasion, Senator Leahy, in a floor statement, remarked, "There seems to be no steps we could take to satisfy Republicans on nominations, because they are using it as a partisan issue to rev up their partisan political base." Sen. Patrick J. Leahy, "Nomination of Mark Steven Davis to be United States District Judge for the Eastern District of Virginia," remarks in the Senate, Congressional Record, daily edition, vol. 154 (June 10, 2008), p. S5416.

[8] As is discussed in greater detail later in this report, most Senators who have cited the Thurmond rule have characterized it as an established practice according to which, at some point in a presidential election year, the Judiciary Committee and the Senate no longer act on judicial nominations — with exceptions sometimes made for nominees who have bipartisan support from Senate committee and party leaders.

[9] Sen. Patrick J. Leahy, remarks in question-and-answer session, at Georgetown [University] Law Forum, following speech entitled, "Ensuring Liberty and Security Through Checks and Balances: A Fresh Start for the Senate Judiciary Committee in the New 110th Congress," Dec. 13, 2006, at [http://www.law.georgetown.edu/webcast/eventDetail.cfm? eventID=246], accessed June 17, 2008.

[10] Sen. Patrick J. Leahy, "Judicial Nominations," remarks in the Senate, Congressional Record, daily edition, vol. 154 (Mar. 3, 2008), p. S 1462.

[11] Sen. Patrick J. Leahy, "Judicial Nominations," remarks in the Senate, Congressional Record, daily edition, vol. 154 (Mar. 7, 2008), p. S1731.

[12] Sen. Patrick J. Leahy, Senate Judiciary Committee webcast of June 12, 2008, executive business meeting, at [http://judiciary.senate.gov/webcast/judiciary06122008-1000.ram], accessed July 25, 2008.

[13] Sen. Harry Reid, "Confirmation of Judges," remarks in the Senate, Congressional Record, daily edition, vol. 154 (Apr. 10, 2008), p. S2829. Senator Reid, however, indicated that it was not his intention to use his understanding of the Thurmond rule to prevent Senate consideration of judicial nominations that had recently been approved by the Senate Judiciary Committee. He said that he had "indicated to the Republican leader that we are going to try to move these nominations along. We are trying to keep up with the average that has gone on in years past without a lot of political bickering." Ibid.

[14] Sen. Harry Reid, "Highway Technical Corrections Act of 2007 — Motion to Proceed," remarks in the Senate, Congressional Record, daily edition, vol. 154 (Apr. 15, 2008), p. S3012.

[15] Sen. Orrin G. Hatch, "The Confirmation Process," Congressional Record, daily edition, vol. 154 (Apr. 1, 2008), p. S2264.

[16] Sen. Jeff Sessions, "Judicial Confirmations," Congressional Record, daily edition, vol. 154 (Apr. 16, 2008), p. S3041.

[17] Sen. Arlen Specter, "Judicial Nominations," remarks in the Senate, Congressional Record, daily edition, vol. 153 (Jan. 4, 2007), p. S27. "The fact of the matter," Senator Specter continued, "is that the Senate has regularly confirmed judges in presidential election years." He noted that in the election year of 1980, "when it is asserted Senator Thurmond inaugurated the so-called rule,"the Senate, after September 1, confirmed 11 district court nominees and 2 circuit court nominees. Ibid., pp. S27-S28.

[18] Sen. Arlen Specter, "Confirmation Process,"remarks in the Senate, Congressional Record, daily edition, vol. 154 (July 17, 2008), p. S6897.

[19] Senator Thurmond, one account reported, "said he told Reagan that he should contact Minority Leader Howard H. Baker Jr. (R.-Tenn.) and all other Republican members of the Senate in an attempt to withhold Senate confirmation of appointments [until after the Nov. 4 election]. 'He said he would be glad to do that,' Thurmond said." "Reagan May Seek to Bar New Carter Nominations," Washington Post, July 17, 1980, p. A15. See also,

"GOP Senators Urged to Stall Appointments," Los Angeles Times, July 17, 1980, p. A19.

[20] "Campaign: GOP," National Journal, vol. 12, July 26, 1980, p. 1248.

[21] One news story reported that in "exchange for Republican support for Breyer," the chairman of the Judiciary Committee, Senator Kennedy, "agreed not to push 17 other Carter judicial nominations pending in the committee." "Breyer Nomination Stalled," Congressional Quarterly Weekly Report, vol. 38, Nov. 29, 1980, p. 3443. Breyer, at the time of his nomination, was the chief majority counsel of the Senate Judiciary Committee.

[22] See Congressional Quarterly Almanac, 1980, vol. 34 (Washington: Congressional Quarterly Inc., 1981), pp. 16A-17A.

[23] Richard L. Lyons, "On Capitol Hill," Washington Post, Sept. 11, 1980, p. A8.

[24] "Transcript of Proceedings, United States Senate, Committee on the Judiciary, Executive Session No. XIV, September 17, 1980," Miller Associates Reporting Service, p. 4. (Copy in archival records of the Senate Judiciary Committee.)

[25] For example, in 1992, Senator Howard Metzenbaum of Ohio, in an exchange with Senator Thurmond at a Senate Judiciary Committee meeting, called the latter "the leader in shutting down entirely the question of judicial nominees in 1980." "Transcript of Proceedings, United States Senate, Committee on the Judiciary, Executive Session, Sept. 12, 1992," Miller Reporting Co. Inc., p. 12. (Copy in archival records of the Senate Judiciary Committee.") In 1996, at a Judiciary Committee meeting, Senator Joseph R. Biden Jr. of Delaware, reportedly said that Senator Thurmond in 1980 "decided that Carter was going to lose and that Reagan would win, so he announced there would be no more judges and shut the whole process down in June." "Hatch Puts Judges on Hold, Unleashing Dem Anger," National Journal's CongressDaily, Sept. 20, 1996, at [http://www.lexisnexis.com], accessed July 22, 2008. See subsequent sections of this report for more detailed discussion of the Senate's processing of judicial nominations in the presidential election years of 1992 and 1996.

[26] Senator Leahy reported said, "I understand under the Strom Thurmond rule that started years ago, that ... in a presidential election year, you tend to slow down on confirming judges appointed by the president. But this goes a little bit beyond." Sen. Patrick J. Leahy, news briefing, Feb. 12, 1997, FDCH Political Transcripts.

[27] "We have followed, in the past," Senator Leahy said, the so-called Thurmond rule of stalling a President's appointments to the judiciary in about the last few months of their term in office. I have never seen the stall start in the first few hours of a President's 4-year term." Sen. Patrick Leahy, "The Crisis In Our Federal Judiciary," remarks in the Senate, Congressional Record, daily edition, vol. 143, Apr. 17, 1997, p. S3391.

[28] Sen. Patrick J. Leahy, "Nomination of Henry W. Saad to be United States Circuit Judge for the Sixth Circuit," remarks in the Senate, Congressional Record, daily edition, vol. 150 (July 22, 2004), p. S8588.

[29] Sen. Orrin G. Hatch, "The Nomination of William Gerry Myers III to be a U.S. Circuit Judge for the Ninth Circuit," remarks in the Senate, Congressional Record, daily edition, vol. 150 (July 19, 2004), pp. S8406-S8412.

[30] "Statement of Chairman Orrin G. Hatch before the United State Senate Committee on the Judiciary," June 3, 2004, at [http://judiciary.senate.gov/member_statement.cfm? id=1211&wit_id=51], accessed June 18, 2008.

[31] Geoff Earle, "Senators Spar over 'Thurmond Rule,'" The Hill, vol. 11, July 21, 2004, p

[32] Ibid.

[33] Ibid. The article, however, singled out only one unnamed Republican staff member, and no Republican Senators, as attesting to this rule or traditional practice. Specifically, the article cited "one senior Republican aide [who] said the tradition was a general understanding that there would be no floor votes on controversial nominees, rather than an understanding that there would be no action on nominees at all." Ibid.

[34] Ibid.

[35] Sen. Mark Hatfield, "Executive Session," remarks in the Senate, Congressional Record, vol. 126, part 21 (Sept. 29, 1980), p. 27758. A fuller discussion of the context of Senator Hatfield's remarks, made on behalf of a three-member Republican panel that had reviewed President Jimmy Carter's judicial and executive branch nominations then before the Senate, is provided below, in the section that discusses Senate processing of judicial nominations in 1980.

[36] Sen. Robert C. Smith, "Nomination of Richard S. Paez and Marsha L. Berzon — Continued," remarks in the Senate, Congressional Record, daily edition, vol. 146 (Mar. 736 (...continued) 2000), p. S 1211.

[37] Ibid.

[38] "Transcript of Proceedings, United States Senate, Committee on the Judiciary, Executive Session, July 20, 2000," Miller Associates Reporting Service, pp. 6-7. (Copy in archival records of Senate Judiciary Committee.)

[39] Lee Davidson, "Hatch Says Lee Appointment May Doom Judiciary Choices," Deseret [Salt Lake City] News, Aug. 4, 2000, p. A7. A fuller discussion of the context of Senator Hatch's remarks, both those made at the July 20, 2000 meeting of the Judiciary Committee (cited in preceding footnote), and those reported on Aug. 4, 2000, is provided below, in the section that discusses Senate processing of judicial nominations in 2000.

[40] An additional controversy that has occasionally marked presidential election years is the creation of new judgeships and the timing of appointments to those new positions. Members of Congress, in debate over judgeship legislation, have sparred with one another and with the President over whether the incumbent President or only his successor would be able to fill the judgeships. See, e.g., Warren Weaver, Jr., "Judgeships Ban Decried By G.O.P.," New York Times, Aug. 10, 1960, p. 18 ("Attorney General William P. Rogers termed 'most regrettable' the apparent decision by Senator Lyndon B. Johnson of Texas, the majority leader, to oppose any increase in the Federal judiciary before Congress adjourns, about Labor Day."); and Lesley Oelsner, "Burger Accuses Congress of Lag on Court Reform," New York Times, Feb. 16, 1976, p. 1 ("The Chief Justice also suggested, without elaboration, that because of Presidential election year politics Congress was failing to act on one particular court problem — the need for dozens of additional judges")

[41] Sheldon Goldman, Picking Federal Judges: Lower Court Selection From Roosevelt Through Reagan (New Haven: Yale University Press, 1997), p. 81. (Hereafter cited as Goldman, Picking Federal Judges.) Goldman's assessment of 1948 may not be correct; the only district court judges confirmed in 1948 were to district courts in the Canal Zone and the Virgin Islands, both of which were territorial courts with limited-term appointments. The Senate returned five other district court nominations in 1948, including one nomination to the district court in Alaska, which, at the time, was a limited-term appointment. The Senate actually confirmed two (not one) court of appeals nominations, but one of the confirmations was for a judge who already served on the court and was confirmed to the position of "chief justice" of the Court of Appeals for the District of Columbia. (At the time, that court, like the U.S. Supreme Court, designated its members as "justices" and had a separate position for chief justice.) Those two

nominations were President Truman's only two nominations to the courts of appeals in 1948.

[42] See, e.g.,"Random Notes in Washington: Spoils Preserved for the Victor," New York Times, Sept. 26, 1960, p. 24, which reported the failure of various judicial and executive branch nominations to be confirmed before the Congress's final adjournment. In an election year, the article commented, the "party controlling the Congress, when it bears a different name, hesitates to confirm the Presidential nominations. There seems to be hope always that the Administration and appointive power will change." See also Abner J. Mikva, "Bench Games: Election Year or Not, the U.S. Senate Too Often Blocks Judicial Nominees for Partisan Or Petty Reasons," Legal Times, Feb. 28, 2000, p. 70.

[43] One scholar, for instance, described the presidential election year of 1976 as one in which "Democrats, in control of the Senate, would be reluctant to confirm judgeships until after the election," ultimately declining to confirm 10 of Republican President Gerald R. Ford's district and appeals court nominations. Goldman, Picking Federal Judges, p. 205. At the final adjournment of the 94th Congress on Oct. 1, 1976, according to one news analysis, "about a dozen lifetime or 15-year federal judgeships were blocked from confirmation — some on substantive grounds, others because they were received late." Senate Democrats, according this analysis, had held up some nominations "because they didn't like the policies or politics of the nominees, or wanted to prevent President Ford — who might not be here next year — from making appointments that possibly could be made by Democrat Jimmy Carter if he wins the presidency on Nov. 2." Spencer Rich, "Ford Nominations to Long- Term Posts Die in Congress," Washington Post, Oct. 3, 1976, p. 8.

[44] Two nominees, one each to a court of appeals and a district court, were also confirmed on Sept. 1, 1960; an additional district court nomination was confirmed on Aug. 27, 1960.

[45] President Ford also withdrew the district court nomination of William Poff on June 7, 1976.

[46] Congressional Quarterly Almanac, 96th Congress, 2nd Session (Washington, DC: Congressional Quarterly Inc., 1981), p. 15-A.

[47] The other two of the 67 district court nominations were withdrawn by President Carter — the first in August, the second in September.

[48] The Judiciary Committee was particularly active in June. The committee held confirmation hearings on both district court and circuit court nominations on June 4 and 9, as well as on district court nominations alone

on June 10 and 19. In addition, at a June 17 meeting, the committee recommended confirmation of 11 nominations — six to district court judgeships, four to the circuit courts (including the nomination of Ruth Bader Ginsburg to the U.S. Court of Appeals for the D.C. Circuit), and one to the U.S. Court of Customs and Patent Appeals. On June 24, the committee voted again on judicial nominations, this time to report favorably eight district court nominations.

[49] "GOP Senators Urged to Stall Appointments," Los Angeles Times, July 17, 1980, p. A 19.

[50] Specifically, it was reported, Senate Republicans had "begun an organized campaign to use various parliamentary stratagems, from committee boycotts to filibusters, to 'slow down or completely stop' Presidential appointments that could outlast the Carter Administration. The action was taken last month by the 41-member Senate Republican Caucus, which appointed a three-member committee to sift 155 Presidential nominations and weed out those whose terms would overlap that of a new President. The primary targets include 13 judicial nominees, as well as nominees to vacancies on the Nuclear Regulatory Commission, the National Labor Relations Board, the Securities and Exchange Commission, the Equal Employment Opportunity Commission and the Legal Services Corporation, among other agencies. Not affected are nominations to advisory boards and those who serve at the pleasure of the President without any fixed term." Martin Tolchin, "Republicans Fight Carter Nominees," New York Times, Sept. 14, 1980, p. 31.

[51] Edward L. Lyons, "On Capitol Hill," Washington Post, Sept. 11, 1980, p. A8.

[52] Ibid.

[53] "Transcript of Proceedings, United States Senate, Committee on the Judiciary, Executive Session No. XIV, Sept. 17, 1980," Miller Associates Reporting Service. (Copy in archival records of the Senate Judiciary Committee.)

[54] "Transcript of Proceedings, United States Senate, Committee on the Judiciary, Executive Session No. XIV, Sept. 17, 1980," Miller Associates Reporting Service, pp. 6-7. (Copy in archival records of the Senate Judiciary Committee.)

[55] "Transcript of Proceedings, United States Senate, Committee on the Judiciary, Executive Session No. XIV, Sept. 17, 1980," Miller Associates Reporting Service, p. 7. (Copy in archival records of Senate Judiciary Committee.) During the remainder of the second session of the 96th

Congress, there was no further Judiciary Committee action on the six judicial nominations held over at the September 17 meeting. After this meeting, the committee voted to report two more lower court nominations before the Senate's sine die adjournment on Dec. 16: it voted on September 24 to report one other district court nomination (one not among the six carried over on September 17), and it voted, on December 2, to report a circuit court nomination. Both of these nominations were confirmed.

[56] Sen. Mark Hatfield, "Executive Session," Congressional Record, vol. 126, part 21 (Sept. 29, 1980), p. 27758.

[57] Ibid.

[58] Ibid.

[59] That same day, the Senate had previously invoked cloture on the Breyer nomination by a 68-28 vote.

[60] One of the circuit court nominations returned at the end of the first session of the 98th Congress, that of Sherman E. Unger to the Court of Appeals for the Federal Circuit, was not resubmitted to the Senate in the second session.

[61] The other unconfirmed nomination was withdrawn by the President in early September.

[62] Prior to the Senate's June 29 adjournment, district court nominations received a Judiciary Committee hearing as late as June 26, a committee vote as late as June 14, and a Senate confirmation vote as late as June 15. The last circuit nomination to be acted on prior to June 29 received a hearing on June 13, a committee vote on June 14, and a Senate confirmation vote on June 15.

[63] P.L. 98-353, 98 Stat. 333.

[64] Philip Smith, "Va. Prosecutor Eyed for Judgeship," Washington Post, July 29, 1984, p. B3.

[65] Linda Greenhouse, "Reagan Names 6 to Federal Appeals Court," New York Times, Aug. 2, 1984, p. A1. Four of the six nominees were confirmed before the Senate's sine die adjournment on October 12, 1984.

[66] At the start of the second session, a Supreme Court nomination — that of Anthony M. Kennedy to be an Associate Justice — also was pending. The Senate Judiciary Committee had already, in December 1987, held confirmation hearings on Judge Kennedy, and it favorably reported his nomination, by a 14-0 vote, on Jan. 27, 1988. A week later, on Feb. 3, the Senate confirmed the nomination by a 97-0 roll call vote. This, it should be noted, was the only Supreme Court nomination pending in the Senate during a presidential election year in the 1980-2004 time period.

[67] "Politics and Judgeships," Los Angeles Times, April 29, 1988, part 2, p. 6.

[68] Ruth Marcus, "Judiciary's 'Slow Pace' Ignites Clash; Thurmond' s Charges Provoke Leahy," Washington Post, June 6, 1988, p. A13. In May, the Judiciary Committee had considered district court nominations on three occasions (voting to report two such nominations on May 12, holding hearings on four nominations on May16, and voting to report two nominations on May 24), without, however, considering any circuit court nominations during the month.

[69] Steven V. Roberts, "Washington Talk: The Senate; Election-Year Ritual Snags Appointment Process," New York Times, June 24, 1988, p. A13.

[70] Ruth Marcus, "Leahy Fires Back at Thurmond; Justice Dept. Delays Blamed for Slow Progress on Nominees," Washington Post, June 14, 1988, p. A2 1. (Hereafter cited as Marcus, "Leahy Fires Back.") Senator Leahy, at this point, was the Democratic member in charge of committee consideration of judicial nominations, in the absence of committee Chairman Joseph R. Biden Jr. of Delaware, who was on medical leave and would not return to chair the committee until September. See "Sen. Biden Back on Job After Brain Operation in Feb.," Los Angeles Times, Sept. 7, 1988, part 1, p. 2.

[71] Marcus, "Leahy Fires Back."

[72] Ibid.

[73] Ibid.

[74] The two most active of these four months in terms of nominations activity were June and August. In June, the committee held three days of hearings on district court nominations, on June 13, 22, and 29, and one day of hearings on a district court and a circuit court nomination, on June 21. In August, prior to the Republican Party's national convention on Aug. 20-23, the committee voted to report two district court nominations on Aug. 3, held hearings on three district court and one circuit court nomination on Aug. 9, held hearings on one circuit court and one territorial district court nomination on Aug. 10, and also on Aug. 10 voted to report one circuit court and one district court nomination.

[75] The nine district court nominations reported by the committee included one to the territorial district court for the Northern Mariana Islands.

[76] The nine district court nominations confirmed by the Senate included one to the territorial district court for the Northern Mariana Islands.

[77] Susan F. Rasky, "Congress Deadlocks Again on Revising Clean Air Act," New York Times, Oct. 5, 1988, p. B6.

[78] Ibid.

[79] Richard Carelli, "Campaign Largely Ignored President's Power to Shape Judiciary," Associated Press, Oct. 28, 1992.

[80] Matthew Brelis, "Bush Pace Faulted on Judges; Chances of Filling Vacancies This Year Seen Slipping Away," Boston Globe, Aug. 16, 1992, p. 29.

[81] Neil A. Lewis, "Waiting for Clinton, Democrats Hold Up Court Confirmations," New York Times, Sept. 1, 1992, p. A1.

[82] M.P. McQueen, "Senate Delays Hispanic Nomination," Newsday, Jul. 4, 1992, p. 10.

[83] Bill McAllister, "Nominee for Judgeship Defends Rights Record: Advocacy Groups' Criticisms Denied," Washington Post, July 23, 1992. According to the same news report, Keating was accused of saying that his job as HUD general counsel was to protect "good Christian landlords." Ibid.

[84] "Transcript of Proceedings, United States Senate, Committee on the Judiciary, Executive Session, Sept. 12, 1992," Miller Reporting Co. Inc., p. 12. (Copy in archival records of the Senate Judiciary Committee.)

[85] Ibid., p. 13. Senator Thurmond, in this exchange, did not dispute the suggestion that he might have used his role as ranking minority member of the Judiciary Committee to prevent the confirmation of some lower court nominations in 1980. His terse reply to Senator Metzenbaum, however, contrasted the number of judicial nominations not confirmed in 1980 (17), with the number then before the Judiciary Committee in 1992 (over 50 — of which 10 court of appeals and 42 district court nominations would soon be returned to the President). He appeared to be conveying the message that if there were any slowdown in processing of judicial nominations in 1980, it was not, in his view, comparable to the slowdown in Judiciary Committee processing of President George H.W. Bush's nominations in 1992.

[86] During the first session of the 104th Congress, the Senate had confirmed 11 circuit court nominations. Two of these, as already discussed, were confirmed on Jan. 2, 1996, the final day of the first session.

[87] The last previous regular session of a Congress in which the Senate did not confirm a circuit court nominee was the first session of the Eighty-third Congress in 1953.

[88] Catherine M. Brennan, "Fourth Circuit Among Courts Facing 'Judicial Emergency'; Long-Term Vacancies on Federal Bench Are Creating Extra Burdens on Overstressed System; Political Posturing Only Adds to the Problem, Daily Record [Baltimore, MD], June 20, 1996, p. 9. The article was evidently referring to the 2 circuit court nominations and 1 district court

nomination confirmed by the Senate on Jan. 2, 1996, and to the 9 circuit court and 44 district court nominations confirmed by the Senate in 1995.

[89] Roger K. Lowe, "Senate Compromise May Allow Confirmation of Federal Judges," Columbus [Ohio] Dispatch, July 14, 1996, p. 3B.

[90] Prior to the Senate votes on July 10 to confirm two district court nominations, Senator. Tom Daschle, the Democratic minority leader, reportedly said that "he and [Senate Majority Leader Trent] Lott have been trying to find a way to take action on as many as possible of the 23 judicial nominations that have been endorsed by the Senate Judiciary Committee." Ibid.

[91] Marcy Gordon, "Senate Still Facing Decisions on Clinton Judgeship Nominations," Associated Press, Oct. 3, 1996, at [http://www.lexis.com], accessed Apr. 25, 2008. In this news story, Senator Tom Daschle of South Dakota, the Senate Democratic leader, faulted the Senate Republican majority for refusing to act on more of President Clinton's judicial nominations, reportedly asserting, "This miserable record will probably be the legacy of the 104th Congress." However, the chairman of the Judiciary Committee, Senator Orrin G. Hatch of Utah, was quoted as insisting that "any objective observer, considering the record rather than the rhetoric, would conclude that this Congress has moved President Clinton's judicial nominations in a fair and responsible manner." Ibid.

[92] The other unconfirmed circuit nomination was withdrawn by the President during the session.

[93] The other unconfirmed district court nomination was withdrawn by the President during the session.

[94] "Transcript of Proceedings, United States Senate, Committee on the Judiciary, Executive Session, July 20, 2000," Miller Reporting Co. Inc., pp. 6-7. (Copy in archival records of the Senate Judiciary Committee.)

[95] Ibid., p. 7.

[96] Ibid., p. 10.

[97] Ibid.

[98] The Senate voted on four nominations which had been reported by the Judiciary Committee on July 27.

[99] Sonya Ross, "President Bypasses Congress, Gives Rights Aide Recess Appointment," Associated Press, Aug. 3, 2000.

[100] Ibid.

[101] Lee Davidson, "Hatch Says Lee Appointment May Doom Judiciary Choices," Deseret [Salt Lake City] News, Aug. 4, 2000, p. A7.

[102] Ibid.

[103] Jim Abrams, "Senator Renews Threat to Block Nominations," Associated Press, Sept. 11, 2000. Senator Inhofe, this story reported, said that President Clinton, in making the August 2000 recess appointments, had broken an agreement he had made with Senate Republicans not to make recess appointments without first consulting them. He called the appointments "just an arrogant defiance of the Senate's prerogative of advice and consent." Ibid. See also "U.S. Senator James Inhofe (R-OK) Holds News Conference Regarding the EPA," FDCH Political Transcripts, Oct. 6, 2000, in which Senator Inhofe discussed his hold on President Clinton's judicial nominations.

[104] Audrey Hudson, "Hill GOP Rips Legislative 'Roadblocks'; Democrats Maneuver to Press Agenda," Washington Times, Sept. 20, 2000, p. A4.

[105] See, e.g., Sen. John Cornyn, "Democratic Leadership's Obstruction," remarks in the Senate, Congressional Record, daily edition, vol. 150 (Apr. 1, 2004), pp. S3525-S3526. ("But unfortunately, as appears to be a growing trend and one where our Democratic colleagues continue to dig in their heels, the answer to every entreaty we might offer, every suggestion we have in terms of creating jobs, in terms of putting people on the bench to decide cases that go unheard because judges are not being confirmed to these posts, we continue to get a consistent response on behalf of our Democratic colleagues of 'no'")

[106] See, e.g., Sen, Patrick J. Leahy, "Nomination of Gary L. Sharpe to be United States District Judge," remarks in the Senate, Congressional Record, daily edition, vol. 150 (Jan. 28, 2004), pp. S304-S307. ("With respect to his extreme judicial nominations, President George W. Bush is the most divisive President in American history. Through these nominees, President Bush is dividing the American people and undermining the fairness and independence of the Federal judiciary on which all Americans depend.")

[107] Quoted in Thomas Ferraro, "Daschle to Block Nominees," Philadelphia Inquirer, Mar. 31, 2004, p. A2.

[108] Sen. John Cornyn, "Misstatements About the Bush Administration," Congressional Record, daily edition, vol. 150 (Mar. 26, 2004), pp. S3203-S3205.

[109] Charles Hurt, "Deal Clears Way for 25 Judicial Nominees," Washington Times, May 19, 2004, p. A3.

[110] The end of July might serve as a useful demarcation point for two reasons. First, the Senate traditionally takes an August recess, and the end of July comes close to marking the end of the legislative work period before that recess in most years. Second, the end of July falls near the time of the

presidential conventions. From 1980 to 1992, one party's convention was held in July, with the other party's national convention held in August; from 1996 to 2008, both conventions were held in August or September (the 2000 Republican National Convention started on July 31). Among other things, Table 3 reveals, for each presidential election year from 1980 to 2004, whether lower court nominations received hearings, committee votes, or Senate floor votes after July.

[111] The patterns illustrated in Tables 2 and 3 above may operate in conjunction with one another. In particular, in 1980, 1984, and 2004, the Judiciary Committee's reporting of nominees after July 31 might have occurred, in some cases, because the committee was considering "consensus" nominees, or, in other cases, because the committee majority, as members of the President's party, might have been willing to report out the President's nominees, whether or not they had bipartisan support.

[112] The significant expansion of the federal judiciary in 1978 offers a useful demarcation when deciding which years to compare. In 1978, Congress enacted legislation that increased the size of the appellate bench to 132 from 97 judgeships; subsequent legislation in 1982, 1984, and 1990 brought the size of the appellate bench to 179 at the end of 2007. Given these expansions of the judiciary, data from before 1977 (the first year of the presidential term in which the above expansion was enacted) may not be easily compared with data after 1977.

[113] One apparent anomaly is that more nominations to the courts of appeals were reported by the Senate in the first year of presidential terms than received hearings; this apparent discrepancy may be due to nominees who received hearings in the first term of two-term presidencies, only to be reported in the second term of a two-term President.

[114] The Senate has, on average, held more hearings for court of appeals nominees in presidential election years (9.0) than in the first year of presidential terms (8.1), but the Senate reported (9.0 in first years; 8.3 in presidential election years) and confirmed (8.5 in first years; 7.3 in presidential election years) more nominees to the courts of appeals in first years of presidential terms than in presidential election years.

[115] The general pattern of adjourning in September or October, and occasionally returning for a lame-duck session, also occurs in midterm election years. In 1978, 1986, 1990, and 1998, the Senate adjourned sine die before congressional elections; in 1982, 1994, and 2006, the Senate returned for lame-duck sessions after the congressional elections. In 2002, the Senate remained in session until November 22, at which point it adjourned sine die.

Such a pattern does not arise in odd-numbered years, when there are no regular congressional or presidential elections. Between 1977 and 2007, the earliest in the year that the first session of any Congress adjourned was November 13, in 1997.

[116] The Senate confirmed one circuit court and five district court nominees on Oct. 8, 1992; it confirmed one circuit court and three district court nominees on Sept. 30, 1993. In the interim, the President nominated (on June 22, 1993) and the Senate confirmed (on Aug. 3, 1993) Ruth Bader Ginsburg to a vacancy on the U.S. Supreme Court.

[117] For number of authorized judgeships, see [http://www.uscourts.gov/history/all_authorized_judgeships.pdf]. Total is derived by adding number of permanent district court judgeships (632) and number of court of appeals judgeships (179). Vacancy data derived from [http://www.uscourts.gov/vacancies/archives.cfm].

[118] The Senate confirmed two district court and one circuit court nominee on July 21, 2000. The circuit court nominee, Roger Gregory, had been first nominated and then recess- appointed by President Clinton, then nominated again by President George W. Bush. The last court of appeals nominee confirmed in the 106th Congress was confirmed on July 21, 2000; the Senate confirmed four district court nominees on Oct. 3, 2000.

[119] For number of authorized judgeships, see [http://www.uscourts.gov/history/all_authorized_judgeships.pdf]. Total is derived by adding number of permanent district court judgeships (651) and number of court of appeals judgeships (179). Vacancy data derived from [http://www.uscourts.gov/vacancies/archives.cfm].

[120] "As I have said on the Senate floor, this is a problem that has been going on for the past two decades. In the last two years of President Reagan's administration, there was a slowdown when Democrats were in charge of the Senate. The slowdown continued during the term of President Bush, the 4 1st President. Then, Republicans retaliated during the term of President Clinton by slowing down the process. We have had very major disputes — I would even call them bitter disputes. Notwithstanding the disrepute of the word 'bitter,' sometimes it is applicable, and I think it is certainly applicable to the filibusters of 2005. During that confrontation between the parties, filibusters were used repeatedly by Democrats. Republicans retaliated in kind with the threat of a so-called nuclear or constitutional option." Sen. Arlen Specter, "Judicial Confirmations," remarks in the Senate, Congressional Record, daily edition, vol. 154 (Apr. 16, 2008), p. S3042. See also Sheldon Goldman, "Judicial Confirmation Wars: Ideology and the

Battle for the Federal Courts," University of Richmond Law Review, vol. 39, March 2005, pp. 871-908.

[121] Ibid.

[122] A Senator's belief in this principle could be a consideration in favor of a slowdown of Senate action on judicial nominations during the election year, whether or not the Senator were of the President's party.

[123] CRS Report RL34405, Role of Home State Senators in the Selection of Lower Federal Court Judges, by Denis Steven Rutkus.

[124] See July 20, 2000, statement of Sen. Orrin G. Hatch, quoted earlier in this report, that the federal judiciary "is at virtually full employment because the Senate has appropriately carried out its advice and consent duties." Sen. Orrin G. Hatch, quoted in Transcript of Proceedings, United States Senate, Committee on the Judiciary, Executive Session, July 20, 2000," Miller Reporting Co. Inc., pp. 6-7. (Copy in archival records of the Senate Judiciary Committee.) See also July 25, 2000, floor statement by Senator Hatch, in which he stated, "The claim that there is a vacancy crisis in the federal courts is simply wrong. Using the Clinton Administration's own standard, the federal judiciary currently is at virtual full employment." Sen. Orrin G. Hatch, "Judicial Nominations," remarks in the Senate, Congressional Record, daily edition, vol. 146 (July 25, 2000), p. S7519.

[125] The separate vacancy rates for the two court categories were 11.7% for the courts of appeals (21 vacancies of 179 judgeships) and 5.9% for the district courts (39 vacancies of 661 judgeships). See [http://www.uscourts.gov /vacancies/070 12000/summary.htm], for vacancy data, and [http://www.uscourts.gov/history/all_authorized_judgeships.pdf], for judgeship data, both accessed Aug. 5, 2008.

[126] This responsibility involves assessing the qualifications of persons to hold lifetime appointments in the third branch of the federal government which is independent of Congress and the President. "The power to name those who occupy the offices of government is the power to shape how and by whom the nation is governed. The division of so critical a power between the president and the Senate all but invites a struggle for primacy between the occupants of the first and second branches and their respective political parties.... " Charles Gardner Geyh, When Courts and Congress Collide: The Struggle for Control of America's Judicial System (Ann Arbor: University of Michigan Press, 2006), p. 172.

[127] Alternately, as discussed earlier, Senators might look at the judicial vacancy rate at that point in the Congress to decide whether, in their view, the Senate had already, in that Congress, confirmed a sufficient number of judicial

nominations. To this end, they could consider whether the judicial vacancy rate had been reduced during the Congress, and whether, at that point, it was at an acceptably low level. An affirmative answer, especially if to both of these questions, could be a consideration for a Senator to favor, or not oppose, a slowdown in Senate processing of judicial nominations.

[128] For a periodically updated listing of nominations by President George W. Bush to the U.S. courts of appeals and district courts during the 110th Congress, and Senate actions taken on those nominations, see CRS Report RL33953, Nominations to Article III Lower Courts by President George W. Bush During the 110th Congress, by Denis Steven Rutkus, Kevin M. Scott, and Maureen Bearden.

[129] Sen. Arlen Specter, "Nominations of Paul G. Gardephe to be United States District Judge for the Southern District of New York and Kiyo A. Matsumoto to be United States District Judge for the Eastern District of New York," remarks in the Senate, Congressional Record, daily edition, (vol 154) July 17, 2008, p. S6893.

[130] See, e.g., Nancy Scherer, Scoring Points: Politicians, Activists, and the Lower Federal Court Appointment Process (Stanford, CA: Stanford University Press, 2005); Lee Epstein and Jeffrey A. Segal, Advice and Consent: The Politics of Judicial Appointments (New York: Oxford University Press, 2005); Sheldon Goldman, "Judicial Confirmation Wars: Ideology and the Battle for the Federal Courts," University of Richmond Law Review, vol. 39, March 2005, pp. 871-908; Stephen B. Burbank, "Politics, Privilege & Power: The Senate's Role in the Appointment of Federal Judges," Judicature, vol. 86, July-August 2002, pp. 24-27; and Elliot E. Slotnick, "A Historical Perspective on Federal Judicial Selection," Judicature, vol. 86, July-August 2002, pp. 13-16.

[131] As of August 4, 2008, the average time to confirmation for President George W. Bush's court of appeals nominees was 350 days, 47% greater than the average time to confirmation for President Clinton's court of appeals nominees (238 days). For data on time to confirmation for court of appeals and district court nominees, see CRS Report RL33953, Nominations to Article III Lower Courts by President George W. Bush During the 110th Congress, by Denis Steven Rutkus, Kevin M. Scott, and Maureen Bearden.

[132] For 2001 vacancy data, see [http://www.uscourts.gov/vacancies/0 1042001/ summary.html]. Judgeship data for 2001 are from [http://www.uscourts.gov/ history/tablek.pdf]. For 2008 vacancy and judgeship data, see

[http://www.uscourts.gov/cfapps/webnovada/CF_FB_301/archived/summary08_0 1_08.html].

[133] One Senator, for example, referring to Robert J. Conrad, Jr., of North Carolina, a nominee to the Fourth Circuit Court of Appeals, said "He was nominated for a judicial emergency. He has the support of both his home Senators, received a unanimous ABA rating of 'well qualified,'' the highest rating you can get. He is a consensus nominee. The Senate unanimously confirmed him for his current district judge seat, and the ABA, then, ranked him unanimously 'well qualified.' The whole ABA 15-member committee voted him the highest rating, unanimously." Sen. Jeff Sessions, "Judicial Confirmations," remarks in the Senate, Congressional Record, daily edition, vol. 154 (Apr. 16, 2008), p. S3041.

[134] According to news reports, an aide to Senator Patrick J. Leahy, chairman of the Judiciary Committee, indicated that a judicial nomination, to be considered a consensus nomination, needed to be approved by the Senate majority leader, the Senate minority leader, and the chairman and ranking minority member of the Judiciary Committee. Al Kamen, "Judicial Vacancies Leave GOP With Empty Feeling," Washington Post, July 6, 2007, p. A13. See also Senator Leahy' s more recent floor remarks, on June 10, 2008, commending President Bush, in certain instances, "for withdrawing controversial nominees and working toward consensus nominees." Sen. Patrick J. Leahy, "Nomination of Mark Steven Davis to be United States District Judge for the Eastern District of Virginia," remarks in the Senate, Congressional Record, daily edition, vol. 154 (June 10, 2008), p. S5417.

[135] In the 110th Congress, it has been noted, "the onus is on the Administration, if it hopes to see its nominee confirmed, not only to consult with the home state Senator but also, through a process of consultation, to select a nominee who is acceptable to both the Administration and the home state Senator." CRS Report RL34405, Role of Home State Senators in the Selection of Lower Federal Court Judges, by Denis Steven Rutkus (quotation under heading, "Consultation Between the President and Home State Senators in the Current Environment").

[136] For example, speaking in support of the confirmation of G. Steven Agee to the Fourth Circuit Court of Appeals, Senator Richard J. Durbin of Illinois said, "he is a consensus nominee. Both Senators Warner and Webb support him. Of the 11 appellate court nominees pending before the Senate, only six can claim the same home State Senator support. That is one of the reasons some of them have been delayed. If we work more toward bipartisan

consensus, more nominations would be approved." Sen. Richard J. Durbin, "Nomination of Michael G. McGinn To Be United States Marshal for the District of Minnesota, Ralph E. Martinez To Be A Member of the Foreign Claims Settlement Commission of the United States, and G. Steven Agee To Be United States Judge for the Fourth Circuit — Continued," remarks in the Senate, Congressional Record, daily edition, vol. 154 (May 20, 2008), pp. S4440-S4441.

[137] Of President George W. Bush's lower court nominees, the shortest time-to-confirmation for a district court judge was 56 days (L. Scott Coogler, Northern District of Alabama, nominated Mar. 27, 2003, confirmed May 22, 2003). The shortest time-to-confirmation for a court of appeals nominee was 63 days (Bobby Shepherd of Arkansas, Eighth Circuit Court of Appeals, nominated May 18, 2006, confirmed July 20, 2006).

[138] For a discussion of the pre-nomination process, see CRS Report RL34405, Role of Home State Senators in the Selection of Lower Federal Court Judges, by Denis Steven Rutkus, pp. 40-41. Typically, but not always, the FBI background check occurs prior to nomination. To take one example of the timing of this process, the nomination of Helene N. White of Michigan, to the Sixth Circuit Court of Appeals, was made on April 15, 2008. From that point, one Senator has noted, "[h]er questionnaire was not received until April 25. The FBI investigation was not begun until April 25. The ABA report cannot be completed until May 19 at the earliest. After Judge White's hearing, which is scheduled hastily for May 7, the committee typically leaves the record open for 1 week, which would close the record on May 14. If there are questions for the record, Judge White would have 1 week to answer those questions, which would bring us to May 21. If the nomination is held over for a week, that would put us into June. Assuming the nomination is not held over for a week, that leaves only 2 days before May 23 for the committee to review her answers, schedule and hold a committee vote, and for the full Senate to vote on her nomination. No circuit court nominee has had hearings prior to their ABA report being received. The ABA report is not expected until at least May 19." Sen. Arlen Specter, "Nomination Process," remarks in the Senate, Congressional Record, daily edition, vol. 154 (May 6, 2008), pp. S3753-S3754.

In: Court Nominations
Editor: Peter C. Kesterhoff, pp. 155-183
ISBN 978-1-60692-556-0

Chapter3

NOMINATIONS TO ARTICLE III LOWER COURTS BY PRESIDENT GEORGE W. BUSH DURING THE 110TH CONGRESS*

Denis Steven Rutkus and Kevin M. Scott and Maureen Bearden

ABSTRACT

This chapter tracks nominations made by President George W. Bush to judgeships on the U.S. courts of appeals, the U.S. district courts, and the U.S. Court of International Trade — the lower courts on which, pursuant to Article III of the Constitution, judges serve "during good Behaviour." It lists and keeps count of all nominations made to these courts during the 110th Congress, including pertinent actions taken by the Senate Judiciary Committee and the full Senate. It also tracks the number of judicial vacancies on the courts (including vacancies classified by the federal judiciary as "judicial emergencies"), the number of nominations pending to fill the vacancies, and the names of the pending nominees. It presents the number of persons nominated by President Bush to each category of lower Article III court during his entire presidency (breaking down each total to show the number confirmed, pending, returned and not re-nominated, and withdrawn). Last, it provides tabular and graphical comparisons of President Bush's lower court nominee statistics with those of the four Presidents who immediately preceded him.

* Excerpted from CRS Report RL33953, dated August 4, 2008.

As of August 4, 2008:

- President Bush had nominated 21 individuals to the U.S. courts of appeals during the 110th Congress, with the Senate having confirmed 10 of them, and with three withdrawn by the President.
- President Bush had nominated 78 individuals to the U.S. district courts during the 110th Congress, with the Senate having confirmed 48 of them, and with one withdrawn by the President.
- There were 10 judicial vacancies on the U.S. courts of appeals, with eight nominations pending to fill these vacancies.
- There were 30 U.S. district court vacancies, with 25 nominations pending to fill these judgeships, and an additional four nominations pending to fill future district court vacancies.
- No vacancies had occurred on the U.S. Court of International Trade during the 110th Congress (and thus no nominations have been made to the court during the Congress).

During the entire presidency of George W. Bush (from January 20, 2001, to August 4, 2008), there have been 370 nominees to Article III lower court judgeships. Of the 370 total nominees, 37 are pending, 314 have received Senate confirmation, nine have been returned to the President in a previous Congress and not resubmitted, and 10 have been withdrawn by the President and not resubmitted.

For corresponding information about President Bush's appeals and district court nominations during earlier Congresses, see CRS Report RL3 1868, U.S. Circuit and District Court Nominations by President George W. Bush During the 107th-109th Congresses, by Denis Steven Rutkus, Kevin M. Scott, and Maureen Bearden.

Introduction

Under Article III of the Constitution of the United States, the appointment of individuals to lifetime positions on the lower federal courts (the U.S. courts of appeals, U.S. district courts, and U.S. Court of International Trade) requires Senate confirmation [1]. In recent years, Congress has expressed increasing interest in the nomination and confirmation process for lower federal court judges [2]. During the 110th Congress, the number of lower court nominations by President George W. Bush that have been confirmed or are likely to be confirmed has been a subject of continuing Senate interest [3].

To provide Congress with a current overview of the lower court appointment process, this chapter tracks the status of certain lower court nominations made by

President George W. Bush during the 110th Congress. The chapter deals primarily with nominations to lower Article III courts (those courts on which judges serve "during good Behaviour"), while also accounting for infrequent nominations to the small number of territorial district judgeships, which have fixed-term appointments [4].

The Article III Lower Courts

Article III, Section 1 of the Constitution provides, in part, that the "judicial Power of the United States shall be vested in one supreme Court, and in such inferior Courts as the Congress may from time to time ordain and establish." It further provides that justices on the Supreme Court and judges on lower courts established by Congress under Article III have what effectively has come to mean life tenure, holding their office "during good Behaviour" [5]. By contrast, judges in various federal courts established by Congress under Article I of the Constitution are appointed for fixed terms [6]. Along with the Supreme Court, the courts that constitute the Article III courts in the federal judicial system are the U.S. courts of appeals, the U.S. district courts, and the U.S. Court of International Trade. The following are thumbnail descriptions of each of the lower Article III courts:

The U.S. Courts of Appeals. These courts take appeals from federal trial court decisions and are empowered to review the decisions of many administrative agencies. Cases presented to these courts are generally considered by judges sitting in three-member panels. Altogether, 178 permanent appellate court judgeships are authorized by law [7]. Courts within the courts of appeals system are often called "circuit courts," because they are divided into 12 geographic circuits and an additional nationwide circuit, the Federal Circuit, which has specialized subject matter jurisdiction. In this chapter, nominations to U.S. courts of appeals judgeships are, at various points, also referred to as "circuit court nominations."

The U.S. District Courts. These are the trial courts of general federal jurisdiction. Each state has at least one district court, while some states have as many as four. There are 674 district court judgeships authorized by law, including those for the District of Columbia and the Commonwealth of Puerto Rico [8].

The U.S. Court of International Trade. This court has original and exclusive jurisdiction over civil actions against the United States, its agencies and officers, and certain civil actions brought by the United States arising out of import transactions and federal statutes affecting international trade. The court is composed of nine judges, no more than five of whom may belong to one political party.

Congress also has established district courts in the territories of Guam, the U.S. Virgin Islands, and the Northern Mariana Islands. Like the U.S. district courts, the territorial courts are trial courts of general federal jurisdiction, while also having jurisdiction over many local matters that, within the 50 states, are handled in state courts. Because they are trial courts of general federal jurisdiction, whose rulings may be appealed to a U.S. court of appeals, [9] the territorial courts can be viewed as a category of court falling within the federal district court system [10]. Territorial courts, however, are not Article III courts, and judicial appointees to these courts serve 10-year terms, with one judgeship each in Guam and the Northern Mariana Islands, and two in the Virgin Islands.

Judicial Nomination Data Tracked

This chapterlists and keeps count of all nominations made to the above-discussed courts during the 110th Congress, including certain actions taken on these nominations by the Senate Judiciary Committee and the full Senate. The chapteralso provides statistics for all of the nominations that President Bush has made to these courts during his entire presidency, starting with the 107th Congress in January 2001 and carrying through to the present. (Thus far in the 110th Congress, no nominations have been made either to the U.S. Court of International Trade or to the territorial district courts, although President Bush made, and the Senate confirmed, nominations to these courts during previous Congresses.)

In the following pages, President Bush's nominations to the lower Article III courts are listed or counted in Tables 1 through 6. Some of these tables, where noted, also keep track of nominations made to the territorial courts. Appendix 1 provides a brief textual overview of the principal steps in the process for appointing lower court judges.

Judicial Nomination Tables for the 110th Congress

Table 1 is a judicial vacancy table. For each type of Article III lower court — circuit, district, and Court of International Trade — it shows the number of judgeships vacant as of the date listed, as well as the number of nominations pending to fill those judgeships. Table 1 also displays the number of nominations pending to fill "future vacancies," which occur when judges in active service announce their retirement to occur on a date that has not yet been reached or when a judge in active service indicates a plan to retire or take senior status upon the confirmation of a successor.

In addition, Table 1 shows how many of these vacancies are classified by the federal judiciary as "judicial emergencies." For the courts of appeals, a judicial emergency is any vacancy in a circuit where there are more than 700 adjusted filings per panel, or any vacancy in a circuit that has existed for more than 18 months and where adjusted filings are between 500 to 700 per panel [11]. For a district court, a judicial emergency is any vacancy in a district where weighted filings exceed 600 per judgeship, or any vacancy in existence more than 18 months where weighted filings are between 430 and 600 per judgeship, or any court with more than one authorized judgeship and only one active judge [12].

Table 1. Vacancies in Article III Lower Court Judgeships (as of August 4, 2008)

Court	Vacancies	Nominations Pending		Judicial Emergencies	
		For Existing Vacancies	For Future Vacancies	Number	Nominees Pending
U.S. Courts of Appeals	10	8	0	7	5
U.S. District Courts	31	25	4	5	4
U.S. Court of International Trade	0	0	0	0	0
Total	41	33	4	12	9

Source: CRS analysis of data provided by the Administrative Office for the United States Courts, available at [http://www.uscourts.gov/judicialvac.html].

Table 2 which lists pending nominations, presents all Article III lower court nominations made during the 110th Congress that were pending as of the date listed.

Table 2. Pending Nominations to the U.S. Courts of Appeals, District Courts, and Court of International Trade in the 110th Congress (as of August 4, 2008)

No.	Name of Nominee	Court	Date		
			Received by Senate	Hearing	Committee Action
Circuit Courts of Appeals					
1	Keisler, Peter D.a	D.C.	1/9/07	b	
2	Conrad, Robert J., Jr.	Fourth	7/17/07		
3	Stone, Shalom D.	Third	7/17/07		
4	Matthews, Steve A.	Fourth	9/6/07		
5	Rosenstein, Rod J.	Fourth	11/15/07		
6	Smith, William E.	First	12/6/07		
7	Conrad, Glen E.	Fourth	5/8/08		
8	Diamond, Paul S.	Third	7/24/08		
District Courts					
1	Farr, Thomas Alvina	E.NC	1/9/07		
2	Rogan, James E.a	C.CA	1/9/07		
3	Dugas, David R.	M.LA	3/19/07		
4	Honaker, Richard H.	WY	3/19/07	2/12/08	
5	Powell, William J.	N.WV	5/24/07		
6	Puryear, Gustavus A., IV	M.TN	6/13/07	2/12/08	
7	Almond, Lincoln D.	RI	11/15/07		
8	Novak, David J.	E.VA	11/15/07	4/3/08	
9	Connolly, Colm F.	DE	2/26/08		
10	Waddoups, Clark	UT	4/29/08		
11	Anello, Michael M.	S.CA	4/30/08		
12	O'Neill, Michael	DDC	6/19/08		
13	Rosen, Jeffrey A.	DDC	6/19/08		
14	Arguello, Christine M.	CO	7/10/08		
15	Brimmer, Philip A.	CO	7/10/08		
16	Goldberg, Gregory E.	CO	7/10/08		
17	Jung, William F.	M.FL	7/10/08		
18	Scriven, Mary S.	M.FL	7/10/08		
19	Dugan, Timothy G.	E.WI	7/15/08		

No	Name of Nominee	Court	Date		
			Received by Senate	Hearing	Committee Action
20	Trenga, Anthony J.	E.VA	7/17/08		
21	Hernandez, Marco A.	OR	7/23/08		
22	Melgren, Eric F.	KS	7/23/08		
23	Goldberg, Mitchell S.	E.PA	7/24/08		
24	Jones, C. Darnell, II	E.PA	7/24/08		
25	Short, Carolyn P.	E.PA	7/24/08		
26	Slomsky, Joel S.	E.PA	7/24/08		
27	Barry, J. Richard	S.MS	7/31/08		
28	Marcelle, Thomas	N.NY	7/31/08		
29	Tharp, John J., Jr.	N.IL	7/31/08		
Court of International Trade					
(There are no pending nominations to the Court of International Trade)					

Source: CRS Judicial Nominations Database.

[a].Renomination of an individual first nominated in the 109th Congress (2005-2006).

[b]The individual received a hearing in the 109th Congress on a nomination to the same position.

The table shows the date each nomination was received by the Senate, the date of any hearing on the nomination before the Judiciary Committee, and the date of any vote by the committee to report the nomination to the Senate. The table also indicates which nominations in the list are renominations — persons nominated to the same judgeship either earlier in the 110th Congress or in a previous Congress. Tables 3 and 4 list all nominations to the circuit courts of appeals and to the district courts, respectively, made by President Bush during the 110th Congress, as of the date listed, and any actions taken on the nominations [13]. The nominations are listed in chronological order according to the date on which each was received by the Senate. The tables show how far along each nomination has progressed in the appointment process, with separate columns indicating the date on which any of the following occurred:

- the Judiciary Committee held a hearing on the nomination
- the committee voted to report or take other action on the nomination, or
- final action was taken on the nomination.

Table 3. President George W. Bush's Nominations to the U.S. Circuit Courts of Appeals During the 110th Congress (as of August 4, 2008)

No.	Name of Nominee	State	Court	Date				Disposition	Vote[a]	Days Elapsed, First Nomination to Final Action[b]
				Nomination Received	Hearing	Committee Action	Final Action			
1	Hardiman, Thomas M.[c]	PA	Third	1/9/07	[e]	3/8/07	3/15/07	Confirmed	95-0	183
2	Keisler, Peter D.[c]	MD	D.C.	1/9/07	[e]					
3	Livingston, Debra A.[c]	NY	Second	1/9/07	4/11/07	5/3/07	5/9/07	Confirmed	91-0	315
4	Smith, N. Randy[c]	ID	Ninth	1/9/07	[e]		1/16/07	Withdrawn	—	—
5	Southwick, Leslie	MS	Fifth	1/9/07	5/10/07	8/2/07	10/24/07	Confirmed	59-38	288
6	Smith, N. Randy[c,d]	ID	Ninth	1/16/07	[e]	2/8/07	2/15/07	Confirmed	94-0	426
7	Kethledge, Raymond M.[c]	MI	Sixth	3/19/07	5/7/08	6/12/08	6/24/08	Confirmed	Voice	727
8	Murphy, Stephen J., III[c]	MI	Sixth	3/19/07		4/	15/08	Withdrawn	—	657
9	Elrod, Jennifer W.	TX	Fifth	3/29/07	7/19/07	9/20/07	10/4/07	Confirmed	Voice	189
10	Conrad, Robert J., Jr.	NC	Fourth	7/17/07						
11	Haynes, Catharina	TX	Fifth	7/17/07	2/21/08	4/3/08	4/10/08	Confirmed	Voice	268
12	Stone, Shalom D.	NJ	Third	7/17/07						
13	Tinder, John D.	IN	Seventh	7/17/07	9/25/07	11/1/07	12/18/07	Confirmed	93-0	154
14	Matthews, Steve A.	SC	Fourth	9/6/07						
15	Getchell, E. Duncan, Jr.	VA	Fourth	9/6/07			1/23/08	Withdrawn	—	139
16	Pratter, Gene E.K.	PA	Third	11/15/07			7/24/08	Withdrawn	—	252
17	Rosenstein, Rod J.	MD	Fourth	11/15/07						

No.	Name of Nominee	State	Court	Date				Disposition	Vote[a]	Days Elapsed, First Nomination to Final Action[b]
				Nomination Received	Hearing	Committee Action	Final Action			
18	Smith, William E.	RI	First	12/6/07						
19	Agee, G. Steven	VA	Fourth	3/13/08	5/1/08	5/12/08	5/20/08	Confirmed	96-0	68
20	White, Helene N.	MI	Sixth	4/15/08	5/7/08	6/12/08	6/24/08	Confirmed	63-32	70
21	Conrad, Glen E.	VA	Fourth	5/8/08						
22	Diamond, Paul S.	PA	Third	7/24/08						

Source: CRS Judicial Nominations Database.

[a]A numerical tally indicates a Senate roll call vote on confirmation (the yeas followed by the nays). "Voice" indicates that the Senate confirmed the nomination by voice vote.

[b]For individuals nominated in a previous Congress, the values displayed in this column report the number of days which elapsed between the date of the first nomination and the date of the final action on the most recent nomination in the 110th Congress.

[c]Renomination of an individual first nominated in the 109th Congress (2005-2006).

[d]Smith was withdrawn as a nominee for a seat vacated by Stephen Trott and renominated, the same day, for a seat vacated by Thomas Nelson.

[e]The individual received a hearing in the 109th Congress on a nomination to the same position. For additional information, see Appendices 1 and 4 in CRS Report RL31868, U.S.

Circuit and District Court Nominations by President George W. Bush During the 107th-109th Congresses, by Denis Steven Rutkus, Kevin M. Scott, and Maureen Bearden.

Table 4. President George W. Bush's Nominations to the U.S. District Courts During the 110th Congress (as of August 4, 2008)

No.	Name of Nominee	Court	Date				Disposition	Vote[a]	Days Elapsed, First Nomination to Final Action[b]
			Nomination Received	Hearing	Committee Action	Final Action			
1	Bailey, John P.[c]	N.WV	1/9/07	2/6/07	3/1/07	3/15/07	Confirmed	Voice	260
2	Baker, Valerie L.[c]	C.CA	1/9/07	[d]	1/25/07	2/1/07	Confirmed	Voice	273
3	Bryant, Vanessa L.[c]	CT	1/9/07	[d]	3/8/07	3/28/07	Confirmed	Voice	427
4	Donohue, Mary O.[c]	N.NY	1/9/07			9/6/07	Withdrawn	—	435
5	Farr, Thomas A.[c]	E.NC	1/9/07						
6	Fischer, Nora B.[c]	W.PA	1/9/07	[d]	2/8/07	2/14/07	Confirmed	97-0	216
7	Frizzell, Gregory K.[c]	N.OK	1/9/07	[d]	1/25/07	2/1/07	Confirmed	99-0	239
8	Gutierrez, Philip S.[c]	C.CA	1/9/07	[d]	1/25/07	1/30/07	Confirmed	97-0	281
9	Howard, Marcia M.[c]	M.FL	1/9/07	[d]	2/8/07	2/15/07	Confirmed	93-0	253
10	Jarvey, John A.[c]	S.IA	1/9/07	[d]	2/8/07	3/8/07	Confirmed	95-0	253
11	Kapala, Frederick J.[c]	N.IL	1/9/07	3/13/07	4/25/07	5/8/07	Confirmed	91-0	154
12	Lioi, Sara E.[c]	N.OH	1/9/07	[d]	2/8/07	3/8/07	Confirmed	Voice	238
13	Mauskopf, Rosslyn R.[c]	E.NY	1/9/07	4/11/07	7/19/07	10/4/07	Confirmed	Voice	428
14	O'Grady, Liam[c] E.V	A	1/9/07	5/10/07	5/24/07	7/9/07	Confirmed	88-0	341
15	O'Neill, Lawrence J.[c]	E.CA	1/9/07	[d]	1/25/07	2/1/07	Confirmed	97-0	183
16	Osteen, William L., Jr.[c]	M.NC	1/9/07	6/20/07	7/19/07	9/10/07	Confirmed	90-0	346
17	Ozerden, Halil S.[c]	S.MS	1/9/07	3/13/07	4/12/07	4/24/07	Confirmed	95-0	231

No.	Name of Nominee	Court	Date				Disposition	Vote[a]	Days Elapsed, First Nomination to Final Action[b]
			Nomination Received	Hearing	Committee Action	Final Action			
18	Reidinger, Martin K.[c]	W.NC	1/9/07	6/20/07	7/19/07	9/10/07	Confirmed	Voice	346
19	Rogan, James E.[c]	C.CA	1/9/07						
20	Schroeder, Thomas D.[c]	M.NC	1/9/07	10/24/07	11/15/07	12/14/07	Confirmed	Voice	441
21	Settle, Benjamin H.[c]	W.WA	1/9/07	3/13/07	4/25/07	6/28/07	Confirmed	99-0	225
22	Van Bokkelen, Joseph S.	N.IN	1/9/07	4/11/07	5/3/07	6/28/07	Confirmed	Voice	170
23	Wood, Lisa G.[c]	S.GA	1/9/07	[d]	1/25/07	1/30/07	Confirmed	97-0	232
24	Wright, Otis D., II[c]	C.CA	1/9/07	2/6/07	3/1/07	3/15/07	Confirmed	Voice	191
25	Wu, George H.[c]	C.CA	1/9/07	2/6/07	3/1/07	3/27/07	Confirmed	96-0	203
26	DeGiusti, Timothy D.	W.OK	2/15/07	6/20/07	7/19/07	8/3/07	Confirmed	96-0	169
27	Sullivan, Richard	S.NY	2/15/07	4/11/07	5/3/07	6/28/07	Confirmed	99-0	133
28	Aycock, Sharion	N.MS	3/19/07	7/19/07	9/6/07	10/4/07	Confirmed	Voice	199
29	Dugas, David R.	M.LA	3/19/07						
30	Hall, James R.	S.GA	3/19/07	2/12/08	3/6/08	4/10/08	Confirmed	Voice	388
31	Honaker, Richard H.	WY	3/19/07	2/12/08					
32	Jones, Richard A.	W.WA	3/19/07	7/19/07	9/6/07	10/4/07	Confirmed	Voice	199
33	Jonker, Robert J.[c]	W.MI	3/19/07	[d]	6/7/07	7/9/07	Confirmed	Voice	376
34	Maloney, Paul L.[c]	W.MI	3/19/07	[d]	5/24/07	7/9/07	Confirmed	Voice	376
35	Neff, Janet T.[c]	W.MI	3/19/07	5/10/07[d]	5/24/07	7/9/07	Confirmed	83-4	376
36	Sammartino, Janis L.	S.CA	3/19/07	6/20/07	7/19/07	9/10/07	Confirmed	90-0	175

Table 4. (Continued)

No.	Name of Nominee	Court	Date				Disposition	Vote[a]	Days Elapsed, First Nomination to Final Action[b]
			Nomination Received	Hearing	Committee Action	Final Action			
37	Powell, William J.	N.WV	5/24/07						
38	Thapar, Amul R.	E.KY	5/24/07	10/24/07	11/15/07	12/13/07	Confirmed	Voice	203
39	Laplante, Joseph N.	NH	6/13/07	10/24/07	11/15/07	12/14/07	Confirmed	Voice	184
40	Puryear, Gustavus A., IV	M.TN	6/13/07	2/12/08					
41	O'Connor, Reed C.	N.TX	6/27/07	10/24/07	11/15/07	11/16/07	Confirmed	Voice	142
42	Dow, Robert M., Jr.	N.IL	7/18/07	9/25/07	10/4/07	11/13/07	Confirmed	86-0	118
43	Anderson, Stanley T.	W.TN	9/6/07	2/21/08	3/6/08	4/10/08	Confirmed	Voice	217
44	Mendez, John A.	E.CA	9/6/07	2/21/08	3/6/08	4/10/08	Confirmed	Voice	217
45	Miller, Brian S.	E.AR	10/16/07	2/12/08	3/6/08	4/10/08	Confirmed	88-0	177
46	Almond, Lincoln D.	RI	11/15/07						
47	Davis, Mark S.	E.VA	11/15/07	4/3/08	4/24/08	6/10/08	Confirmed	94-0	208
48	Kays, David G.	W.MO	11/15/07	4/3/08	4/24/08	6/10/08	Confirmed	Voice	208
49	Novak, David J.	E.VA	11/15/07	4/3/08					
50	Short, Carolyn P.	E.PA	11/15/07			7/24/08	Withdrawn[c]	—	—
51	Limbaugh, Stephen N., Jr.	E.MO	12/6/07	4/3/08	4/24/08	6/10/08	Confirmed	Voice	187
52	Snow, G. Murray	AZ	12/11/07	5/1/08	5/22/08	6/26/08	Confirmed	Voice	198
53	Suddaby, Glenn T.	N.NY	12/11/07	6/11/08	6/26/08	7/22/08	Confirmed	Voice	224
54	Lawrence, William T.	S.IN	2/14/08	5/1/08	5/22/08	6/26/08	Confirmed	97-0	133
55	Connolly, Colm F.	DE	2/26/08						

No.	Name of Nominee	Court	Date				Disposition	Vote[a]	Days Elapsed, First Nomination to Final Action[b]
			Nomination Received	Hearing	Committee Action	Final Action			
56	Matsumoto, Kiyo A.	E.NY	3/11/08	6/11/08	6/26/08	7/17/08	Confirmed	Voice	128
57	Seibel, Cathy	S.NY	3/11/08	6/11/08	6/26/08	7/22/08	Confirmed	Voice	133
58	Murphy, Stephen J., III	E.MI	4/15/08	5/7/08	6/12/08	6/24/08	Confirmed	Voice	70
59	Gardephe, Paul G.	S.NY	4/29/08	6/11/08	6/26/08	7/17/08	Confirmed	Voice	79
60	Waddoups, Clark	UT	4/29/08						
61	Anello, Michael M.	S.CA	4/30/08						
62	O'Neill, Michael	DC	6/19/08						
63	Rosen, Jeffrey A.	DC	6/19/08						
64	Arguello, Christine M.	CO	7/10/08						
65	Brimmer, Philip A.	CO	7/10/08						
66	Goldberg, Gregory E.	CO	7/10/08						
67	Jung, William F.	M.FL	7/10/08						
68	Scriven, Mary S.	M.FL	7/10/08						
69	Dugan, Timothy G.	E.WI	7/15/08						
70	Trenga, Anthony J.	E.VA	7/17/08						
71	Hernandez, Marco A.	OR	7/23/08						
72	Melgren, Eric F.	KS	7/23/08						
73	Goldberg, Mitchell S.	E.PA	7/24/08						
74	Jones, C. Darnell, II	E.PA	7/24/08						

Table 4. (Continued)

No.	Name of Nominee	Court	Date				Disposition	Vote[a]	Days Elapsed, First Nomination to Final Action[b]
			Nomination Received	Hearing	Committee Action	Final Action			
75	Short, Carolyn P.[f]	E.PA	7/24/08						
76	Slomsky, Joel S.	E.PA	7/24/08						
77	Barry, J. Richard	S.MS	7/31/08						
78	Marcelle, Thomas	N.NY	7/31/08						
79	Tharp, John J., Jr.	N.IL	7/31/08						

Source: CRS Judicial Nominations Database.

a. A numerical tally indicates a Senate roll call vote on confirmation (the yeas followed by the nays). "Voice" indicates that the Senate confirmed the nomination by voice vote.

b. For individuals nominated in a previous Congress, the values displayed in this column report the number of days which elapsed between the date of the first nomination and the date of the final action on the most recent nomination in the 110th Congress.

c. Renomination of an individual first nominated in the 109th Congress (2005-2006).

d. The individual received a hearing in the 109th Congress on a nomination to the same position. For additional information, see Appendices 5 and 8 in CRS Report RL31868, U.S. Circuit and District Court Nominations by President George W. Bush During the 107th-109th Congresses, by Denis Steven Rutkus, Kevin M. Scott, and Maureen Bearden.

e This nomination was made to fill a district court judgeship upon the elevation of U.S. district court judge Gene E.K. Pratter to the Third Circuit. (See in Table 3, above, the November 15, 2007, nomination of Pratter to the Third Circuit.) When the Pratter nomination to the Third Circuit was withdrawn on July 24, 2008, the district judgeship in question no longer needed to be filled; accordingly, the Short nomination was withdrawn, also on July 24. That same day, President Bush renominated Short to a different district judgeship in the same judicial district.

f Renomination of an individual nominated earlier in the 110th Congress to a different judgeship in the same judicial district. See in this table the November 15, 2007, nomination of Short, the withdrawal of that nomination on July 24, 2008, and preceding table note explaining the need for that nomination to be withdrawn.

Table 5. President George W. Bush's Nominations to the U.S. Court of International Trade During the 110th Congress (as of August 4, 2008)

No	Name of Nominee	State	Court	Date				
				Nomination Received	Hearing	Committee Action	Final Action	Days Elapsed, FirstNomination to Final Action
	Thus far, during the 110th Congress, there have been no nominations to this court							

Source: CRS Judicial Nominations Database.

When final action has occurred on a nomination, the nature of the action is indicated in another column, under the heading "Disposition." (For each nomination, one of four kinds of disposition is possible — confirmation by the Senate, return of the nomination to the President, withdrawal by the President, and rejection by the Senate. During George W. Bush's presidency, however, the Senate has never voted to reject a judicial nomination.) An additional column, for nominations receiving a Senate confirmation vote, indicates whether the vote was by roll call (by supplying the roll call tally) or by voice vote.

A final column in Tables 3 and 4 presents time-span information for nominations having received final action in the 110th Congress. Specifically, for each such nomination, the column measures the number of days that elapsed between a nominee's first nomination to a particular court and the final action on this (the most recent) nomination. In some cases, a nominee has been nominated only once by President Bush for a judgeship, and the time span measured for such a nominee in the final column in Tables 3 and 4 is the number of days that elapsed between the date during the 110th Congress that the nomination was received in the Senate and the date it received final action. However, in other cases, a judicial nominee in the 110th Congress has been nominated more than once, with one or more nominations of that person having been made in an earlier Congress. For such a nominee, the final column in Tables 3 and 4 measures the number of days that elapsed between the nominee's first nomination in the earlier Congress and the date that the nominee's nomination in the 110th Congress received final action [14].

Table 3 shows that, thus far in the 110th Congress, President Bush has nominated 21 individuals to circuit court judgeships,15 eight of whom have been confirmed by the Senate, and the nominations of three were withdrawn by the President and not resubmitted [16]. Table 4 shows that, thus far in the 110th Congress, the President has nominated 78 individuals to district court judgeships [17] Of those 78, 48 have been confirmed, and the nomination of one was withdrawn by the President and not resubmitted [18].

Table 5, for the present, is an empty table, which exists to account for any future nominations that President Bush might make to the U.S. Court of International Trade. (Thus far during the 110th Congress, no nominations have been made to this court.) The table is of the same format as Tables 3 and 4. Accordingly, in the event any nominations are made to the court, the table will list actions on the nominations by the Judiciary Committee and the Senate, any other final action taken, and number of days elapsed between the date of nomination and date of final action.

Table 6 presents the total number of persons nominated by President Bush to each category of lower Article III court during his entire presidency.

Table 6. President George W. Bush's Nominees to Article III Lower Courts: A Numerical Breakdown According to Status of Their Most Recent Nomination

Court	Confirmed	Pending	Returned, Not Renominated	Withdrawn	Total
Courts of Appeals	61	8	8	6	83
District Courtsa	251	29	1	4	285
Court of International Trade	2	0	0	0	2
Total	314	37	9	10	370

Source: CRS Judicial Nominations Database.

[a] Does not include three nominees to the territorial district courts, all of whom were confirmed prior to the 110th Congress. Judges on those courts are appointed to renewable 10-year terms. There have been no nominations to the territorial district courts in the 110th Congress.

The table also breaks down each numerical total, showing, as of the date listed, the number of nominees whose most recent nominations were (1) confirmed; (2) pending in the Senate; (3) returned to the President, at the end of a Congress or at the start of a Senate recess of more than 30 days, and not re-submitted; or (4) withdrawn by the President.

This table counts nominees to a particular judgeship only once, even if they were nominated to their judgeship more than once [19].

Table 7 places the judicial nominee numbers of the George W. Bush presidency in the context of the last five Presidents.

Table 7. Article III U.S. District Courts and Courts of Appeals: Number of Nominees, Number Confirmed, and Percent of Nominees Confirmed, Five Most Recent Presidents (as of August 4, 2008)

President	Court of Appeals			District Courts[a]		Tot	al[b]		
	Confirmed	Nominees	Percent	Confirmed	Nominees	Percent	Confirmed	Nominees	Percent
Jimmy Carter	56	60	93.3%	202	218	92.7%	258	278	92.8%
Ronald Reagan	83	94	88.3%	290	306	94.8%	373	400	93.3%
George H.W. Bush	42	53	79.2%	148	191	77.5%	190	244	77.9%
Bill Clinton	65	90	72.2%	305	350	87.1%	370	440	84.1%
George W. Bush (through August 4, 2008)	61	83	73.5%	251	285	88.1%	312	368	84.8%

Comparison of the nominee statistics of the two-term Presidents in this group (Reagan, Clinton, and George W. Bush) reveal the following:

- The percentage of George W. Bush's nominees confirmed to the circuit courts (73.5% as of August 4, 2008) is relatively close to the confirmation percentages for Clinton nominees (72.2% for circuit courts), but well below that for Reagan nominees (88.3% for circuit courts).
- The percentage of George W. Bush's nominees confirmed to the district courts (88.1% as of August 4, 2008) is slightly more than the confirmation percentage for Clinton nominees (87.1%), but less than that for Reagan nominees (94.8%).
- The *number* of Bush nominees confirmed to the circuit courts (61) is somewhat below the number of confirmed Clinton circuit nominees (65) and well below the number of confirmed Reagan circuit nominees (83), while the number of Bush nominees confirmed to the district courts (251) is well below the confirmed district court nominee numbers of both Presidents Clinton and Reagan (305 and 290, respectively).

To put Senate consideration of President George W. Bush's lower court nominees in additional historical context, Figures 1 (courts of appeals) and 2 (district courts) illustrate the average number of days that have elapsed from first nomination to final action for judicial nominations for each of the last five Presidents. Both Figures 1 and 2 separate confirmed nominees from those who were not confirmed by the Senate (those who were rejected by the Senate or withdrawn by the President, or whose most recent nomination was returned by the Senate and not resubmitted by the President).

Compared with recent Administrations, Figure 1 shows that President George W. Bush's appeals nominees experienced, on average, the highest number of days elapsed from first nomination to final Senate action. The data presented in Figure 1 also reflect consistently increasing average time to final action for confirmed nominees over each of the last three presidencies and increasing average time to final action for unconfirmed nominees over each of the last four presidencies. The average time to final action for President George W. Bush's confirmed nominees to the courts of appeals, 350 days, is 47% greater than the average time to final action for President Clinton's confirmed nominees to the courts of appeals and 407% greater than the average time to final action for President Carter's confirmed nominees to the courts of appeals.

The average time to final action for President George W. Bush's unconfirmed nominees to the courts of appeals (not including those currently pending in the

Senate), 859 days, is 96% greater than the average time to final action for President Clinton's unconfirmed court of appeals nominees and 341% greater than the average time to final action for President Carter's unconfirmed court of appeals nominees. The average time to final action for President George W. Bush's confirmed nominees to the courts of appeals, 350 days, is 47% greater than the average time to final action for President Clinton's confirmed nominees to the courts of appeals and 407% greater than the average time to final action for President Carter's confirmed nominees to the courts of appeals.

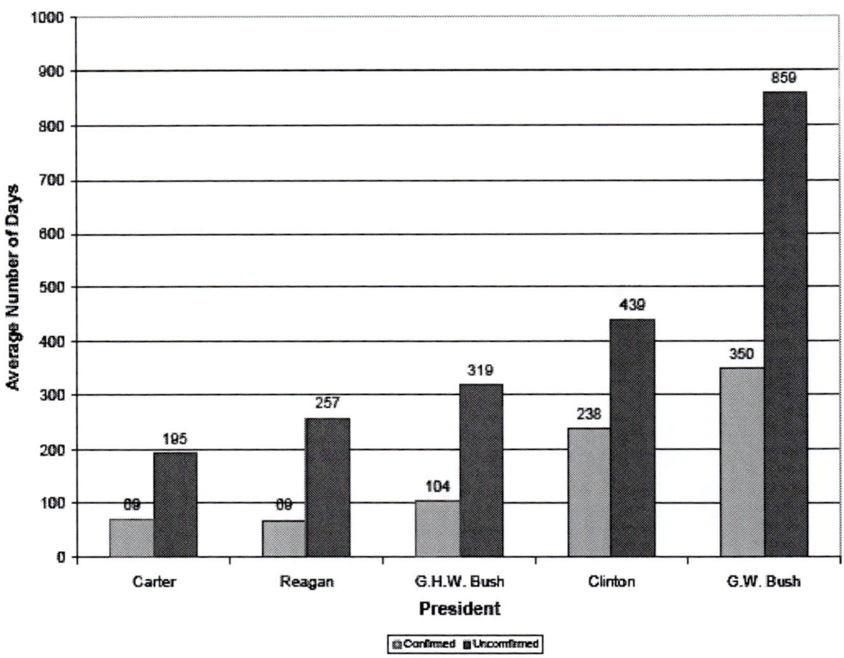

Source: CRS Judicial Nominations Database. Numbers atop the bars indicate the average number of days to final action. Unconfirmed nominees include those whose nominations were rejected by the Senate, withdrawn by the President, or returned to the President and not resubmitted. Data are current as of August 4, 2008, and do not include any nominees pending as of that date.

Figure 1. Average Number of Days From First Nomination to Final Senate Action, Nominees to the U.S. Courts of Appeals, January 20, 1977-August 4, 2008.

The average time to final action for President George W. Bush's unconfirmed nominees to the courts of appeals (not including those currently pending in the Senate), 859 days, is 96% greater than the average time to final action for

President Clinton's unconfirmed court of appeals nominees and 341% greater than the average time to final action for President Carter's unconfirmed court of appeals nominees.

Many of the patterns observed in time to final action for court of appeals nominees can also be observed in time to final action for district court nominees. Compared with recent Administrations, Figure 2 shows that President George W. Bush's district nominees experienced, on average, the highest number of days elapsed from first nomination to final Senate action. The data presented in Figure 2 also demonstrate consistently increasing average time to final action for confirmed nominees over each of the last three presidencies and increasing average time to final action for unconfirmed nominees over each of the last two presidencies.

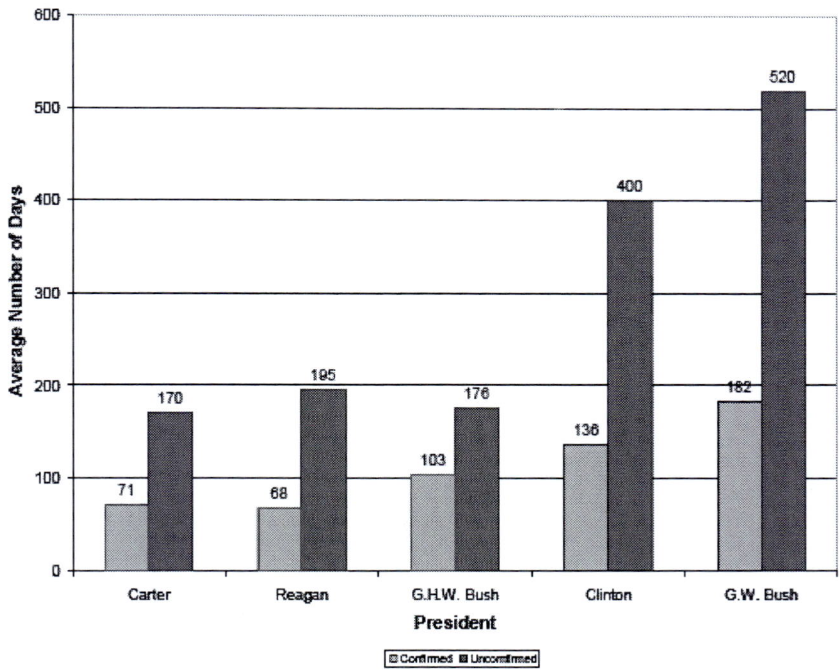

Source: CRS Judicial Nominations Database. Numbers atop the bars indicate the average number of days to final action. Unconfirmed nominees include those whose nominations were rejected by the Senate, withdrawn by the President, or returned to the President and not resubmitted. Data are current as of August 4, 2008, and do not include any nominees pending as of that date.

Figure 2. Average Number of Days from First Nomination to Final Senate Action, Nominees to the Article III U.S. District Courts, January 20, 1977-August 4, 2008.

The average time to final action for President George W. Bush's confirmed nominees to the district courts, 182 days, is 34% greater than the average time to final action for President Clinton's confirmed nominees to the district courts and 156% greater than the average time to final action for President Carter's confirmed nominees to the district courts. The average time to final action for President George W. Bush's unconfirmed nominees to the district courts (not including those currently pending in the Senate), 520 days, is 30% greater than the average time to final action for President Clinton's unconfirmed district court nominees and 206% greater than the average time to final action for President Carter's unconfirmed district court nominees.

APPENDIX. THE APPOINTMENT PROCESS FOR NOMINATIONS TO ARTICLE III JUDGESHIPS

Under the Constitution of the United States, the President and the Senate share the responsibility for filling vacancies in the federal judiciary [20]. While it is the President who nominates persons to fill federal judgeships, the appointment of each nominee also requires Senate confirmation. Although not mentioned in the Constitution, the Senate Judiciary Committee also plays an important role midway in the process — after the President selects, but before the Senate as a whole considers, the nominee. It is the Judiciary Committee in the Senate that has committee jurisdiction over most federal judicial nominations — namely, those to the Supreme Court, the courts of appeals, the district courts (including the territorial district courts), the U.S. Court of International Trade, and the U.S. Court of Federal Claims [21].

The need for the President to make a nomination to an Article III court judgeship arises when a vacancy occurs on the court, due to the death, retirement, or resignation of a judge (or when a judge announces the intention to retire or resign) [22]. In considering judicial candidates for possible nomination, the President frequently receives recommendations from U.S. Senators [23]. By longstanding custom, dating back to the mid-1800s, Senators of the President's party have provided Presidents such advice, recommending candidates for judgeships situated in their states or linked by tradition to their states [24]. Also by custom, Senators not of the President's party play a consultative role and may convey to the President their views about candidates under consideration for judgeships in their states [25]. The judgeships for which a Senator ordinarily recommends nominees, or is consulted, are those in the U.S. district court or courts which geographically fall within the Senator's state and the U.S. court of appeals circuit of which the Senator's state is a geographic part — provided the circuit judgeship historically has been associated with the Senator's state [26].

After selecting someone to fill a judicial vacancy, the President formally submits a nomination in writing to the Senate [27]. Usually on the same day it is received by the Senate, the nomination is referred to the Judiciary Committee. The committee's first formal public step is to hold a hearing on a nomination. The committee subsequently meets again to vote on whether to report the nomination to the full Senate. A committee vote to report (even a vote to report with an unfavorable recommendation) sends the nomination forward to be considered by the Senate as a whole, while a vote against reporting (historically, a very rare occurrence) prevents the nomination from going forward, and in effect defeats the nomination in committee. The next step in the appointment process occurs when the Senate votes to confirm or disapprove the nomination. A vote to confirm requires a simple majority of Senators present and voting.

If the Senate votes to confirm the nomination, the Secretary of the Senate then attests to a resolution of confirmation and transmits it to the White House [28]. In turn, the President signs a document, called a commission, officially appointing the individual to the court. The signed commission is then "returned to the Justice Department for engraving the date of appointment (determined by the actual day the president signs the commission) and for the signature of the attorney general and the placing of the Justice Department seal" [29] Once the President has signed the commission, the incoming judge is eligible to be sworn into office. The new judge actually takes two oaths of office — a judicial oath, as required by the Judiciary Act of 1789, and a constitutional oath, which, as required by Article VI of the Constitution, is administered to Members of Congress and all executive and judicial officers.

As with nominations in general, judicial nominations sometimes fail to advance through each procedural step in the appointment process. After referral to committee, a nomination might not receive a hearing or, after receiving a hearing, might not receive a committee vote on whether it should be reported. Even if favorably reported by committee, a nomination might not receive a vote by the Senate on whether to confirm. The majority leader might not schedule a vote, or some Senators might oppose taking such a vote and a "super-majority" of three-fifths of the full membership of the Senate would be needed to invoke cloture on the nomination [30]. If a nomination fails to receive a Senate vote on confirmation, it ultimately will be either withdrawn by the President or returned to the President by the Secretary of the Senate upon a Senate adjournment or recess of more than 30 days [31]. The Senate may, by unanimous consent, carry nominations over a recess of more than 30 days.

REFERENCES

[1] For an overview of the process for appointing lower court judges (and the respective roles played in that process by the President, the Senate Judiciary Committee, and the full Senate), see the Appendix.

[2] See, for example, Nancy Scherer, *Scoring Points: Politicians, Activists, and the Lower Federal Court Appointment Process* (Stanford, CA: Stanford University Press, 2005); Lee Epstein and Jeffrey A. Segal, *Advice and Consent: The Politics of Judicial Appointments* (New York: Oxford University Press, 2005); Sheldon Goldman, "Judicial Confirmation Wars: Ideology and the Battle for the Federal Courts," *University of Richmond Law Review*, vol. 39, March 2005, pp. 871-908; Stephen B. Burbank, "Politics, Privilege and Power: The Senate's Role in the Appointment of Federal Judges," *Judicature*, vol. 86, July-August 2002, pp. 24-27; and Elliot E. Slotnick, "A Historical Perspective on Federal Judicial Selection," *Judicature*, vol. 86, July-August 2002, pp. 13-16.

[3] See, for instance, the floor remarks of the Senate Republican Leader, Sen. Mitch McConnell of Kentucky, on June 5, 2008, and of the chairman of the Senate Judiciary Committee, Sen. Patrick J. Leahy (D-VT), on June 10, 2008, expressing contrasting views on whether a sufficient number of judicial nominations had been confirmed by that point in the 110th Congress. Sen. Mitch McConnell, "Judicial Nominations," *Congressional Record*, daily edition, vol. 154, June 5, 2008, p. S5128; and Sen. Patrick J. Leahy, "Nomination of Mark Steven Davis to be United States District Judge for the Eastern District of Virginia," *Congressional Record*, vol. 154, June 10, 2008, pp. S5413-S5416.

[4] For a detailed narrative and statistical analysis of President George W. Bush's lower court nominations during the first six years of his presidency, see CRS Report RL3 1868, *U.S. Circuit and District Court Nominations by President George W. Bush During the 107th-109th Congresses*, by Denis Steven Rutkus, Kevin M. Scott, and Maureen Bearden.

[5] Pursuant to this constitutional language, Article III judges may hold office for as long as they live or until they voluntarily leave office. A President has no power to remove them from office. Article III judges may be removed by

Congress only through the process of impeachment by the House and conviction by the Senate.

[6] Citing the power to do so in Article I of the Constitution, Congress, in separate statutes, has created four courts of specialized subject matter jurisdiction — the U.S. Court of Federal Claims, the U.S. Tax Court, the U.S. Court of Appeals for Veterans Claims, and the Court of Appeals for the Armed Forces — and has authorized 15-year judicial tenure in these courts.

[7] On January 7, 2008, President George W. Bush signed H.R. 660, the Court Security Improvement Act of 2007 (P.L. 110-77, 121 Stat. 2534). Among other things, the act decreased the number of judgeships in the D.C. Circuit Court of Appeals from 12 to 11 and, effective January 21, 2009, increased the number of judgeships on the Ninth Circuit Court of Appeals from 28 to 29. Accordingly, there are 178 judgeships on the courts of appeals until January 21, 2009, when, barring any other adjustment, that number will rise to 179.

[8] The 674 total consists of 663 permanently authorized judgeships and 11 "temporary" judgeships (which, pursuant to statute, temporarily increase the *number* of judgeships for specified judicial districts. These districts revert back to the permanently authorized number of judgeships at a future time fixed by the statute — typically, when, after a specified number of years, a judgeship in the district is vacated).

[9] Decisions of the U.S. District Courts for the District of Guam and the District of the Northern Mariana Islands are appealed to the Ninth Circuit Court of Appeals. Decisions of the U.S. District Court for the District of Virgin Islands are appealed to the Third Circuit Court of Appeals.

[10] For instance, the federal judiciary subsumes territorial courts under the heading of "District Courts" in various places on its website, at [http://www.uscourts.gov]. In one link on the website, entitled "Authorized Judgeships," accessed via [http://www.uscourts.gov/ judicialvac.html], the judiciary lists the number of authorized judgeships, respectively, on the Supreme Court, the circuit courts, the district courts, and the Court of International Trade. The link, under the heading of "District Courts," provides an "Article III" subheading (with 674 judgeships) and a "Territorial Court" sub-heading (with 4 judgeships), and, in an adjacent column, 678 is shown to be total number of judgeships for the "District Courts" heading.

[11] "Adjusted filings" eliminate reinstated cases and weight *pro se* appeals as one-third of a case. All other cases have a weight of one. The number of

adjusted filings in a given year is then divided by the number of three-judge panels on a circuit (e.g., a circuit with 7 authorized judgeships has 2.33 panels). Adjusted filings data are updated every three months.

[12] "Weighted filings" use a system developed by the Federal Judicial Center to account for how much of a judge's time each case type should take. Like adjusted filings data, it is an annual measure of court workload updated every three months. According to the Administrative Office for the United States Courts, "average civil cases or criminal defendants each receive a weight of approximately 1.0; for more time-consuming cases, higher weights are assessed (e.g., a death-penalty habeas corpus case is assigned a weight of 12.89); and cases demanding relatively little time from judges receive lower weights (e.g., a defaulted student loan case is assigned a weight of 0.031)." See [http://www.uscourts.gov/ library/fcmstat/ cmsexpl06.html].

[13] In the event any nominations are made to the territorial district courts, they will be listed in Table 4, and treated as falling within the category of district court nominations, even though, as discussed above, they are not Article III court nominations. Thus far during the 110th Congress, no nominations have been made to the territorial courts.

[14] For a person nominated for the first time to a judgeship during the 110th Congress, only to be re-nominated during the 110th Congress, the final column in Tables 3 and 4 shows, if final action has occurred on the last nomination, the time elapsed between date of first nomination and date of final action on the last nomination.

[15] While Table 3 lists 22 nominations to the courts of appeals, the number of persons nominated is 21. The 20 nominations include two of the same person, N. Randy Smith. As Table 3 shows, Smith's first nomination in the 110th Congress to a particular seat on the Ninth Circuit was withdrawn on the same day that he was renominated for a different Ninth Circuit seat.

[16] Thus far in the 110th Congress, the nominations of four court of appeals nominees have been withdrawn. However, as explained in the preceding footnote, one of these individuals was renominated.

[17] While Table 4 lists 79 nominations to the district courts, the number of persons nominated is 78. The 78 nominations include two of the same person, Carolyn P. Short. As Table 4 shows, Short's first nomination in the 110th Congress to a particular seat on the Eastern District of Pennsylvania was withdrawn on the same day that she was renominated for a different Eastern District of Pennsylvania seat.

[18] Thus far in the 11 0th Congress, the nominations of two district court nominees have been withdrawn. However, as explained in the preceding footnote, one of these individuals was renominated.

[19] Some of President Bush's nominees were nominated to a circuit or district judgeship more than once within a Congress, or nominated to the judgeship in more than one Congress. For a listing of these nominees, as well as other Presidents' nominees to the circuit and district courts whose nominations were resubmitted from 1977 through 2006, See CRS Report RL33839, *Returns and Resubmissions of Nominees to the U.S. Courts of Appeals and District Courts, 1977-2006*, by Kevin M. Scott.

[20] Article II, Section 2, clause 2 of the Constitution provides that the President "shall nominate, and by and with the Advice and Consent of the Senate, shall appoint ... Judges of the supreme Court, and all other Officers of the United States, whose Appointments are not herein otherwise provided for, and which shall be established by Law...."

[21] Nominations to the Court of Appeals for the Armed Forces fall within the jurisdiction of the Senate Armed Services Committee; nominations to the U.S. Tax Court fall within the Jurisdiction of the Senate Finance Committee; and nominations to the Court of Appeals for Veterans Claims fall within the jurisdiction of the Senate Veterans' Affairs Committee.

[22] A vacancy also would occur if a judge were removed by Congress through the impeachment process, but historically such occurrences have been extremely rare. Specifically, in our nation's history, "there have been 15 impeachment trials in the Senate, 11 against judges. Seven trials have resulted in convictions, all against judges." CRS Report RL32935, *Congressional Oversight of Judges and Justices*, by Elizabeth B. Bazan and Morton Rosenberg.

[23] See CRS Report RL34405, *Role of Home State Senators in the Selection of Lower Federal Court Judges*, by Denis Steven Rutkus.

[24] A scholar on the Senate's role in judicial appointments, writing in 1953, described the "well-established custom, which has prevailed since about 1840," wherein U.S. district judges "are normally selected by senators from the state in which the district is situated, provided they belong to the same party as the President." By contrast, the President was said to have "a much freer hand in the selection of judges to the circuit courts of appeals, whose districts cover several states...." Joseph P. Harris, *The Advice and Consent of the Senate* (Berkeley, CA: University of California Press, 1953; reprint, New York: Greenwood Press, 1968), p. 314, (page citations are to the reprint edition). See also, for more recent discussion of

the continuing role played by Senators in recommending judicial candidates, Sheldon Goldman, *Picking Federal Judges: Lower Court Selection from Roosevelt Through Reagan* (New Haven, CT: Yale University Press, 1997) (in each presidency chapter, under the heading "Senators and Selection").

[25] See CRS Report RL32013, *The History of the Blue Slip in the Senate Committee on the Judiciary, 1917-Present*, by Mitchel A. Sollenberger. See also Elliot E. Slotnick, "A Historical Perspective on Federal Judicial Selection," *Judicature,* vol. 86, July-August 2002, where, at p. 13, the author observes that the blue slip procedure of the Senate Judiciary Committee "has worked to ensure that home state senators of both parties, whether or not they are of the president's party, have some say when judges are being nominated from their state."

[26] A President is generally believed inclined to avoid selecting a judicial nominee opposed by a home-state Senator of the President's party — given the custom of "senatorial courtesy," wherein the Senate, as a collegial body, customarily supports Senators in disputes with the President over judicial appointments in their state. Two scholars have written that, as a result of this custom, Senators of the President's party "who object to a district judgeship in their home state have a virtual veto over the nomination." Robert A. Carp and Ronald Stidham, *Judicial Process in America*, 3d ed. (Washington: CQ Press, 1996), p. 247.

[27] For a detailed examination of the procedures followed by Senate committees and the full Senate in considering nominations in general, see CRS Report RL3 1980, *Senate Consideration of Presidential Nominations: Committee and Floor Procedure*, by Elizabeth Rybicki. For a diagrammatic overview of procedures followed by the Senate Judiciary Committee and the full Senate in considering district and circuit court nominations, see CRS Report RS2 1735, *U.S. District and Circuit Court Nominations: A Diagram of Customary Procedures*, by Mitchel A. Sollenberger.

[28] If, on the other hand, the Senate votes in the negative on whether to confirm, the nomination is defeated, and a resolution of disapproval is forwarded to the President.

[29] Sheldon Goldman, *Picking Federal Judges: Lower Court Selection from Roosevelt Through Reagan* (New Haven, CT: Yale University Press, 1997), p. 12.

[30] See CRS Report RL32878, *Cloture Attempts on Nominations*, by Richard S. Beth and Betsy Palmer.

[31] Rule XXXI, paragraph 6, *Standing Rules of the Senate,* provides, in part, that "if the Senate shall adjourn or take a recess for more than thirty days, all nominations pending and not finally acted upon at the time of taking such adjournment or recess shall be returned by the Secretary to the President and shall not again be considered unless they shall again be made to the Senate by the President."

INDEX

A

B

C

D

E

F

G

H

I

J

K

L

M

N

O

P

T

U

V

W